Justine Ford is a true crime author, t
journalist. Her first forays into crime
top-rating TV series *Australia's Most W* ... has covered
the Melbourne gangland wars and scores of chilling homicides and missing persons cases. Justine has won the trust of many families who are victims of crime or whose loved ones have gone missing. She has also developed deep access to police all over Australia, enabling her to share crucial, never-before-published case information with the public. Justine has written five books and is an executive producer of the TV adaptation of her book, *The Good Cop*, about Australia's most successful homicide detective, Ron Iddles.

www.justineford.net

Also by Justine Ford

Missing You
One Piece of the Puzzle
Unsolved Australia
The Good Cop

UNSOLVED AUSTRALIA

LOST BOYS, GONE GIRLS

JUSTINE FORD

MACMILLAN
Pan Macmillan Australia

Some of the people in this book have had their names changed to protect their identities.

First published 2019 in Macmillan by Pan Macmillan Australia Pty Ltd
1 Market Street, Sydney, New South Wales, Australia, 2000

Cataloguing-in-Publication entry is available
from the National Library of Australia
http://catalogue.nla.gov.au

Typeset in 12.5/16 pt Bembo by Midland Typesetters, Australia
Printed by McPherson's Printing Group
Cover images and model used for illustrative purposes only.

The author and the publisher have made every effort to contact copyright holders for material used in this book. Any person or organisation that may have been overlooked should contact the publisher.

Aboriginal and Torres Strait Islander people should be aware that this book may contain images or names of people now deceased.

The paper in this book is FSC® certified. FSC® promotes environmentally responsible, socially beneficial and economically viable management of the world's forests.

For the men of books,
Angus Fontaine and John Timlin

CONTENTS

UNSOLVED AUSTRALIA

Photo courtesy Simon Schluter/*The Age*

FOREWORD

In February 2017, I retired from Victoria Police after forty-two years. Twenty-five of those were spent at Victoria Police Homicide Squad.

During those twenty-five years, I investigated more than 320 homicides with a success rate of more than 95 per cent. The cases which still concern me are those which remain unsolved. The very first homicide I attended was the murder of Maria James in 1980. She was stabbed sixty-eight times in her bookshop in High Street, Thornbury, and her murder remains unsolved today. However, that could change at any moment, as it is my view that there is always someone in the community who holds the key to solving every crime.

Over my time at Homicide I was regularly 'on call' to respond to suspicious deaths in Victoria. This included overnight, weekends and public holidays, and often it was in the early hours of the morning when the phone rang. I was acutely aware that the conversation could involve another victim who had lost their life at the hands of a fellow human being or the report of a suspicious missing person. Devastation for a family and lives changed forever would nearly always follow. The expectation of these families and the community was that professional investigators would solve the mystery.

Once called out, the investigation was underway. There may be a result in hours, it may take years, or it may never be solved. However, immediate thoughts went to who was at the crime scene, was it adequately protected, what did we know about the victim, had an offender been apprehended? It was routine to arrange other homicide detectives, crime scene services, the pathologist and, of course, to notify the coroner.

Three fundamental questions are always front of mind for homicide detectives. Who was the victim, what was the cause of death and what was the motive? Investigators are generally confident that once they have the answers to these questions, an arrest should be possible.

Experience has shown us that 98 per cent of homicides are committed by someone known to the victim and it is rare that there is no connection between the victim and perpetrator. I have also learned over my career that most killers, and indeed those who commit serious crimes, eventually tell someone. It is about finding who they told or creating an environment in which people feel comfortable contacting police with vital information.

I have often said homicide investigations are like jigsaw puzzles. Some have a limited number of pieces and are easily solved, others have hundreds of pieces and are much harder to fit together. Then there are those homicide investigations where one or two pieces of the puzzle are missing, and they often become the unsolved cold cases. These are the cases that linger in the memory of the investigators, the media and the public.

Unsolved homicide cases often become computer files or 'box' files with a simple number. We should never lose sight of the fact that they represent a life taken in tragic circumstances. Detectives strive to provide a voice for the victim.

All police services in Australia have cold case units, and among the cases they investigate are some of the most famous and well publicised unsolved homicides in Australian history. Dedicated detectives have the same mission: to bring answers and resolution to the families who have lost loved ones.

While investigations grind on, it is often through media and news articles or books that the crucial facts emerge. The old saying, 'An ounce of information is worth a tonne of investigation' remains true today. Someone in the community holds the key to solving all the crimes written about in this compelling book, *Unsolved Australia: Lost Boys, Gone Girls*, by Justine Ford.

This book is written with compassion and understanding for the victims and their families in the hope that answers will emerge. Justine Ford has a genuine desire to find the missing pieces of puzzling jigsaws.

Without journalists and the media, the last homicide I investigated would never have been solved.

In 2013, a persistent and dedicated young journalist, Tammy Mills, wrote a feature article on the unsolved murder of sixteen-year-old Shepparton girl Michelle Buckingham, who had been stabbed to death and left on the side of a lonely country road. As a result of the article, information was provided which led to the arrest and subsequent conviction of the accused, thirty years after the terrible crime.

Families need hope and investigators should remember that failure should never be an option.

Ron Iddles OAM

INTRODUCTION

Welcome back, armchair detectives!

In the tradition of the first book in this series, *Unsolved Australia: Lost Boys, Gone Girls* takes an in-depth look at mysterious missing persons cases, unsolved murders and a perplexing case of unidentified remains. Once again, you might hold the key to solving one of these cases. Perhaps you've seen one of the missing people in the book, or know the identity of the man whose skeletonised body was found at a Melbourne dockyard in 1990. Maybe you know something about a decades-old murder featured in these pages and feel ready to come forward with information. Or do you have an inkling about one of the recent cases? You might think your information is insignificant, but the police ask you to let them be the judge. Come forward anonymously if you wish and remember, sometimes it only takes one piece of the puzzle to crack a case!

In *Unsolved Australia: Lost Boys, Gone Girls*, you will hear from people missing a son, daughter, former lover, brother, sister or friend. No matter how much time has passed, they all remain desperate for answers and want us to remember their loved ones the way they really were, not as mere statistics.

Throughout the writing of this book, I have been privileged to interview more of Australia's most extraordinary detectives – the kind who never give up. None of them seeks the limelight yet each knows the media can help solve crime. When the first *Unsolved Australia* went to print, case information was circulated in newspapers, magazines, on television, radio and online, with one extract attracting two thousand clicks per minute at one point! As you are about to read, the media, when used properly, can be a powerful investigative tool. In the world of crime there are many wonderful journalists who use their work for good every day. Some of them are featured in this book.

On that note, I have included half a dozen profiles of leading professionals in the crime solution space, including a top investigative journalist, a podcast phenomenon, a forensic anthropologist/criminologist, two former missing persons investigators – one who is now a private investigator, and the other a keynote speaker and PTSD survivor – and a famous forensic psychologist. Conducting these interviews was very inspiring, and I'm sure you'll enjoy reading them.

Right now, however, it's time for *Unsolved Australia: Lost Boys, Gone Girls* to take you deep into some of this country's most mysterious unsolved crimes and missing persons cases. Meet the families, follow the twists and turns, consider the clues and, if you can, help our humble heroes crack these frustrating cases once and for all.

Justine

AN OUTBACK WHODUNNIT

THE BAFFLING DISAPPEARANCE OF **PADDY MORIARTY**

MISSING

NORTHERN TERRITORY 2018

WHAT HAPPENED TO PADDY?

Patrick (Paddy) Moriarty was last sighted at dusk on **16 December 2017** when he left the **Larrimah Hotel** on his red quad bike with his dog 'Kellie'.

Paddy is 70 years of age, approximately **178cm tall with black and grey hair**. He was last seen wearing a **singlet, dark shorts, silver watch and black thongs.**

NT Police are investigating the circumstances surrounding his disappearance.

Kellie is a red and brown female kelpie about 12 months old.

If you have information regarding the whereabouts of this missing person, please contact Crime Stoppers on

1800 333 000

www.nt.crimestoppers.com.au

CRIME STOPPERS 1800 333 000

FOLLOW YOUR INSTINCTS

Missing man and his dog: Paddy Moriarty and Kellie

Photo courtesy Northern Territory Police

'He was a personality that just stood out . . . He had a charisma about him.'
Barry Sharpe, Paddy's friend

Had the suspected murder of Paddy Moriarty taken place in a more genteel location – the drawing room of an Edwardian mansion or aboard a trans-continental train – you'd be forgiven for thinking it was a mystery torn straight from the pages of an Agatha Christie novel.

For the tale of Paddy's disappearance has all the ingredients of a classic whodunnit – an out-of-character disappearance, a detective consumed by the case, colourful local characters, and long-held rivalries.

It is set, however, in a tiny outback village that is home to little more than a pub, a pie shop and a tip.

And all those places figure in this tragic story which, unlike an Agatha Christie novel, is true.

Paddy Moriarty's strange disappearance from the tiny town of Larrimah, five hundred kilometres south of Darwin, has had the whole country talking. It has featured in national news and current affairs segments, newspapers, and even the medium du jour – a podcast.

'He was a terrific bloke, one of the best blokes living in this town, bar none,' says Barry Sharpe, the former owner of the gloriously quirky bush pub the Larrimah Pink Panther Hotel, which has – no surprise here – a giant Pink Panther out the front. The pub is also home to the Big Stubby and has a zoo full

Larrimah: tiny town, big news
Photo courtesy Northern Territory Police

of rescued wildlife – including a three-and-a-half-metre saltwater croc called Sneaky Sam.

Paddy Moriarty worked for Barry, but they were also best mates. 'I've known him a long time, since before he came to Larrimah,' says Barry, who met Paddy years earlier in Daly Waters, another roadside community an hour or so south of Larrimah.

In his late teens Paddy emigrated to Australia from Ireland with nothing more than a few bob in his pocket, a sense of adventure and a cheeky grin. It was 1966 and he could not have found a place less like the gentle green hills surrounding his hometown of Limerick than the remote, hot, dusty and dangerous Northern Territory outback. But in this new land he could create the kind of life he wanted, far from the crushing poverty of his childhood. There was plenty of work in the Top End for someone who wasn't afraid to get their hands dirty, and Paddy became a sought-after stock worker, known as a 'ringer' in the Northern Territory.

Paddy lived by himself but was never short of company. In the decade he spent in Larrimah, which has a population of twelve, people gravitated towards the cheerful Irishman. Aside from the locals, Larrimah attracted a steady influx of tourists and truck drivers along the Stuart Highway, and if Paddy liked you, he was always up for a bit of banter and a laugh.

There was much about life in Larrimah that suited Paddy, who was a stickler for routine. Every morning he put his red kelpie cross, Kellie, on the back of his shiny red quad bike and drove to the pub where he cleaned the toilets and did odd jobs. When the clock struck midday he downed tools, put his debit card on the bar and withdrew twenty dollars. He then used his card to buy four cans of XXXX Gold beer. Once he'd drunk them he'd use the cash he'd already withdrawn to buy four more. It was a funny system, but it was Paddy's way.

With eight beers under his belt, Paddy – who bore more than a passing resemblance to the late country singer Smoky Dawson – would turn to his dog and say, 'All right, it's time to go!' Kellie would then jump on the back of Paddy's bike and they'd ride the two hundred metres home and settle in for the night. He'd had one-year-old Kellie for a couple of months; prior to that a border collie named Rover had been his faithful companion for sixteen years.

One day, when Paddy failed to turn up at the pub, his mate Barry knew something was up. Paddy was not at home either, and nor was Kellie, whose lead was inside the house. Knowing better than anyone that Paddy was a creature of habit and would not go anywhere without telling him, Barry reported him missing at four o'clock in the afternoon on Tuesday, 19 December 2017.

As his fears mounted, Barry called the police twice more and asked them to send the sergeant from the nearest police station in Mataranka to investigate, which they did. It took Sergeant Tom Chalk about an hour to drive to Larrimah and when he arrived locals were searching the bushland for their neighbour. A search and rescue team, police tactical response officers and emergency services volunteers joined in. The hope was that Paddy and Kellie might still be found alive. Even as the mercury soared and hope started to fade, the searchers did not stop scouring the bush on foot, on motorbikes and from the air.

Local police also contacted the Missing Persons Unit in Darwin, and officers there conducted proof of life checks of Paddy's bank accounts, phone and Medicare records. They found that Paddy had not used any of his accounts and there was no evidence he had travelled anywhere either. On paper, his life seemed to have come to a standstill. When the sun went down on Saturday, 23 December, police reluctantly called off the search. Paddy had a heart condition and was on medication at the time of his disappearance and could not have survived any longer in the elements. His friends were devastated.

The investigation, however, was far from over, and was promptly handed to the Northern Territory Major Crime Squad. Paddy Moriarty's disappearance had been deemed suspicious.

Detective Sergeant Matt Allen was in a plane on the tarmac at Darwin Airport when he got the call to come back to work. He'd just returned from the Gold Coast where he'd celebrated his fortieth birthday, and even though he still had remaining leave, he set off straightaway for Larrimah with four other investigators. It was a five-hour drive along the Stuart Highway, scrubby and lumped on either side with termite mounds.

Matt was concerned that by the time he heard about Paddy's disappearance, the 'golden hour' of police investigation – the short window of time in which leads are hot and a case might be solved quickly – had come and gone. Days had passed, and if Paddy had met with foul play there had been plenty of time to cover it up. 'We were a week behind the game,' Matt says. 'Anything can happen in that time.'

By the time Matt and his team arrived on Saturday, 23 December, detectives from Katherine, around two hours' drive from Larrimah, had been canvassing the locals, asking where they'd been at the time of Paddy's disappearance. If anyone was wondering how the police were treating Paddy's disappearance, it was clear they now feared it was murder. But it was not going to be an easy investigation and the remoteness of the location was just one of the challenges. 'There was no mobile phone coverage and no CCTV,' Matt says. 'So it was completely old school policing without technology.'

On their first night in Larrimah, the Major Crime Squad detectives bunkered down at the visiting officers' quarters and a motel in Mataranka, ready to kickstart their own investigation after breakfast. 'On Sunday we started early and got statements from everybody, probably in a bit more detail,' Matt says. He learned that some of the locals believed Paddy had been 'done in' and some suspected their neighbours.

The following day – which was Christmas Eve – a forensics team flew from Darwin to conduct a thorough examination of Paddy's house, his Toyota Hilux and his yard. They found nothing to suggest Paddy had intended to go anywhere. 'There was no sign of a disturbance in his home,' Matt says. 'He had food in the dog bowl. He had his reading glasses on the table and the bushie hat and peak hats he always wore were in the house, as well as his money and cards.'

So Paddy's disappearance had apparently not been motivated by robbery. Had he gone away with a woman, perhaps? 'Paddy had no wife or girlfriend and no kids that we know of,' Matt says. 'There were rumours that he may have had kids with someone but investigations were unable to confirm this. We did checks with Births, Deaths and Marriages. No one's come forward in any capacity to say he's their father.'

On Christmas Day the detectives reviewed the information that had been gathered so far and took statements from Larrimah locals at Mataranka Police Station. When Matt asked one of the locals to sign and date a document, the man asked Matt for the date. 'It's bloody Christmas, mate!' Matt replied, thinking how easy it was to lose track of time in a place like this, where every searingly hot day blends into the last. Not only that, but with Paddy missing, who could feel festive? It was only when the family of the officer in charge shared some Christmas ham that the locals' spirits lifted, if only for five minutes.

★

Three days later, on Thursday, 28 December, the police launched a second, more refined search. Sadly, this time they were looking for the remains of Paddy and his dog. The searchers worked shoulder to shoulder, inch by inch. 'We were also looking for thongs, clothing, a watch, anything,' Matt says. 'We wanted to find anything that was foreign to the area. Nothing of interest to us turned up.'

Mounted police looking for Paddy and his dog
Photo courtesy Northern Territory Police

The search lasted three long days in the stifling heat and humidity. 'We covered eighty-five square kilometres,' Matt says. 'Again, there were motorbikes, a helicopter, foot and vehicle searches.' Mounted police joined in on later searches too. Matt himself went up in the chopper to have a good look at the terrain. 'It was featureless,' he says. The intense rains of the wet season hadn't yet begun so the ground below was easy to see, free from the vegetation that would overgrow the area in the following months. 'Back then the visibility was really good.'

Yet there was no sign of Paddy or his dog.

On Thursday, 4 January, the police focused on the local tip because Paddy used to walk his dog to that area down a little bush track. As well as being a central part of the town, the tip was the closest Larrimah landmark to Paddy's house, about one kilometre away. Even though no one had suggested anything of value might be found at the tip, Matt says, 'It would have been completely remiss of us not to search there.' A local business donated the use of its excavator and locals helped sift through the mounds of stinking refuse. 'We basically tipped the tip out but we didn't find anything of relevance,' Matt adds. Police also searched a dam about a kilometre west of Larrimah. 'Again, we didn't have any information that items of interest would be located [at the dam]; it was a process of elimination.'

Matt had to consider all the non-suspicious explanations for Paddy's disappearance too. 'Had the dog been hit by a car? Had Paddy been hit by a car?' he asked himself. But there was no evidence of a road accident and no one reported having seen anything unusual. 'Had he wandered off looking for the dog and tripped over? Had he had a heart attack? Had pigs gotten to him?' Even if Paddy and Kellie had been ravaged by wild pigs, Matt believes they would at least have found some clothing or a thong. 'We can't say for sure but we're confident if he was there we would have found him.'

If Paddy and Kellie could not be found *above* ground, perhaps they had slipped below. The investigators did not find any mineshafts in the area, but there were rumours of sinkholes and claims that indigenous people avoided the area for that reason. 'Sinkholes of various sizes were located in certain areas, but they were not that prevalent,' Matt says. 'There were some in which you could sprain your ankle and some where you could fall down.' But in the sinkholes they found, there was no sign of Paddy.

There were also unusual places left over from when Larrimah was home to a World War Two army staging camp, which the police also searched. 'There were forty-four-gallon drums everywhere and some concrete pads which were foundations for a bore or a military structure,' Matt says. But Paddy and Kellie were found neither in nor under them. If their bodies had been hidden, it was somewhere the police had not yet looked.

Police believe one of the strongest indicators that someone else was involved in Paddy's disappearance is that it was unlikely he planned to go out on the night he went missing. 'According to locals, no one had ever seen him walking his dog at night,' Matt says. 'And after eight to ten beers you're going to want to go home, put your feet up and not walk your dog.'

So did someone go to Paddy's house that night and ask, lure, or force him out? Possibly.

Matt's theory that Paddy had planned to stay home was further strengthened by something that had happened earlier at the pub. A tourist, drawn to Kellie and her wagging tail, had engaged in a friendly conversation with Paddy. The tourist, who'd travelled from Katherine, had some scraps left over from a cooked chicken they'd bought in Woolworths. 'They gave the scraps to Paddy for his dog at dusk when he was leaving the pub,' Matt says. 'That's really relevant because we found the cooked chook in its wrapper in the microwave with the date of 16 December on it.' It told Matt that whatever happened to Paddy took place that night. No Territorian in their right mind would leave chicken out of the fridge for very long as it would turn in the heat, so it looked like Paddy was about to warm it up. 'I just can't tell you what happened after that,' Matt says.

So if Paddy met with foul play, who was responsible? And why would anyone want to harm him? It might come as a surprise to learn that such a jovial, knockabout character could have rubbed someone up the wrong way, but sometimes he did. 'He spoke his mind,' Matt says. 'Over the years tourists have pulled up and parked out the front of his home and if he didn't like where they'd parked he'd let them know.'

The chicken tells the story: Police believe this cooked chook is a clue to Paddy's disappearance
Photo courtesy Northern Territory Police

Paddy's outspokenness didn't end there. 'If he didn't like you, he'd let you know, before or after a few beers.'

Among the locals who Paddy did not like was Fran Hodgetts, the septuagenarian owner of a pie and scone shop called Fran's Homemade Devonshire Tea House across the road from Paddy's place. Fran is well known on the tourist trail for her homemade buffalo and camel pies. Paddy, however, had made no secret of the fact that he didn't care for Fran's pies and had even said so in an ABC television interview seven years prior to his disappearance. 'They had an ongoing feud to the point where Paddy allegedly affected Fran's business,' Matt says. 'It wasn't that they didn't like each other; they hated each other.'

Adding fuel to the fire, Barry's pub had started selling pies and scones. It was all fair trade according to both Barry and Paddy, but Fran did not see it that way, particularly when Paddy erected a sign outside his house which promoted the 'best pies in town' over at the Pink Panther. Yet while Fran is the first to admit to the animosity between her and Paddy, she has consistently maintained that she had nothing to do with his disappearance. 'I don't know anything,' she says. 'I don't know what happened to him. I didn't even know he was missing 'til the 21st [of December].'

Theirs had been a uniquely outback feud. 'On the 12th of December [2016],' Fran alleges, 'he threw a kangaroo under my bedroom window.' She says it wasn't the first time. 'In 2017 he threw two dead kangaroos under my shop window. He didn't like me but I didn't like him either. But I didn't do nothing to him.'

Matt has investigated the disagreements and says while there are persons of interest in and outside Larrimah, he can't discuss who they are or why they are persons of interest. Yes, Fran has been 'looked at', but so has everyone else in Paddy's life. That's just the way homicide investigations work. 'Just because you're having a feud doesn't mean you're going to kill someone,' Matt says. If it did, Larrimah would be a ghost town because there have been feuds aplenty. Paddy even remarked on how the locals didn't get on in his 2011 ABC interview. Over the years, rival progress associations have clashed, neighbours have yelled abuse at each other and pet peacocks have been fed to Sneaky Sam. But Paddy has not ended up in the croc's jaws, as reporters have speculated. 'If a croc has an opportunity to eat an adult, it's unlikely to swallow him up in one fell swoop,' Matt says. 'He'll likely store some away for a later time.' Matt adds that the detectives regularly inspected Sneaky Sam's cage 'from the outside', but Paddy wasn't there.

Fran has found the whole ordeal surrounding the investigation into Paddy's death so stressful that she believes it has contributed to her recent diagnosis of breast cancer. And by pure coincidence, Paddy's disappearance is not the only such case to have taken place in her orbit. She was one of the last people to see missing New Zealander Jamie Herdman, who disappeared from Daly Waters in 2006 after stopping in Larrimah on the way. Fran reported the sighting to police and cannot believe her life has been touched by another missing persons investigation.

Fran – who has lived in Larrimah for forty-five years – urges us not to listen to the rumours surrounding Paddy's disappearance. She has her own theories about what happened to him but does not believe he was murdered. She thinks it is more likely Paddy met with misadventure in the bush; perhaps he tried to stop his dog chasing a kangaroo. 'I reckon he's got lost and frightened and had a heart attack. I don't believe anyone's done anything to him,' she says. 'The pigs have him now.'

Whatever happened to Paddy Moriarty and Kellie, his friends remain in limbo. They are grieving, but without a body they cannot properly farewell the spirited, straight-talking Irishman.

These days it is hard for Barry Sharpe – who has sold the pub – to talk much about his old mate. He is content to say a few words but the pain of his loss is still overwhelming. Paddy might have agitated Fran, but to friends like Barry he was the heart and soul of the town – a good bloke who brought joy and laughter into people's lives. 'He was a personality that just stood out,' Barry says. 'He had a charisma about him.'

Barry's best hope of finding out what happened to his friend is Matt Allen, who sometimes makes the long trek to and from Larrimah on the promise of fresh information. Matt says the dog adds 'another dimension' to the investigation and might be the key to solving it. 'If you're going to cause harm to a person, that's horrific, but if you're going to harm an animal, that plays on the heart too,' he says. Matt wonders if Kellie was dropped off at a dog shelter and he's calling on animal lovers who read this book to spread the word. 'Not just in the Northern Territory but across the country. We need the support of the public to put the word out.'

Alternatively, perhaps someone driving along the Stuart Highway at the time of Paddy's disappearance could help. 'We need to capture cars with cameras or tourists who stopped and took happy snaps on the 16th of December 2017, trucks with dash cams and tourists on Greyhound buses,' Matt says. If anyone at all saw Paddy and his kelpie cross in town that day, Matt wants to hear from them. 'People will know if they saw him,' Matt says. 'They'd think, *I remember Paddy*!'

The disappearance of the unforgettable Paddy Moriarty is such a mystery that Matt also welcomes information that may seem inconsequential so he can investigate it. 'We want to hear from anyone and everyone, it doesn't matter what rumour or innuendo it is, come and talk to us,' he says. 'I'm very open for anyone to give me ideas, including local residents with suggestions of where to look in the remote country that surrounds Larrimah.' Perhaps the killer might even confide in someone. 'It's very hard to keep a secret, so if anyone out there hears what happened to Paddy and Kellie from someone, please give us a ring.'

Until Matt finds the answers, he'll keep clocking up the kilometres on the Stuart Highway, the case constantly ticking over in

Consumed: officer in charge, Detective Sergeant Matt Allen
Photo courtesy Northern Territory Police

his mind. 'I haven't stopped thinking about it,' he says. 'There're a couple of detectives working full-time on it and we communicate regularly after hours. It's such an intriguing matter that it's completely consumed me.'

Such is the effect of an unsolved mystery – it frustrates those seeking answers as well as those left behind.

Paddy Moriarty might have divided opinion in Larrimah, but no one would say they wanted it to end in his death. So spare him a thought if you're passing through. Stop at the Pink Panther for a refreshing cold beer then head over to Fran's Homemade Devonshire Tea House for her famous cakes and scones, or try her new specialty, camel and buffalo sausages in freshly baked bread rolls. Keep Larrimah – and the fond memories of Paddy Moriarty – alive.

'He's just so missed,' Barry says. 'Now we don't have Paddy to cheer us up.'

MISSING IN MITTA VALLEY

NARELLE FRASER'S SEARCH FOR **LORRAINE CARTER**

Victim of foul play: Lorraine Carter

Photo courtesy Allen and June Yardley

'It was a typical domestic violence situation and there were two people with mental health issues. It was just the road to nowhere.'

Narelle Fraser, former detective, Victoria Police Homicide Squad Missing Persons Unit

Start a meaningful conversation with an ex-cop and you'll soon discover there's an unsolved case that haunts them all. For Narelle Fraser, it's the sudden disappearance of Lorraine Carter, a vulnerable, intellectually delayed woman who disappeared from a crumbling Victorian farmhouse in 2002.

Narelle believes Lorraine was murdered, but the case never went to trial and Lorraine's body was never found.

The crusading former detective hopes that someone reading this book will not only have crucial information about Lorraine's disappearance, but that they will finally lead police to her body.

In April 2002, Melbourne millionaires Paul King and his wife Margaret Wales-King went missing in an intriguing case the media dubbed the 'Society Murders'. It was the start of a period of extreme busy-ness for the Victoria Police Homicide Squad Missing Persons Unit. 'I hadn't been there very long and there were a whole lot of big jobs almost one after the other,' Narelle says. 'It was pretty full-on.' Investigators in the Missing Persons Unit took it in turns to lead the surfeit of troubling cases, and the disappearance of Lorraine Carter was handed to the squad's newest recruit, Detective Senior Constable Narelle Fraser. It would not be as high profile as the 'Society Murders', but Narelle knew it was no less important.

The Homicide Squad's analyst, who reviewed all the missing persons reports that filtered in overnight, had thought Lorraine's disappearance looked suspicious, as did the boss. The moment the report landed on Narelle's desk, she felt the investigation's success or failure was up to her. 'When it's your job, you just step up a little because you want to try to find this person,' she says. 'I'm not saying you don't work as hard on other jobs but you're the one who takes the reins. You take control.'

Lorraine Carter was born in 1958. 'She had a lot of complications when she was born,' Narelle says. 'She had a harelip, a cleft palate, hearing problems and intellectual difficulties. You could tell by looking at Lorraine that she was vulnerable.'

The forty-three-year-old was reportedly last seen in the Mitta Valley in northern Victoria on Monday, 15 July 2002, and local detectives had kickstarted the investigation. They did everything they could but needed someone with more resources and expertise to investigate Lorraine's disappearance further. Enter the Homicide Squad Missing Persons Unit and Narelle Fraser.

The early police checks had revealed Lorraine did not have a driver's licence, that there was nothing to suggest she'd gone anywhere on public transport, and she hadn't arranged for a passport to go overseas. What heightened the possibility of foul play was that Lorraine had been in frequent contact with the counselling and respite services of the Department of Human Services. When Narelle and her team found this out, they knew it was a bad omen.

As Narelle discovered, even though Lorraine lived with her husband, Murray Carter, it was her father who had reported her missing. 'We thought that was a bit unusual,' she says. 'The husband had told the local detectives the last time he'd seen her was on 15 July 2002. He said she'd walked out in the morning.' Narelle knew there would be more to the story, but rather than speak to Lorraine's husband straightaway, she first sought background information from Lorraine's parents, Allen and June Yardley.

Before the rot set in: Lorraine at Phillip Island when she was single
Photo courtesy Allen and June Yardley

Narelle learned that Allen had made the missing persons report on Wednesday, 17 July at his local police station, Knox, in Melbourne's east. 'He was very concerned about a phone call he got from Murray the day before saying, "Have you heard from Lorraine?" The hackles had gone up on Allen's and his wife June's necks and they thought something was wrong.' And there was good reason for that. 'Lorraine had called them many times to say, "He's belted me", "I'm frightened" or "He tried to kill me".' Lorraine's parents tried calling her mobile phone but there was no answer. Murray said that when Lorraine left the house she had not taken the mobile phone with her.

Narelle and a fellow detective spent around three hours at Allen and June Yardley's house, where they noticed countless framed photos of Lorraine. 'They absolutely adored her,' Narelle says. The Yardleys had always been close to their daughter and had tried to protect her from a world which can be cruel to those who are different. 'She went to a special school and was bullied and teased,' Narelle says. 'She was assessed as being a child who'd never attain an intellectual level above that of a ten-year-old.' But with the love and support of her parents, Lorraine achieved much more than that, and even though she relied on a disability pension she proudly held part-time jobs.

The Yardleys had much more to tell the police. Before Lorraine met her husband she'd lived at home with her parents, who made sure her needs were met. It was a big decision for them to take an overseas holiday one year, and even then they made sure carers popped in to give Lorraine the extra help she needed. When the carers turned up, Lorraine would often be feeding or grooming her beloved lap dog. 'That little dog, Chloe, was the love of her life,' Narelle says. Yet when Lorraine went missing, she didn't take the dog with her. 'Her parents knew that was something she would never do.'

During her conversation with Allen and June, Narelle also learned that Lorraine had always been unlucky in love. 'But I'll give you the tip, the minute she met Murray, she became unluckier,' Narelle says. 'Because of her vulnerability she was an easy target for someone who wanted to manipulate somebody.'

In 1998, June and Allen had bought a caravan on Phillip Island, and because Lorraine loved it so much the family-of-three frequently took trips there. It was a community in which Lorraine enjoyed a heightened level of independence and where the shopkeepers always treated her with kindness. Looking back, Narelle believes that buying the caravan was 'the worst thing the family ever did' because Murray also lived in the caravan park and that's where Lorraine met him.

Around 2000, Lorraine and Murray formed an intense romantic relationship. 'It was like any other relationship in the beginning; you can't get enough of each other,' Narelle says. 'It was really full-on. She was in love.'

However, as time went by, the dynamic between Lorraine and Murray began to shift. 'Poor old Lorraine,' Narelle says. 'When she met Murray she used to ring her mum and dad two or three times a day. They were so close. But when Murray came on the scene, hello, hello, things changed and contacting them became intermittent.'

When Narelle inquired about Murray's past she discovered he had form. 'He'd been in jail for five years, which is quite a long time,' she says. 'He'd done a robbery with violence where he'd hit a shop owner over the head with a spanner. He'd also done car thefts.'

Before he met Lorraine, Murray had been married for around thirty-five years. 'They separated in the late nineties because he'd had a brain aneurysm and it changed his personality,' Narelle says. 'He had a streak of violence and was a bit of a player and had apparently had a couple of affairs.' In other words, Narelle says, he wasn't a 'top bloke' to begin with, but his wife – with whom Murray had two daughters – supported him for as long as she could after the aneurysm led to mental health issues. Life was far from rosy and Murray apparently ostracised his wife from her family. 'She described him as very controlling, of finances in particular, and she had to almost beg for money when she needed it.

'It got to the point where the wife and daughters couldn't deal with it anymore,' Narelle says. 'He'd fly off the handle and become embarrassing and would yell and was sort of uncontrollable and became abusive.' Not surprisingly, after starting a relationship with Lorraine, history repeated itself. 'Looking back, you can see the same habits,' says Narelle. 'He was very controlling of her and ostracised her from her family, and she no longer saw her friends as much. It was as though she was a piece of property that could be manipulated.'

And yet, convinced that Murray was in love with her, in 2001 Lorraine moved with him to Cape Patterson, a small seaside town near Wonthaggi, where the relationship went further downhill. 'Things started to become more public and turn very sour and very violent very quickly,' Narelle says. 'The neighbours reported hearing loud arguing, yelling and screaming, and would see the police turn up a lot. People were noticing injuries to her, bruising. Her mum and dad would visit and they were horrified at the deterioration in her physical and mental health.'

Bur rather than leave Murray, Lorraine decided to marry him, and there was nothing her parents could do about it because she

The biggest mistake of her life: the day Lorraine got married
Photo courtesy Allen and June Yardley

was an adult. 'They were telling her, "We think you're making a mistake,"' Narelle says. 'But she wanted it to work and she wanted to be married. He began to control her so much that he arranged the whole wedding, and even her dress. Fancy organising her dress!'

As if the situation were not volatile enough, it got worse. 'Apparently, straight after the wedding Murray's violence escalated,' Narelle says, shuddering when she thinks about how frightened Lorraine must have been. 'It's a world I couldn't relate to. I've only ever got love and support from my husband.' Narelle then learned that six weeks after the wedding Lorraine made a distressing phone call about Murray to her mum. 'She told her he'd been hitting her with a chair. She was thinking about doing herself in and had spoken to her mum about suicidal thoughts. You want your daughter to experience lovely married life, but it was a disaster.'

Narelle pauses, as if to gain strength, as she recounts the heartbreaking story. 'The neighbours rescued her on a number of occasions and rang her parents,' she says. 'She'd received a hell of a hiding one time, there were scratches and bruises on her face. It was swollen. Once she said she'd been thrown across a room and thrown against a cupboard. The neighbours saw that skin had been ripped. There was raw skin with bruising.'

Lorraine was petite and couldn't have defended herself if she'd tried. Her husband, on the other hand, was strong and rotund.

'He was about five foot nine or five foot ten but a big bloke with a pot belly.'

The police tried to help but it must have been frustrating. 'The police would go around and do what they had to do but she would always go back to him,' Narelle says. 'She'd say, "This is what I deserve. I brought this all on myself."' Narelle cannot hide her disgust at the kinds of men who treat women like this. 'These animals talk to their partners in this way so they believe it,' she says.

There was other professional intervention, too. 'She went to CASA (Victorian Centre Against Sexual Assault) because he was abusing her sexually,' Narelle reveals. 'You name it, Lorraine experienced it.'

Narelle says Murray also tried to convince Lorraine to commit a crime in relation to an alleged offence against her when she was younger. 'Apparently she told one counsellor that he was pressuring her to apply for victims of crime compensation. She couldn't understand the form so he filled it out. She told the counsellor she didn't want the money but he did.' She also told a counsellor he was so controlling of her finances that she never saw her pension or had money in her purse. 'Honestly, when I talk about it, it makes me angry,' Narelle fumes.

In April 2002, Lorraine and Murray moved again, this time to Eskdale in the remote Mitta Valley where Murray's family owned a run-down farmhouse. There was no electricity or gas, but it was rent-free. 'The farmhouse was in the middle of nowhere, about five hundred metres from the road and about five kilometres to the closest town,' says Narelle. 'From a domestic violence point of view, what a perfect place if you want to belt your wife senseless.'

Once again, Allen and June received numerous distressing calls from their daughter. 'She was in fear,' Narelle says. Lorraine kept her mobile phone close in the knowledge that her parents were only a phone call away. 'Imagine how they felt when they heard what was happening to their only child,' says Narelle. 'She said one time he had thrown her to the floor and one time she'd wet herself while he was trying to choke her.'

On Tuesday, 9 July 2002, June called her daughter to tell her about the death of a family friend. 'Lorraine was very upset and didn't have enough money for a card,' Narelle says. 'She asked her mum to buy one on her behalf. That was the last time June ever spoke to her.'

One week later, on Tuesday, 16 July, Murray called Lorraine's parents to ask if they'd seen or heard from her, telling them she'd walked out of the house the previous day. 'He said they'd had an argument and Lorraine threw coffee over him and said, "I don't need you pricks anymore," whatever that meant,' says Narelle. Murray also told Lorraine's parents she'd left her medication behind but had taken a calico bag which June had made for her, along with one hundred and fifty dollars. Narelle finds that unlikely given that the week before Lorraine hadn't even had enough money for a card. Apparently Lorraine had also left her mobile phone at home, which Narelle says was entirely out of character because, 'It was her security blanket and she never went anywhere without it.'

From four hundred helpless kilometres away, Allen immediately called the police in Tallangatta, the closest police station to Lorraine's house. He asked them to go over and speak with Murray to check if everything was okay. Allen said he was worried about Lorraine and told the police about the nerve-racking conversation he'd just had. 'The police spoke to Murray and he told the same story but said this time that she had one hundred and ninety dollars in her purse,' Narelle says.

Two days later, on Thursday, 18 July, Murray made another suspicious move. 'He attended Centrelink and requested a single person's pension, telling Centrelink his wife's left him,' Narelle says, adding, 'You get more money as a single than a couple. And he withdrew her pension.'

Murray told the police he'd gone to the local store to ask the shopkeepers if they'd seen Lorraine, but they said he'd done no such thing. He did not contact Lorraine's friends to tell them she was missing, either. When Narelle met Lorraine's friends, she found them to be 'beautiful, loving people' who cared deeply about Lorraine. They would have wanted to have known she was missing.

But it was the Yardleys Narelle felt most sorry for as they told her the terrible events surrounding their daughter's disappearance. 'To have your daughter taken away from you by an animal who's manipulating and controlling, it doesn't get much sadder,' Narelle says. 'I felt so sorry for Allen and June. I wanted to find Lorraine and put them at peace.'

But under what circumstances might Narelle have found her? 'I was thinking I didn't like the chances of finding her alive,' she says. 'It was a typical domestic violence situation and there were two people with mental health issues. It was just the road to nowhere. I believe on that day we all thought the same thing, but we didn't say it.'

Cherished photo: this glamour shot of Lorraine, aged forty, was a gift from her mum June. Lorraine had cared for June during a short illness so June purchased a photo session as a thank you.
Photo courtesy Allen and June Yardley

As Narelle's team carried out other inquiries, she and a colleague went to see Murray at home. 'It was an isolated farmhouse, a dump of a place. It gave me the creeps,' Narelle says. 'It was cold, it was dilapidated, it was very run-down. It was a hole. He had her just where he wanted her.' The Homicide Squad Missing Persons Unit executed a warrant to search the house while Narelle focused her attentions on Murray. 'I couldn't stand him from the moment I met him,' she says, recalling how she poked a finger at his chest and said what was on her mind. 'I'm gonna get you, you prick, if it's the last thing I do.'

Narelle knows her words flew in the face of her training, but she is unrepentant. 'I said it because of what he'd done to Lorraine – which had all been recorded and was indisputable – and what he'd done to her family,' she says. Narelle believes that with no evidence to suggest Lorraine was alive after 15 July 2002, she was probably killed on that day.

While searching the property, the police found Lorraine's calico bag in a wardrobe. She had not taken it with her after all. 'We spent a good month looking in every nook and cranny, going down every rabbit burrow we could to find any evidence she was alive, but there was none,' says Narelle. 'We even checked the contents of the vacuum cleaner. We thought we might find hair, we might find jewellery – something to indicate if he'd tried to clean a crime scene, but we didn't find anything.'

On the subject of Lorraine's jewellery, the investigators later discovered that on Wednesday, 4 September, Murray had pawned some of it. 'He told the salesperson his wife had left him,' says Narelle, confirming her hunch that the motive for Lorraine's disappearance was money. She recalls Murray's interest in obtaining victims of crime compensation and the fact that he took Lorraine's pension. 'What he spent it on, I'll never know. It was a terrible place to live in.'

As the hunt for clues continued, search and rescue officers looked in the river and explored the property and surrounding bushland from a chopper. 'We were hoping her body might be somewhere or that we'd find some clothing, but we found nothing,' Narelle says. Aware that Murray had grown up in the area, she figures he knew it intimately. 'Looking back, he could have gone up into the hills to some secluded little place and disposed of her. I believe she's buried somewhere on Mitta Mountain.'

Yet Murray consistently maintained his innocence. 'We interviewed Murray and he said he didn't do it,' Narelle says. 'We had no evidence to prove he did – but we had no evidence to prove he didn't, either.' Without evidence – and with fresh cases demanding their attention – Narelle and her team headed back to St Kilda Road. Narelle found returning to headquarters without having located Lorraine's body or evidence that Murray had killed her 'hard to accept'.

The months went by and then, in July 2003, a year after Lorraine had gone missing, Narelle received unexpected news. 'We were notified that Murray had suicided,' she says. When Narelle read Murray's suicide note, in which he 'blamed police for sending him to his grave and said he didn't kill Lorraine' she had to admit to 'a smidgen of doubt' that Murray was culpable. As an investigator, she knew to keep an open mind. Then Narelle realised there was probably another reason why he hadn't wanted to confess. 'I suppose it was his way of being in charge and controlling until the very end.'

When cops are described as 'dogged' it means they are the kinds of police who go the extra mile to crack a case. They are the investigators who spend sleepless nights wondering, *Is there something I missed?* They are the cops who struggle to accept it when they cannot find the answers. Narelle Fraser was one of these cops. On top of that, she was on the verge of her own personal nightmare – a diagnosis of post-traumatic stress disorder (PTSD) – from all the unspeakable crimes she'd investigated over the years. Policing is not for the faint-hearted and even the toughest investigators – such as those who dare to point their finger at a suspect's chest – can be broken too.

What made this case especially challenging was that Narelle had grown fond of Lorraine's parents. She felt they regarded her as a second daughter, especially as there had been only six months age difference between herself and Lorraine. 'I felt they adored me, but I adored them and I felt so responsible that I hadn't found Lorraine,' she says. It was that sense of failed responsibility that Narelle now knows is a common warning sign of PTSD in police and other people who suffer from the disorder. 'You feel responsible for people's happiness or sadness. I felt that it was my fault I couldn't give them the happiness they deserved.'

Every week, when Allen called for an update, Narelle felt as though she was disappointing him. 'He was so lovely,' Narelle says. 'He'd say, "Hello love, have you had any luck today?" I'd say, "No, sorry, Allen," and I'd feel so guilty every time.'

At a memorial service for Lorraine, Narelle could no longer disguise her pain. She sat at the back of the church during the service in which Allen delivered a moving eulogy. 'He said how blessed they were to have had such a lovely daughter,' Narelle says, adding that minutes into the ceremony she broke down. 'The tears started and I couldn't stop crying. It was very embarrassing. It's something that, as a police person, you don't want to do: cry. You had to remain professional and this was not professional. I could not control it. It was humiliating.' Yet how fortunate the Yardleys were to have had a detective on the case who felt so strongly about it, about their daughter, and about them. If that is unprofessional, it is commendable.

In 2004, the suspected death of Lorraine Carter went to an inquest before Coroner Phillip Byrne. After examining the evidence, he found it was a case of foul play, as Narelle had suspected all along. His Honour stated that 'although her body has never been found, Lorraine Joy Carter is no longer alive. I further conclude her husband Murray Carter, in spite of his protestations of innocence, was implicated (in all likelihood alone) in her death.'

Narelle felt vindicated by the coroner's findings. 'Aneurysm or not, Murray was an arrogant bully who picked on a vulnerable woman who only wanted to be loved and return that love,' she says. 'The price she paid was to be beaten to a pulp, abused and ultimately murdered because she loved and trusted him.'

Yet to this day, the precise cause of Lorraine's death remains unknown, as does the location of her body, and without those final pieces of the puzzle it will continue to gnaw at Narelle. 'There's a lot of regrets in a lot of jobs,' she says. 'To be able to put a family's mind at ease is very rewarding, so they can move on a bit, but with this job they're still wondering.'

These days, Allen and June Yardley live in a retirement village from where they call Narelle, who is no longer in the police force, for a friendly chat once a year. Approaching ninety, they would still like to find their daughter to give her the respectful burial she deserves. Perhaps her killer told someone what he had done, or perhaps one day someone will stumble upon Lorraine's remains on Mitta Mountain.

PROFILE

NARELLE FRASER

FORMER VICTORIA POLICE DETECTIVE, PTSD SURVIVOR, KEYNOTE SPEAKER

Photo courtesy James Penlidis

The Woman Who Saw Too Much

I was a counsellor at Lifeline when I was in my mid-twenties. A lot of people called Lifeline because they wanted to commit suicide. When that happened we'd ring the police and say, 'Can you go and help them?' I remember thinking, *God, what a fantastic job to be able to talk to people face to face and offer them support*. That's where I got my interest in joining the police force. My application was accepted and I started at the [Victoria] Police Academy in April 1987.

Seeing dead bodies can come as a shock. When you're at the police academy you have to go to the mortuary at the Coroners Court of Victoria on week three or four. I sort of wanted to go but I knew it would affect me. You walk in and the smell hits you. It's almost like you're on the slab yourself. ▶

We went into the room where they kept the bodies in drawers. The guy in charge said, 'If anyone's going to get upset seeing a deceased baby, don't look to your right.' I looked. I thought I'd faint or be sick and had to leave the room for a while. I was so distressed but I eventually went back in; I just didn't look at the baby again. I got over it but they are the sorts of things that get ingrained in your mind.

I graduated from the Police Academy in August 1987. I was twenty-seven. I was very excited and like, bring it on! I felt I would be a good policewoman because I was honest and fair, but the main thing was that I could help people. But nothing prepared me for my first training station, which was St Kilda.

St Kilda was another world. I'd never seen such sadness, such trauma, such cruelty. It was a real shock to the system, but I also saw there were so many opportunities to help people, especially the prostitutes. I thought, *You poor things, how did life get you to this point?*

I went to Carlton Police Station as a constable in 1992 and saw something I'll never forget. I got called out to a report of a woman acting a bit strangely at a 7-Eleven store. The proprietor of the store didn't know if the woman had stolen anything. It was about 4 am and I was working on the divisional van with a trainee. When we got there I didn't know if the woman had a mental illness or was drugged. I spoke to her gently and said we wanted to help her. I looked in her bag which contained makeup, little hairsprays and deodorant. From working in St Kilda it was clear to me that she was a prostitute. We got talking and I told her my name was Narelle and she told me her name was Julie. I said, 'How about I take you home, Julie?' She said, 'You'd take me home?' She was really surprised. I said, 'Yeah, why not?' So we drove her home. ▶

Half an hour later we got a call from someone around the corner from the 7-Eleven. When we got there someone was writhing in the gutter, screaming. The trainee went as white as a ghost. I said, 'You stay here. Get the firies and ambos!' I raced to the person in the gutter. They were so black from the fire I couldn't tell if they were male or female. I bent down and said help was on its way. The person whispered to me, 'Narelle, it's Julie.' She had strapped the miniature aerosols to her body, poured petrol over herself and set herself on fire.

When the firies came, everyone was very distressed. The firies sprayed a very fine mist of water over her. While I was leaning down, holding her hand, all her skin was coming off onto my hands and uniform.

Julie was taken off in an ambulance and the ambos told me she probably wouldn't survive. My supervising sergeant told me to go and tell her parents what had happened, and I said, 'I can't, I reek of fire and human flesh, and I've got her skin all over me.' But I had to follow the sergeant's orders. I felt bad to be at her parents' house. It was very difficult. Afterwards I remember myself and the trainee holding hands to comfort each other in the divvy van.

As the ambos had predicted, Julie died. I had trouble sleeping for a week after that. It was so traumatic. I couldn't go to a barbecue for a while because the smell brought it all back. I thought I'd better harden up if I was to survive in this job.

One of the sergeants at Carlton thought I'd suit working with sexually abused women and children at the Community Policing Squad at Broadmeadows. I realised it was my forte and I did it for five years. I'm not sure why it interested me; I wasn't abused as a child, but I was drawn to help with the upper end of suffering.

A detective's job came up at the Rape Squad and I got it. I saw an enormous amount of suffering while I was at the Rape Squad but I thought I suited the role because of my compassion and empathy. I'd listen, and victims felt they could talk to me. They showed incredible strength – to go through all that trauma and then have to tell strangers in court about their most terrible, intimate experiences. It was humiliating and embarrassing for them.

I think rape is about power. Of course it's also about sex, but rapists put women in a vulnerable position and get to do what they want, which is where the power element comes in. Men are inherently stronger, they can overpower women quite easily.

We found quite a lot of sex offenders had priors for cruelty to animals and pyromania. I'm not a psychologist but I noticed that many sex offenders go from animals and fires to women. I don't get it.

We arrested a suspect over a series of violent rapes involving teenage girls and that morning I was sick with diarrhoea. It was one of many arrests I was involved in, but looking back I realise I had anxiety. I was very stressed about the interview because I was a female in a male-dominated world, and the hope was that I could get a confession and DNA. Looking back, I now realise it was the first time it was obvious I was not managing.

After four years at the Rape Squad I joined the Homicide Squad Missing Persons Unit. I needed a break and thought that to arrest and charge someone with the worst offence against a human – murder – would be very rewarding. Of course it wasn't a break at all; quite the opposite. What was I thinking?

I'll never forget Maria Korp. We found her car in the hot February sun four days after she went missing ►

in February 2005. We could smell something emanating from the car from at least seventy to eighty metres away. The car was full of condensation but Maria was not in the front or back seat so we knew she must be in the boot. I'll never forget the smell. She was decomposing. That's what had caused the condensation.

She was in the foetal position. The sergeant said, 'I think we need to check she's dead.' I said, 'I'll go in.' I climbed into the boot. She was so vulnerable. She was so alone. She would have been petrified. I checked for signs of life and there was nothing. On a whim I decided to put my head on her chest and it moved up and down. I yelled out, 'She's alive! She's alive!' I accompanied her in the ambulance to the hospital, hoping she'd make a miracle recovery, but she died after about six months in a coma.

I don't believe what I've seen is unusual. Maybe not everyone has gone into the boot of a car where someone is decomposing but all police have seen assault and rape victims and some have dug up a body. I hope the next time people see police out having a coffee, instead of judging them and saying, 'Those bloody lazy police,' they give them a break. You don't know what kind of day they've had.

I also found the body of a woman hidden at a rubbish tip. After making the discovery I walked away and sat on a rock. I was so ashamed because I was upset and I thought that was a weakness.

I didn't start to noticeably unravel until after I left the Homicide Squad Missing Persons Unit. A couple of years later I started working in the Sexual Offences and Child Abuse Investigation Team in Bendigo. There were two jobs there that undid me. The first was a child porn job. I'd done hundreds by that stage. We executed a warrant and found 1,700 videos of child pornography. ▶

It was off the scale. I'd never seen anything like it before. We had to watch them over two days. It affected me so badly. I had reactions I'd never had before.

The next week I had to go to a committal hearing. It was May 2012. It was a rape case and I had to sit behind the victim in court. She was being hammered by the defence team and I remember thinking, *I am responsible for this.* The next I remember I was in a coffee shop, having a coffee. I didn't know how I'd got there or what I was meant to be doing. I later found out I was suffering from amnesia. I just thought I was stressed but then a doctor diagnosed me with post-traumatic stress disorder (PTSD) and sent me to a psychologist.

There had been so many warning signs but I'd ignored them. I used to shake really badly to the point where I couldn't read my own writing. I'd become socially withdrawn from my friends and family. Everywhere I went there were reminders of the terrible things I'd seen. Dogs and horses brought back shocking memories of the child porn videos. I'd see little girls with dolls and it would remind me of SIDS (Sudden Infant Death Syndrome) cases I'd been to. I'd be cooking and I'd think of the kids I'd encountered who'd been abused with kitchen utensils. I had nightmares and unbelievable anger to the point that I thought my head was going to burst. My hypervigilance was out of control too; I saw danger everywhere. It got to the point where I walked, talked, dreamed and thought everything 'police'. I couldn't escape.

The doctor and the psychologist saved my life. My doctor has a lovely personality and empathy, and my psychologist has been a rock in a lot of ways. One of the forms of therapy I've done is called EMDR, which stands for eye movement desensitisation and reprocessing. ▶

It's based around the belief that emotional trauma gets locked into the nervous system. EMDR unlocks the trauma and allows the brain to process it.

I also did an amazing PTSD course at the Austin Hospital. Up until then I hadn't really accepted the diagnosis that I was sick. The PTSD course taught me the importance of mindfulness and meditation. The other thing that is important is stability at home. My husband's a beautiful person. He and my two sisters and lovely girlfriends have all supported me. I don't think they have any idea how much they've helped.

In 2014, I left the police force. It was sad but as they say, when one door closes another one opens. I taught investigative techniques and human rights for a while then someone said, 'You tell a really good story, Narelle. Why don't you come and talk to Probus [a social group for retirees]?' It evolved from there and I became an accidental mental health advocate! I'd never thought I would talk in front of a group but now people from all kinds of groups and organisations pay money to hear me speak. I have to pinch myself. Seriously, I love it!

I call my talks 'It's Not a Crime to be Stressed'. I open each talk with something hard-hitting like, 'Imagine being in the boot of a car with a decomposing body and finding out the person is alive.' Then I say I was a member of Victoria Police for twenty-seven years and I saw a lot. But in the end I saw too much.

I tell the audience that stress is a normal human emotion. I explain that I lost my job because I ignored the signs. I'd also been worried about the stigma attached to being stressed. Then I talk about jobs I worked on like the 'Society Murders' (the 2002 murders of wealthy socialites Paul King and Margaret Wales-King). I also tell ▶

the audience funny things like how I arrested someone using my finger as a pretend gun and how I found a man in a panel van with a sheep! Yes, he was doing exactly what you're thinking.

My message is a serious one, though, and it is about looking after your mental health. Don't be ashamed of having a mental health issue because it causes an enormous amount of damage and it doesn't have to be like that. I am much better now and, if you get the right help, you can be too.

For more information or to book Narelle as a keynote speaker, go to www.narellefraser.com

THE SEARCH FOR THE SERVERS OF THE DIVINE PLAN

FRESH EYES ON THE VANISHING OF **CHANTELLE MCDOUGALL, LEELA MCDOUGALL, TONY POPIC** AND **GARY FELTON**

Missing cult members (top left to right): Chantelle McDougall, Gary Felton, Tony Popic, Leela McDougall (front)

Photo courtesy Jim and Catherine McDougall

'If it is one person who has gone missing, you ask: Are they missing, murdered or is it that they don't want to be found? But when it's four people including a little girl . . . You've got to think something might be wrong.'

Barry McIntosh, family member and former detective, Victoria Police

Spiritual gurus come in all shapes and sizes. There are those with menacing stares, some with jazzed-up hairdos and others who turn themselves out like guests at the Last Supper. Cult leader Simon Kadwill, however, resembled none of those, and would not have looked out of place in front of a giant whiteboard at a middle-management conference.

Despite his appearance of buttoned-up normality, English-born Simon Kadwill had charisma, a prerequisite for any cult leader worth his weight in joss sticks. Not that he was naturally social. He ran his cult – 'The Truth Fellowship' – from a computer in his bedroom in the remote Western Australian town of Nannup. He told his followers the end was nigh, and in the three weeks before his last confirmed contact with the outside world he neither chatted online nor ventured out in public.

It was from Nannup that Simon, his younger partner Chantelle, their six-year-old daughter Leela and their friend Tony Popic went missing in late 2007. At an inquest ten years later, the lifestyle of the self-styled spiritual leader was scrutinised as a coroner examined what part, if any, Simon's beliefs played in the group's disappearance. As you might expect, there was talk of faraway realms, suicide pacts and polygamy.

Yet despite the outlandish nature of this tale, at its heart is a group of missing people – a family, in effect – whose disappearance still needs to be explained. Here, Chantelle's salt-of-the-earth parents, Catherine and Jim McDougall, give us an insight into their daughter's life. And for the first time we hear from Catherine's brother, a distinguished former homicide detective from Victoria, who has done some investigating of his own.

The last thing Jim and Catherine McDougall would have expected was for their daughter Chantelle to join a cult. The youngest of three, Chantelle grew up playing with dogs and riding horses on a four-acre property near the dairy town of Tangambalanga in north-eastern Victoria, not far from the New South Wales border. Family life was happy, stable and supportive, and Chantelle's outgoing and entertaining personality was a source of joy in the household. 'She was a character, actually,' Catherine says. 'She was always making jokes and we loved her sense of humour.'

Not surprisingly, Chantelle was drawn to the dramatic arts. Her mum adds, 'She used to do dancing, hip hop, tap and jazz when she was sixteen or seventeen, so she'd always be flipping round the living room!'

Chantelle had hoped to study acting at university after leaving school but was not offered a place. It was disappointing, but while she considered an alternative career she went to live with her grandfather in Melbourne where she taught swimming and worked as a lifeguard. Then the future of this vibrant young woman changed in ways no one had anticipated. 'It went downhill from there because she met this Simon Kadwill,' Catherine says.

It all started in an ashram. Catherine's stepsister, who lived in Melbourne, asked Chantelle if she'd like to go on a retreat with her. Chantelle accepted out of idle curiosity but found herself mesmerised by the alternative teachings of a spiritual leader her mother had never heard of. 'She rang up and started talking to us about this "Dr Bob",' Catherine says.

After a while, Catherine feared her daughter was being drawn into a kooky New Age world. She rang a youth line in the phonebook and said, 'This is the situation, it's a bit strange.' Catherine recalls the youth line counsellor advising her that all she could do was keep the lines of communication open. Catherine took the counsellor's advice and maintained regular phone conversations with Chantelle, ever-mindful not to push her away. 'I didn't knock what she said but I questioned it. It all sounded a bit weird to me.'

It was around this time that Chantelle, accompanied by her boyfriend, also called Simon, first encountered Simon Kadwill, another New Age guru who was addressing a spiritual seminar. All talk of Dr Bob faded, and Simon Kadwill became the object of Chantelle's fascination. Catherine recalls that next thing, Chantelle was saying, 'I'm going to live in Upwey to be a babysitter for this guy Simon Kadwill and his partner.' Chantelle's boyfriend Simon went to live with Kadwill and his partner too. What worried the McDougalls most about the new arrangement was the way in which Chantelle had so quickly adopted her new employer's philosophies, which seemed to have a doomsday element to them. 'She used to say we don't need many worldly possessions, we're going to be looked after and we're going to be on another plane – an astral plane, or something like that. I was thinking, *Oh my God!*'

Catherine decided to see for herself what was going on. 'I visited her with the little boy and everything seemed to be okay,' she says. 'She seemed reasonably well, but things were a bit strained.' Still, Catherine did not criticise Chantelle and kept her daughter close, as she'd been advised.

Soon, though, Chantelle had more staggering news. Simon Kadwill had apparently persuaded her to move to Western Australia, but not before a peculiar, solo stop-off. 'She came and said,

"I'm going to Alice Springs first to save the Aborigines from the bad spirits,"' Catherine says. 'So she went to Alice Springs and lived in a tent and then moved into a container.' Catherine knows how strange that sounds but is so used to the oddity of the situation that the words roll easily off her tongue. The shipping container was a long way from the comfortable family life Chantelle had enjoyed back in Victoria but Chantelle set it up like a tiny flat and endured the oppressive heat inside. She gave up on protecting people from bad spirits, however, and waited tables at a steak joint instead.

After around six months, Chantelle moved to Perth. She told her mum she would have stayed longer except there was 'too much bad energy' in Alice Springs. Living with Simon Kadwill, his partner Deborah and their son, Chantelle helped out with the babysitting but also worked in various part-time jobs, mostly as a waitress. 'She seemed to be happy and enjoying her adventures,' Catherine says, and remembers thinking, *Perhaps everything will be all right after all?*

In 1999 Simon Kadwill and Deborah split up and Simon went back to England. Chantelle, Deborah and her son moved into a house in the Perth suburb of Floreat. Around that time a young woman named Justine, who Chantelle and Deborah had met at a spiritual event, visited England where she followed Simon's spiritual leadership and later became his lover.

Towards the end of that year, Chantelle and her boyfriend broke up and she flew to England to visit Simon Kadwill. After returning to Perth, Chantelle organised the paperwork for a visa so that Simon could legally return to Australia – which he did, with Justine. For a while, Simon, Chantelle, Justine, Simon's ex-girlfriend Deborah and her son lived in the Floreat house.

Not long after arriving back in Australia, Chantelle had some news she couldn't wait to share with her parents. 'Chantelle fell pregnant just after she came back from England,' Catherine says. 'She rang up to tell us. She was very excited about it.' So who was the father of the unborn baby? Apparently it was Simon Kadwill, who was almost thirty-nine. 'We never really liked him but by then she was an older adult, she was twenty-one or twenty-two and you can't run their lives,' says Catherine.

But hadn't Simon been in a relationship with two other women in the household? 'I think Simon used to visit them all,' Catherine says. 'They stayed in the bedrooms and he lived in the shed out the back.' It sounded to Catherine like something straight out of Utah, but again she kept her counsel.

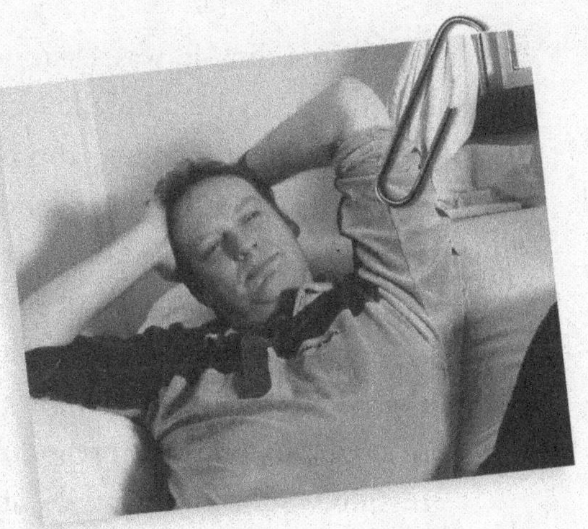

Rare photo: Gary Felton, aka Simon Kadwill
Photo courtesy Jim and Catherine McDougall

In September 2001, Chantelle gave birth to a healthy baby girl but did not name the father on the birth certificate. She called the baby Leela, the Sanskrit word for 'play'. Six weeks later, Catherine flew to Perth for ten days and stayed at a backpackers' hostel not far from where her daughter and granddaughter were living. At the time, Chantelle was babysitting Simon's son again, and Catherine spent time with them all in the park. 'It was lovely,' she says, 'and Leela was so cute and quite adorable.'

During her stay, Catherine didn't see much of Simon, who stayed in his own quarters most of the time. 'Chantelle said he'd be asleep all day and talking to people overseas about their beliefs at night,' Catherine recalls. One of those beliefs, apparently, was that humans came from Mars, or similar. 'He asked me when I was there visiting after Leela was born, what planet I was from,' Catherine says. 'I just sort of looked at him and said, "I dunno, Planet Earth!!" I thought, *We'll see where this goes.*'

After returning home, Catherine kept up her regular phone calls to Chantelle. In many ways they enjoyed normal mother–daughter conversations but it was clear to Catherine that Chantelle was under Simon Kadwill's spell.

By 2002 the other occupants of the house had left and Chantelle had made a gentle, likeable friend named Tony Popic who was also charmed by Simon Kadwill. 'He was having a few problems and was a bit vulnerable so he got sucked in too,' Catherine says. In the past, Tony had been a senior fruit and vegetable buyer for a supermarket chain but after attending a New Age seminar in 1996 he became entranced by unorthodox spiritual beliefs.

In 2003 Simon, Chantelle and Leela moved together into a house in Denmark, on the south coast of Western Australia, where they caught up with Tony, who had also moved to the township. Catherine says that Chantelle was a loving and attentive mum who took Leela to playgroups and Christmas parties 'like normal children'. To outsiders, there was no indication that there was anything unusual about their lifestyle.

Later that year, though, the family and Tony moved into a farmhouse in Nannup, a few minutes' drive from Denmark. 'Simon didn't like the vibe [in Denmark] or some damn thing,' Catherine says. Nannup, home to just a few hundred people, was out of the way, which suited Simon for a while. 'He wanted it to be away from people and he didn't want people to influence their ideas,' Catherine adds.

Despite Chantelle's far-flung new home, nothing could keep her parents away. Catherine and Jim had bought a campervan and visited Nannup in 2005 while they were on a trip around Australia. With no spare rooms at the farmhouse, the McDougalls stayed in a cabin at the local caravan park but visited their daughter and now four-year-old granddaughter each day. They found the township friendly and quaint, populated with 'alternative lifestyle people'. Yet, despite its appeal, Catherine wished her daughter did not live in such an isolated place and says she used to think, *Oh my God, what is she doing here?*

The farmhouse was old and basic with an outside shower, but Chantelle had lovingly decorated it with furniture and small treasures she'd found in op shops. 'She kept the house immaculate inside and out,' Catherine says. 'She mowed the lawn. Simon had a bad back and wouldn't do anything.' Chantelle had also arranged for new carpet to be laid and had sewn curtains on a second-hand sewing machine. As Nannup was such a hot town she'd also installed a bathtub for Leela and renovated the bathroom. Chantelle took on several part-time jobs too – at the pub, the fish and chip shop, and as a swimming teacher at the local pool. Despite the workload, she always put Leela first and took her to karate and ballet lessons. 'She was really quite an amazing girl,' Catherine says of her daughter, who also fit well into the community. 'She was so well-liked in the town and got on with everyone.'

Isolated: the Nannup farmhouse
Photo courtesy Jim and Catherine McDougall

Simon, Chantelle and Leela lived inside the house and their friend Tony slept out the back in his caravan. In a way, it was reassuring to Catherine and Jim that Tony was there. 'Tony was a lovely guy,' Catherine says. 'He was very quiet but always very nice.' Yet when they visited, the McDougalls rarely saw him.

Simon also kept to himself. 'He'd come out of his room, have dinner, then go back,' Catherine says. 'He'd only talk to you occasionally to get you interested in his beliefs but we didn't start conversations about that.' Was there a reason he played the loner? 'We were told he'd had a hard life and a tough upbringing. We don't know the details. But that is no excuse to be that weird.'

'He was a remote, hide-out sort of a guy,' Jim McDougall says. The retired auto-electrician never bought Simon's doomsday beliefs and didn't mind saying so. 'I was probably a bit abrupt and probably said it was bullshit. He told me to keep away from Leela because I'd contaminate her.'

'He didn't want us to have anything to do with her,' Catherine continues. 'He used to tell us we'd poison her mind and we'd have to be careful what we said.' Yet one night Simon made the unusual decision to allow Leela to stay overnight with her grandparents at the caravan park. The McDougalls read her bedtime stories and Leela slept soundly all night.

Two days later, however, when it was time for Catherine and Jim to leave, Simon did not want Leela to say goodbye to the grandparents who had driven thousands of kilometres across Australia to visit her and her mother. 'He held her tight and wouldn't let her give me a cuddle or a kiss,' Catherine says. 'She was screaming and yelling.' The memory still haunts them.

Catherine and Jim returned to Nannup once more together. They could tell Simon didn't want them there, but they would never give up on Chantelle or Leela. 'You worry about your daughter when your daughter's twenty and he's forty-something, but that was the least of our worries,' Jim says.

Mother and daughter: Chantelle and Leela McDougall
Photo courtesy Jim and Catherine McDougall

In May 2007, not long before the group disappeared, Catherine flew over to see Chantelle and Leela by herself. Once again she stayed at the caravan park but when she dropped in at the farmhouse she had a feeling something was going on. The feeling intensified when one day Simon fetched the mail. Inside an envelope was a passport for Leela. Catherine asked Simon why Leela needed a passport but didn't receive a proper answer. She decided not to press the point.

Another day, Chantelle asked her mum if Leela could stay with her in the cabin that night. Catherine was delighted at the opportunity to spend one-on-one time with her granddaughter and hoped Chantelle would enjoy a night off from mum duties. Catherine and Leela had great fun, telling stories and eating cake with buttery pink frosting. The next day started well too, with the six-year-old running and dancing around an old amphitheatre in the town centre. Later, when Chantelle turned up, the three generations of McDougalls visited a maze together.

Unfortunately, the sense of normality was short-lived. When Catherine asked Chantelle if she'd had an early night, Chantelle said she hadn't; they'd had visitors. 'I thought it was strange,' Catherine says, 'because Chantelle had said nothing about having people over. Then, when she asked Chantelle who the visitors were, her daughter refused to say. *Why the secrecy?* Catherine wondered. There was also the matter of Leela's new passport. 'I thought, *What's going on?* I really felt uneasy.'

When it was time to leave, Catherine felt sick. She knew something was afoot, but no one would tell her what. In the car on the way back to Busselton, she fell apart. 'I burst into tears because I knew something was happening,' Catherine says.

Her instincts turned out to be right because a few weeks later Chantelle called to say they were going to live in Brazil. *Brazil!* thought Catherine, and asked Chantelle why. Chantelle replied that they were going to help people with the same beliefs who lived in a commune there. After that, mother and daughter spoke several more times on the phone. 'She was packing things and she just seemed like someone who was going on a trip and was happy about it,' Catherine says.

The conversation Catherine remembers most, though, took place on Saturday, 14 July 2007, when she said to Chantelle,

'You have to write as soon as you get there to let us know you're okay and give us your address.' Chantelle assured her mum that she would. 'That was the last we heard from her.'

After three or four weeks with no word from their daughter, the McDougalls figured something must have happened. They found out that a plane bound for Brazil had crashed but were relieved to discover that none of the names of the group were on the flight manifest. After six weeks, Jim started searching online for communes in Brazil and contacted the police there. 'They said as it was such a big place they'd be hard to find there.' This was not what the McDougalls wanted to hear.

Catherine wondered if the authorities in Australia could help and asked her brother – Senior Sergeant Barry McIntosh, one of Wodonga's top cops at the time – what she should do. He suggested she report them missing at their local police station. During Barry McIntosh's career in the police force he'd spent years as an investigator in Victoria's elite squads, including the Homicide Squad. There, he'd worked on some of Australia's most notorious murder cases, including the Frankston serial killings; the cemetery stabbing of Mersina Halvagis; and the murder of Shepparton man Rocky Iaria, whose body was found wrapped in plastic in someone else's double grave. Barry McIntosh was a cop who knew how to lead a case, and a cop who knew how to solve one. The only problem – and it was a major one – was that he came from a different jurisdiction, so there was little he was allowed to do.

The local policeman who took the missing persons report quickly sent the information to police in Western Australia. His initial inquiries returned some information about the missing group, including that their dogs had been sold and Chantelle's car had been sold at a car yard. He also found out that Chantelle had left the car yard in another vehicle. Who was in that car? And did they have something to do with the group's disappearance?

Even though the group had left Nannup as they'd said they would, checks with airlines and the Immigration Department showed they had neither flown to Brazil, nor attempted to. Perhaps they were going somewhere else first. But where? What troubled Jim the most was that wherever Chantelle went she always told her mum because they were so close. 'That's what's so bizarre,' he says. 'It doesn't make any sense.'

'The first investigation didn't come back with much,' Catherine says. This was despite the Western Australia Police Force carrying out more than four hundred inquiries in a bid to find the group. 'There were no leads, really. The CCTV at the airport . . . there was nothing. We just didn't know what to think.'

It eventually emerged that before leaving Nannup the group had finalised some of their affairs. Tony had visited his parents in Manjimup, around sixty kilometres south-east of Nannup, to say goodbye. He told them Simon was going to Brazil and would be followed by Chantelle and Leela. He said he was thinking about going to Alice Springs, although Chantelle had told her mum that Tony was going to Brazil too. After visiting his parents, Tony sold his ute and, a few days later, gave his brother Joseph power of attorney over his affairs.

Chantelle arranged for the final electricity meter reading at the farmhouse and for the phone to be disconnected. As her family had already discovered, she sold her car at a car yard and three dachshund puppies, from a litter born to the group's mature dachshunds, to a pet shop. A woman named Carolyn was going to buy the remaining puppies and had been organising to do so with Simon. She said she would collect them at the end of July 2007 but, in an email to her on Sunday, 24 June,

Simon said she would need to pick them up on Sunday, 15 July because the family was leaving for Brazil earlier than anticipated. After that, Carolyn made the arrangements with Chantelle because Simon's emails started bouncing back. No one heard from him again.

When Carolyn called on Saturday, 14 July, to confirm she was picking up the dogs the next day, Chantelle told her she would have to get them that very day because she and Leela were about to leave the property. Simon, apparently, had already gone. When Carolyn arrived at the farmhouse, the furniture inside gave the impression the occupants were not ready to leave at all. Chantelle told Carolyn they were leaving some items behind and that she was going to spend three days in Perth.

Carolyn thought Leela might like to farewell the puppies but she was apparently unwell and in the caravan with Tony. A short while later, Chantelle walked into another room in the house, and reappeared looking uneasy, claiming that Leela might need to go to the hospital. It was strange because the room Chantelle had gone into was nowhere near the caravan where her sick daughter was supposed to be.

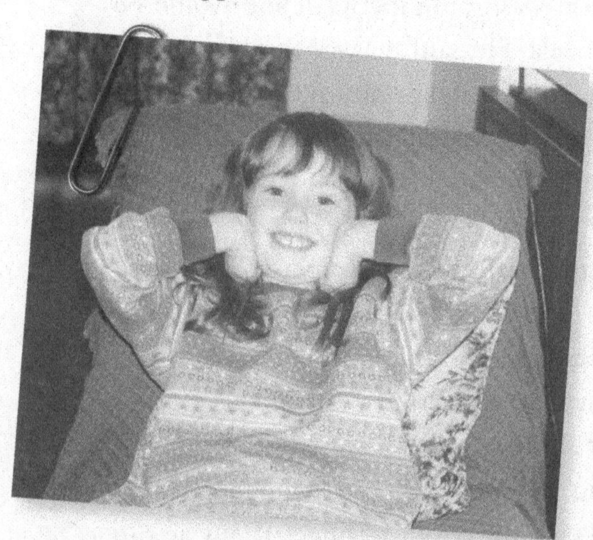

Leela, just before she went missing
Photo courtesy Jim and Catherine McDougall

On the way home, Carolyn realised she had not paid all the money owing for the sale of the pups. She called Chantelle to fix things up and found out that Leela had not needed to go to hospital after all. That was good news.

The next day, Carolyn left a message on Chantelle's answering machine, but she never called back. Instead, an angry-sounding woman later returned the call, demanding to know who Carolyn was and whether she knew Chantelle.

Who was that caller? And why the rage?

The owners of the Nannup farmhouse, Lyndon and Elizabeth Crouch, had no idea their house was being vacated until Monday, 16 July 2007, when they turned up to do some work on the property and Lyndon found a letter on the back doorstep. It was from Chantelle, who said they'd left the property because EMF waves were preventing them from sleeping. When the Crouches had subdivided the property they'd installed a transformer about ninety metres from the house, and Simon was convinced its electromagnetic frequencies were making him ill.

Chantelle's letter, which was apologetic in tone, said they had moved to Brazil and could not take all their furniture. They gave the Crouches permission to do as they saw fit with the items they'd left behind, which included a fridge, a plasma television, a DVD player and the beds. It appeared the group had taken their linen and their clothes.

In his caravan, Tony Popic had also left a note, giving the Crouches permission to keep the van and its contents. On the same day, Tony's brother Joseph received Tony's bank statements, superannuation and power of attorney forms in the mail. In an accompanying letter Tony apologised for being a 'crap' brother.

After that, it was radio silence from the group.

As time marched on, with no evidence emerging to show that the group had flown to Brazil, the question arose: What if they'd travelled under aliases? It sounded far-fetched but, as it transpired, Simon Kadwill was not Simon Kadwill at all. About two years after the group went missing, the McDougalls found out that Simon's real name was Gary Felton.

Years later at the inquest, the McDougalls were rocked by other revelations about their daughter's partner, including that he'd been convicted of fraud back in England. The inquest also brought to light that while he was working for a software company he had stolen the birth certificate of a man named Simon Kadwill and was later issued a passport in that name.

The McDougalls wished they'd known about the stolen identity, but as different investigators had been assigned to the case over the years, they had often relied on journalists to keep them up to date. 'We found out bits and pieces but we didn't really know much,' Catherine says. So it was at that inquest before Coroner Barry King in December 2017 – and in May 2018 when he handed down his report – that the McDougalls gained their clearest insight to date into their daughter's life with Gary Felton, aka Simon Kadwill.

In his report, Coroner King outlined how Simon (as His Honour referred to him) had embarked on a spiritual pilgrimage in the 1990s which, predictably, included a visit to India, where he met his erstwhile partner Deborah. After moving to Melbourne he ran a website called 'The Truth Fellowship' and peddled his beliefs in chat rooms. He also wrote two books called *The New Call: Servers of the Divine Plan* and *Rare Insights*. They were the kinds of books that might attract both people seeking enlightenment and lost souls. A quick glance at Google's book reviews is illuminating. One reviewer says, 'One of the best books in the last 100 years to be written by a human hand. Life changing.' Another was not so enthusiastic: 'It's all rather toxic, and will attract marginal immature types. Don't waste your time.'

The coroner said that he 'briefly skimmed over Simon's books' and 'recognised elements of Christianity and Buddhism, including Zen Buddhism, but there were also quotations from Tolstoy and Thoreau cited.' His Honour stated, 'The language used, especially in *The New Call*, is grandiose and replete with hyperbole and unsupported assertions, some of which appeared bizarre to me.'

At the heart of Simon's teachings was the belief that through death some people could ascend from the physical world to a higher dimension. That wasn't so strange in itself, considering most religions believe in some sort of afterlife, but other aspects sounded like science fiction. WAPOL behaviour analyst, Dr Kristine Giesen, produced a report for the coroner in which she wrote of Simon's beliefs: 'Further, this new level of consciousness is apparently extra-terrestrial in entity and capable of interplanetary travel. For those few who are ready for the ascension process and essentially waiting, they find living on earth as being toxic and polluted, and that there is nothing left but murder, hatred and putrefaction.' Other things she wrote were even more ominous than that. 'They believe that we are heading towards an Armageddon; a judgment day; the end of the world . . .' According to the doctrine, we were meant to meet our maker in December 2012.

Like a lot of end-of-the-world types, Simon did believe in God, but that was probably the most mainstream of his beliefs, which Simon's one-time lover Justine further brought to light at the inquest. 'Some "way out" aspects were a belief in star seeds, walk-ins and reptilians, which are concepts quite popular in niche areas on the internet,' the coroner said, summarising part of Justine's evidence. 'It was a mishmash of many things but also included belief in aliens, which is what star seeds and walk-ins were.'

To each their own under normal circumstances, but with four people missing after ten years the question was whether Simon's beliefs had something to do with the group's disappearance. Or had something else happened to them?

By June 2017, Barry McIntosh had retired from the force and was running his own business, and thought it prudent to ask if he could look at the documents WA Police had prepared in time for the inquest. He found the system quite different from that in Victoria. 'I was labouring under the misapprehension that an inquest brief would have been compiled,' says Barry. 'I was expecting IR's [information reports] and the whole shooting match.' There was, however, a very detailed report from a Senior Sergeant Greg Balfour, identifying what had been missed and the issues he saw. He had reviewed the case in 2014, and then led a reinvestigation into it.

The coroner agreed to let Barry look at the document – known as the Omega Report – at Wodonga Magistrates' Court. He later viewed a separate file containing the information reports. Soon, he too identified areas he thought needed to be further investigated prior to the inquest and wrote to the coroner and the investigator to make his recommendations. Most of what troubled Barry – who stresses that his suggestions were intended as constructive and not critical – harked back to the original investigation, which was illuminated in Senior Sergeant Balfour's insightful report.

One event that troubled Barry McIntosh took place in 2007, when a woman and her son were walking along a bush track at Pelican Point, Bunbury, where the son was testing his metal detector. After happening upon some clothes and other personal belongings, they discovered two sand mounds, which the coroner later described as 'similar to what is seen on new graves at a cemetery'. On top of one of the mounds was a pair of girl's underpants. The woman told police in Bunbury what she'd seen but her concerns were dismissed and by the time the case was reinvestigated years later the area was covered in weeds. Did the mounds have anything to do with the group's disappearance? Perhaps, but who would know?

Something else worried Barry too. In October 2007, a prisoner who was part of a group of inmates working under the supervision of a prison officer found a woman's t-shirt in bushland near Northcliffe in the south-west of Western Australia. There was also the unmistakable odour of dead flesh. Barry understands that the area, in which there was a walking track and a large, flat rock with distinctive etchings, is no longer as accessible to the public as it was then.

After receiving the report, police from Pemberton seized the t-shirt, which they suspected had been there for some years. The shirt was meant to be forensically tested but it never was and no one knows what happened to it. 'In fairness to [the police],' says Barry, 'they may not have known there were four people missing when they went there.'

Barry understands that during the original investigation, the police did not speak to the prisoner who did his civic duty in reporting the clothing and the foul smell. 'It would have been just as easy to accept that it was probably a dead animal and leave it at that,' he says. 'But the prisoner did feel it necessary to report it, which makes me think the description of the clothing by the police as being old may not be accurate.' He says the timing of the finding also fit the timeline of the group's disappearance.

The police did attempt to search the area again, but it was more than seven years later, after Senior Sergeant Balfour had launched his reinvestigation and spoken to the police officers who'd originally attended the scene. One of the officers felt sure that he could locate the area again and in February 2015 he returned with other police to try and find it. By this time vegetation had grown and a bushfire had swept through the area, so they couldn't be sure if they were in the right spot. The following month the police conducted a line search but the effects of the fires made it difficult. Large trees had fallen down and the searchers feared that if bodies were beneath them they might never be found.

Barry wondered if the area had been the location of some kind of suicide pact. This had to be considered because, in early June 2007, Simon had written in an email to a follower named Sheryl in the US that the group was planning to take their own lives in the bush using a fast-acting drug. Simon added that after he, Chantelle and Leela died, Tony was to bury them, then kill himself. Simon indicated, however, that Chantelle was putting it off, suggesting she had gone off the boil about the idea. It was not the only time that Simon, who complained of depression, wrote of wanting to end it all. He and the other adult members of the group had been prescribed antidepressants before they disappeared and perhaps it's because they planned to kill themselves. Simon had been prescribed several other drugs too, which could have been combined to end life.

There was also the possibility the group had been cultivating a hallucinogenic plant called ayahuasca, more often taken in a jungle setting under the guidance of a shaman by people who believe it induces spiritual and personal enlightenment. When Catherine last visited the Nannup farmhouse in May 2007, she'd noticed a plant she did not recognise, which Chantelle said was from Brazil. Catherine recalled there being up to ten of the plants growing in a mini-hothouse. Barry showed her photos of the psychoactive plant to see if it could be eliminated from the inquiry but, due to the time that had passed, Catherine couldn't be sure. Despite this, Barry says, 'Ayahuasca plants can be purchased online in Australia, and, given that Chantelle had said they were from Brazil, I think it's more than likely the plants were ayahuasca.'

Could the plants have been used in a psychedelic prelude to a group suicide in Northcliffe? Maybe yes, maybe no, but either way Northcliffe – where the clothing was found and the smell of dead flesh reported – was of investigative significance. Here's why. On Thursday, 12 July, a man made a call from the landline at the Nannup farmhouse to book a train ticket under the name of J Roberts for travel between Bridgetown and Northcliffe on Sunday, 15 July, but the trip was not taken. In his letter to the coroner, Barry wrote, 'I believe this trip, in particular the end destination, has significant relevance. I note also that the Nannup residence is situated in Roberts Road.' So was the name Roberts an alias inspired by the nearest street sign? Quite possibly.

What's certain is that whoever bought the ticket paid for it that day in cash at the Manjimup Visitor Centre. Not only had Tony been visiting his family there but the person who bought the ticket gave their contact number as the landline at the Nannup farmhouse. Forty-year-old Tony might not have used that ticket to get to Northcliffe, but it appears to Barry that he got there in the end.

On Sunday, 15 July a trip under the name of Roberts was taken from Bunbury to Perth. Tony had been in Bunbury (just over an hour and a half's drive from Manjimup) on 12 July, where he'd pled guilty to a charge of disorderly behaviour after exposing himself to a male plain-clothes police officer in a toilet block that day. Barry says Tony's mobile phone 'pinged' at 5.30 pm from the towers at inner-city Northbridge and that there was other evidence to strongly suggest it was he who made the trip. Among that evidence is that the trip started in Bunbury; the same name of Roberts and the phone number of the Nannup farmhouse were used in the second booking; Tony's phone called at least one gay-friendly accommodation place in Perth; Tony's driver's licence was used to book into Underground Backpackers, a hostel in Northbridge; and his phone was used to order a pizza that night, as well as to book a taxi for the next day under the name of Tony. It is Barry's view that Tony Popic – whose pizza with the lot was dropped off near a gay beat in King's Park – had attempted to enjoy one last hoorah before travelling on to Northcliffe where, now that his affairs were in order, he could end his life.

The following morning at 6.35, Tony's phone called Transwa, the state's regional train network. At 6.54 am, a taxi driver took a man calling himself Tony from Underground Backpackers to the East Perth train station. The taxi arrived at 7.09 am. Seven minutes earlier a ticket had been purchased under the name of Roberts from Perth to Bunbury, with a bus connection to Northcliffe. It may simply be that either the taxi meter or the train station clock was wrong because Barry finds it likely that Tony purchased this ticket and was the person who took the trip. In his letter to the coroner, Barry stated, 'I believe this travel was undertaken by Popic and that Northcliffe may well be his final resting place and coincided with the intended travel, not undertaken, on 15 July 2007.'

There was other curious travel on 16 July too. A ticket had been purchased at East Perth train station on 13 July under the name J Robwerts (probably a typo), from Perth to Kalgoorlie. A man used the ticket at East Perth at 7.15 am on 16 July to travel at least one way to Kalgoorlie. Could it have been Simon Kadwill?

Had he met up with Tony at the train station early that morning? And if he was going to Kalgoorlie, why? In Barry's opinion, considering that Simon Kadwill disappeared from view on 24 June, he doubts it was him.

While the coroner did not reach the same conclusions about the mysterious travel as Barry, he said, 'The identities of the persons (who) travelled to Northcliffe as J Roberts and to Kalgoorlie as J Robwerts on 16 July 2007 is a mystery within a mystery.'

Among the many matters examined at the inquest, Coroner King looked at the events leading up to the group going missing. He considered whether Simon's purported fears about the EMF waves from the transformer on the Nannup property were a motivating factor. When the trench for the transformer was dug in April 2007 Simon had told the electrician the electromagnetic field was making him sick and that he wanted to move away, perhaps to Brazil. Yet curiously he had indicated to his online follower Sheryl, who had tried to convince him to go there, that he did not want to. The coroner noted, 'He rejected the idea and held to a spiritual hopelessness that was consuming him, and telling her that he would be physically incapable of making the trip without months of therapy first.' During proceedings, Dr Giesen suggested the story about going to Brazil might even have been 'a ruse'.

Another reason why Simon might have left Nannup could have been to do with a 2004 visit from Chantelle's ex-boyfriend Simon, who she complained about to the police. His Honour stated that the ex-boyfriend told officers during a car journey 'that the group were part of a cult and that Simon [Kadwill], who was the leader of a cult, was a fake and that his real name was Gary Felton'.

One of those police officers had picked up Simon Kadwill for speeding in 2007 and found him 'nervous and uncomfortable about answering questions about where he came from'. His Honour said that when the policeman got wind of the group leaving the farmhouse in 2007 'he concluded that they had all left in a hurry because of his contact with [Chantelle's ex-boyfriend] Simon on 5 May 2007'. Supporting that theory is the fact that Chantelle applied for Leela's passport the day after the officer stopped Kadwill for speeding.

There had also been more talk of suicide. In June 2007, the month after Simon Kadwill's email to Sheryl about a group suicide, he had written to her saying that when he went offline he was going to kill himself. On that occasion he did not, but it should also be noted that as well as complaining to others of depression, one of the medications he was taking around this time was an antipsychotic drug.

It is also worth noting that on 24 June 2007, the last time anyone outside the group was known to have had contact with Simon, a follower from Canada called Alixander Fominoff – who had visited Simon a few years earlier with another supporter by the name of Kirk Helgason – used pentobarbital to take his own life. Just over a year later, Kirk and his girlfriend Christina Parrott used the same method to kill themselves, but not before Christina deposited twelve thousand dollars into Chantelle's bank account in Australia. Suicide notes left by the couple conveyed a belief that they had gone to a higher plane.

Perhaps Simon had stockpiled his medication to reach that plane himself?

Clouding matters about the disappearance were possible sightings of the four, which were also included in the coroner's report. One of the sightings took place about seven months after the group went missing. A Nannup local who had known Chantelle and Leela for over two years said she saw a woman and a little girl who looked like them going into a shoe shop in Busselton in February 2008.

In April that same year a woman, responding to images in the media, reported seeing a man and a woman shopping for a wheelchair in the Perth suburb of O'Connor. Was it Simon and Chantelle? Apparently the man needed back surgery, and Simon did have a bad back. Police contacted Perth hospitals, but at the time in question none of the missing adults in the group had been patients there.

On the same day, there was a sighting of a man and a girl who resembled Tony and Leela in a bottle shop in Bassendean, another Perth suburb. The shop had surveillance footage but it's understood the police did not download it.

In June 2008 a Busselton woman smiled at a little girl in a queue at a newsagent. It seemed to aggravate the man accompanying the little girl, who he called Leela. When the woman saw photos of the missing four in the paper the next day she thought the girl in the newsagency was the missing girl in the photo and that the adult with her looked like one of the men. But sadly, another investigative opportunity was missed. 'Investigators did not inquire as to whether CCTV footage was available in the vicinity of the newsagent,' His Honour said.

After seeing a story on television in 2011, a man called to report that in 2007 he had met a man named Tony at a tavern in King River, near Albany in the state's south-east, and that he was apparently accompanied by another man, a woman and a girl. That witness later told police that Tony had said the other man was a spiritual leader.

Later publicity led to a man coming forward in 2014. The man ran a petting zoo and fun park near the south-western WA town of Dunsborough and told police that in 2008 he'd seen a woman and a girl who looked like photos run in the media of Chantelle and Leela. It was possible he also saw someone matching the description of either Simon or Tony.

So if any of these sightings were of members of the group, could they simply have been travelling around the southern part of Western Australia? It's possible, but they did not use their bank accounts after they disappeared, and Chantelle had a balance of almost seven thousand dollars. If you intended to start a new life, you probably wouldn't leave that much money in the bank. Having said that, they could have been mobile for a little while because before leaving Nannup, Chantelle had cashed cheques and withdrawn money from her account, and had around six thousand dollars in her kick.

So what had happened to the four? Were they living undercover somewhere in Australia? Had they found another way to get to Brazil? Was it a suicide pact? Or something else?

Coroner King, after praising Senior Sergeant Balfour's 'admirably comprehensive report', stated that the investigator had submitted evidence from which an inference could be drawn that the missing people were now dead. That evidence included the facts that the group: had not used their bank accounts; had not been recorded as having left Australia; and had 'spiritual beliefs about ascending to a higher plane through death'.

Senior Sergeant Balfour had also submitted significant and lengthy evidence to the contrary, suggesting the group might have faked their own disappearances to 'give the impression that they are dead'. That evidence included: 'Simon's coercive influence over Chantelle and Tony, suggesting that he could convince them to disappear with him'; the six thousand dollars which Chantelle had withdrawn from the bank and acquired through the sale of her pets, 'giving the financial means to pay for short term living expenses'; and even 'the possibility that members of the group left Australia on a cargo ship from Fremantle', which was not excluded. His Honour explained it was Senior Sergeant Balfour's conclusion that 'in the circumstances, there were not sufficient grounds to be reasonably satisfied that the members of the group are dead'.

Before revealing his own conclusion, the coroner made a number of comments including that, 'There appears to have been no reasonable basis for the group to have committed suicide and then to have hidden the fact after the event.' He noted that the overseas followers who'd committed suicide had left notes of explanation. 'It seems to me that, if Simon had truly been motivated to end his life by his desire to be considered a spiritual leader, making his ascension known would have been a powerful message.'

In conclusion, he stated, 'There are reasonable bases to ground a belief that Chantelle, Leela and Tony are dead, especially the fact that they have not been in touch with their respective families for over ten years. There is also evidence, especially the evidence relating to Simon's apparent despondency and his belief in ascension, which would, if accepted, support a conclusion that Simon is dead.

'However, given the nature and quantity of evidence inconsistent with any of their deaths, I cannot be satisfied to the required standard of proof that any one of them is dead,' the coroner continued. 'For the sake of clarity, I must add that my conclusion does not mean that I have found that any of them is alive. I must also emphasise that my conclusion is based on the evidence presently available.'

The inquest had been a harrowing ordeal for the McDougalls but the findings gave them more food for thought. Catherine does not tend to believe her daughter is still alive, but without proof she has hope. 'Some days my mind goes, *I hope they're somewhere and alive*, but I think maybe they've got to this plane they talked about all the time.'

Knowing that the handling of missing persons reports had vastly improved in his own state, Barry suggested that Western Australia's missing persons reporting system could also be improved so that more thorough investigations are undertaken at the start. He says that it is crucial that when a family fears a case may be suspicious, the police investigate straightaway and with an open mind. 'If you have a closed mind and treat it just as a missing persons file, you can get tripped up,' Barry says. 'If it is one person who has gone missing, you need to ask: Are they missing, murdered or is it that they don't want to be found? But when it's four people including a little girl . . . it's not that easy to hide four people. You've got to think something might be wrong.'

Barry made seventeen targeted requests to the coroner and Western Australia Police on behalf of his family. They are the kinds of suggestions that only an experienced detective would know to make, and they call for further investigation of key elements of the case including: following up the reports made to Pemberton and Bunbury Police; speaking to witnesses to determine any likelihood they assisted the group with their disappearance; making inquiries as to whether the medicines prescribed to Simon had been fully dispensed and what quantities of medication he may have possessed; consideration of Luminol testing at the Nannup house and caravan; and additional inquiries into personal documents belonging to Chantelle which Barry was told had been found in the Nannup tip.

Unfortunately, if there had been a body or bodies near Northcliffe, we may never know due to the destruction caused by the fire that swept through the area. Similarly, if bodies had been buried in shallow graves at Picnic Point they may never be found. But that doesn't mean more can't be done. Barry would be grateful for the opportunity to spend a couple of weeks at least poring over all the police files, as there is still much he has not seen. 'If I got the opportunity to sit down with the entire file, I'm sure I could find other areas of investigation that could be followed up,' he says.

Barry does not want to step on any toes but has already followed up on one missed investigative opportunity himself. After the inquest – having learned that the original investigators had not spoken to the prison officer who'd supervised the inmates at Northcliffe – Barry decided to track him down. His hope was that the officer could confirm the location where the prisoner noticed the t-shirt and smell of decomposition. 'I eventually found the prison officer and got the coordinates of the right spot, ten to twelve years later,' he says, now certain that the police who'd tried to find the location in 2015 were off the mark, as they'd suspected. 'They'd gone to the wrong place,' Barry says, aware he might now have the bombshell information needed to finally crack the case. He also made the further revelation that, 'The prison officer I spoke to believes there were actually two pieces of clothing: the t-shirt and a pair of jeans, but he's not entirely sure due to the passage of time.'

Until the disappearances can be explained, Barry believes they should be viewed as suspicious. 'I think one of the problems when talking about the missing four is that it strips away the fact that this was probably a murder,' he says. If that is so, how does he think it went down? 'My gut feeling is that whatever happened, Chantelle wouldn't have known. She was not the kind of individual who'd see anything happen to her daughter. She's too much of a family person to have that occur. I firmly believe she thought she was going overseas because she'd applied for a passport for Leela; you wouldn't do that if you were planning on topping yourself in bushes somewhere. So I think it was probably a murder-suicide of some type and the bodies are somewhere nearby in WA.'

Crusader: former top cop Barry McIntosh wants answers for his family
Photo courtesy Barry McIntosh

As we consider the gravity of this theory, we should not forget Barry's own pain at the loss of two family members which he says is something he's learned to rein in. 'I've seen enough misery and stuff over the years that I don't allow myself really to dwell on it,' he says. 'It's one of those things. There's probably nothing I can do now to change things. Sometimes I wish I'd gone to WA to make my own inquiries, but I just assumed the right things were being done by the people there.'

His heart goes out to his sister Catherine and brother-in-law Jim. 'I don't know how they've kept their sanity, to be quite honest, to have to go through life not knowing what happened and where their loved ones are,' he says. 'They know if they don't keep it in the media no one will do anything about it. But every time you put it in the media, they relive it.' Barry adds that he doesn't think he would have coped so well under similar circumstances, saying, 'I don't know how many times a day it would cross your mind. That'd send me nuts, I think.'

Jim admits there are times when coping with Chantelle and Leela's disappearance is harder now than it was at the start. Sometimes, when he lets his mind wander, he compares what might have happened to his daughter and granddaughter with the fate of cult members overseas. 'All the American ones killed themselves,' he says, with thoughts of Jonestown and Heaven's Gate springing to mind. Yet, despite the passage of time, he holds out hope that Chantelle and Leela are still alive, grimly adding, 'The odds are less than fifty-fifty.'

'I get this feeling that I'm never going to know what happened to them,' Catherine says. But if Chantelle is still alive, she has this direct message for her: 'I absolutely love you to bits and I miss you so much. Could you please contact me somehow and let me know you're all right?' If that is not possible, perhaps someone else will feel moved to come forward with information to ease the family's suffering. 'Simon Kadwill' had followers around the world and, as we know, some of them visited his house. Perhaps they hold the key to this mystery but haven't yet realised. Or perhaps whoever picked up Chantelle from the car yard can help.

So where to from here? Barry, who strongly suspects others helped the group execute their final plans, hopes that when the time comes for him to ask, the Western Australia Police will allow him to view all their files on the case, dating back to 2007. It is not so that he can sit in judgement, but because after thirty-five years in the force he understands the value of a fresh set of eyes. And yes, it's also because two of those missing are people he loves.

THE COMPASSIONATE GIRL

THE PRESENCE OF **LIZ HERFORT'S** ABSENCE

Not to be forgotten: Liz Herfort, missing since 1980

Photo courtesy Janie McGough

'I just had this feeling that Liz wasn't coming home. I never wanted to acknowledge it but I had a full appreciation that might be the case.'

Alistair Herfort, Liz's brother

In 1980 Maria James was stabbed sixty-eight times in her flat at the back of her second-hand bookshop in Melbourne. The people of Victoria were floored – why would anyone want to kill a devoted mother of two children, and in such a frenzy? The media was saturated with appeals from police, theories about the murder, and news of possible suspects.

Soon another unusual case came along and stole the public's attention, with the disappearance of baby Azaria Chamberlain in Australia's exotic red centre. This case produced an endless stream of fascinating clues and red herrings and saw punters weighing in on whether or not they thought Azaria's mother Lindy Chamberlain had killed her own baby. Eventually, Lindy was convicted of Azaria's murder but was ultimately cleared. As a coroner later found, a dingo had taken her baby, as Lindy had said all along.

There were other mysterious disappearances that year, as well as other homicides. But not all of those who went missing or were murdered have remained in the public consciousness for so long.

Take Liz Herfort, for example. She went missing from Canberra in 1980, but have you ever heard of her? There was press coverage at the time but, with little known about the circumstances surrounding her disappearance, the media focus was limited and short-lived. It meant that after a few weeks the only people talking about the missing eighteen-year-old were her family, friends, the police, and perhaps her abductor. Liz's family felt the public had forgotten her, but perhaps it was more the case that they never got to know her.

Reliving memories that are both joyous and painful, Liz Herfort's siblings, Janie and Alistair, want to properly introduce us to the sister they adored. They want us to know what made Liz tick, understand the impact on them of her loss and, if possible, provide answers to the still-baffling mystery of her disappearance.

When Liz Herfort was two she moved into her sister Janie's bedroom. Five-year-old Janie fumed about it for a while but it didn't take long for the pair to become inseparable. 'When we were really little we used to sleep in the same bed for warmth and cuddles,' Janie remembers. By the time Janie was seven and Liz was four they used to talk for as long as they could after their mum Anne had turned off the light. 'Sometimes I'd tell her a story when we were going to sleep and the next night she'd want to know what happened next. It went on and on forever. It wasn't just my story, we were both in it.'

Inseparable: Janie, aged five, and Liz, aged two
Photo courtesy Janie McGough

Janie always looked out for her little sister. 'I felt quite protective towards her,' she says. 'As much as I'd get bossy with her when she didn't pick up her clothes, I was always concerned about her wellbeing. I felt it was my job.' Janie was especially protective after the family unit broke down in 1972 and they moved from place to place.

The sisters had an older brother, Duncan, and a younger one, Alistair, who was three years younger than Liz. Having a younger brother gave Liz the chance to act as a guiding influence this time, and it was a job she relished. As a fan of contemporary folk rock, she even shaped Alistair's taste in music. 'For my ninth birthday she gave me Neil Young's *Harvest* album because I was listening to Olivia Newton-John at the time,' he says with a laugh.

Liz was tender and kind, too. 'She had a lot of compassion for other people,' Alistair says. 'She was very, very sensitive and aware of my feelings about the world around me, particularly after the family separation.' Such was the level of Liz's empathy that when her siblings cried, she did too. 'I respected her so much as a person, as my mentor, and as my sister,' Alistair recalls.

Moved by her brother's words, Janie rises from her chair to embrace him. 'Liz was the nicest person in the family, really,' she says.

At sixteen, Liz, who was not academically minded and had left school early, started dating her first serious boyfriend. Dave was a couple of years older than Liz and everyone in the Herfort family gave him the tick of approval. The young couple had much in common, particularly their love of nature. 'From when she was young, Liz was very much into plants and growing things,' Janie says. 'Dave was very into orchids and he got Liz into orchids as well.'

By the time Liz was eighteen, she and Dave set off together to explore Australia, one vine at a time. Janie remembers going to visit them in Young, the cherry capital of New South Wales. Liz was fit and tanned from picking fruit and would sleep in a tent beneath the stars at night. It wasn't everyone's cup of tea but it suited Liz and Dave. 'She was a wholemeal girl and they lived a pretty rustic life,' Janie says. 'They were kind of hippies.'

Alistair, who was living with his father in Bermagui on the New South Wales south coast at the time, also recalls how easily Liz and Dave could reject creature comforts. After driving their 1968 HR Holden station wagon all the way to Bermagui for a visit, they didn't even stay inside the house. 'They had a bed there but they stayed on the state reserve across the road, looking over the ocean,' Alistair says.

For Liz and Dave, there was nothing nicer than waking to the sound of crashing waves.

There are worse places to pick fruit than Bowen on Queensland's Whitsunday Coast. Picture unspoiled beaches, succulent tropical fruit and a charming, village atmosphere in the town centre, and you can see why Liz was drawn to it. She and Dave went there to pick tomatoes, but after a while Liz started to wonder about the future of their relationship.

Taking time out to reflect, Liz went alone to Canberra where she planned to stay with her mum Anne for a couple of weeks before returning to Bowen to keep working. By this time Janie was living in a nearby village with her partner and recalls that when Liz came to Canberra she wasn't sure about Dave's commitment. But a week later, Liz was buoyant. 'She got a letter from Dave a few days before she disappeared saying he was happy and that he loved her,' Janie says.

In their mum's backyard: Janie (left) and Liz
Photo courtesy Janie McGough

All was well in the world – for a few days, at least.

On Friday, 13 June 1980, Liz and Janie chatted on the phone, though Janie was at work so she couldn't talk for long. She'd been hoping to see Liz that afternoon and was disappointed to hear that she was catching up with friends and wouldn't be home when Janie dropped by after she left the office. Still, the sisters made plans to see Bette Midler in *The Rose* at the drive-in the next night. Even though they were looking forward to it – and other plans they had made for the week ahead – neither of the sisters seemed ready to end the call. Janie says, 'I just remember her saying, "Okay then, see you later." It was like she would have liked to have seen me if I could have gotten to Mum's earlier. I just felt I wasn't quite finished with the conversation or she wasn't quite finished with the conversation.'

The next day – Saturday, 14 June – Janie called Liz to confirm their night at the drive-in. Their mum answered the phone, talking fast. 'She said, "Liz didn't come home, I'm worried,"' Janie recalls. *Surely nothing bad has happened*, Janie thought, *because Liz was with her friends*. But Anne was on edge and asked Janie to come over and start phoning Liz's friends to see if they knew where she was. Janie says, 'I thought, *Naughty thing. She's stayed out and didn't tell anyone.*'

But as Janie discovered when she called Liz's friends one by one, they had no idea where Liz was either. The most they knew was that she'd last been seen in the company of a trusted male friend, but he wasn't home when Janie first called.

Desperate to find her daughter, Anne called the police. 'Mum thought it didn't feel good,' Janie says.

Eventually, Janie spoke to the friend who was the last to see Liz at the bar. He didn't know she was missing and recalled the events of the previous night. 'They were both going home and he knew she'd run out of money,' Janie says. Their plan was to walk to the bus stop together and he would pay Liz's fare home. But after stopping to go to the toilet, Liz vanished. 'He waited for quite some time and thought she'd left,' Janie says. Eventually he went home by himself, assuming Liz was all right.

By the Saturday afternoon, Liz's friends and family were in a panic. 'I just had this feeling that was getting worse,' Janie says. She stayed overnight at her mum's where they waited by the phone for news of Liz. 'I just kept telling myself she was going to show up. It didn't make sense. She had to be somewhere.'

One of Anne's friends suggested lighting candles for Liz until she came home, but Janie was against it. 'I said, "No, that's a bad idea, because when a candle goes out we're all going to freak out."' Despite Janie's reservations, Anne lit candles all around the house, including one in Liz's old bedroom.

Meanwhile, in Bermagui, Alistair was having a barbecue with his mates to celebrate his sixteenth birthday. But when a knock sounded on the door of the house Alistair shared with his dad, Norm, it wasn't another friend on the doorstep; it was the police. 'They were there to tell Dad that Mum had reported Liz missing, and had we heard from her?' he says. 'I just heard Dad say, "What? She didn't come home?"' Alistair's friends left as he retreated to his bedroom, trying to get his head around what he'd heard. 'I just had this feeling that Liz wasn't coming home. I never wanted to acknowledge it but I had a full appreciation that might be the case.'

Back in Canberra, nothing could settle Janie's nerves. 'I was saying mantras to get to sleep because I was so freaked out,' she says. She eventually dozed off but awoke with the feeling that something was terribly wrong. She got up and walked around the house in a trance, checking that all the candles were still alight. So far so good, until she opened the door to Liz's room. There, the candle had gone out.

Sick with worry over his daughter's disappearance, Norm drove from Bermagui to Canberra to find out if he could help with the search. Alistair didn't accompany him at first and was billeted with a family he barely knew. 'It was surreal,' he says. 'I was going to school and trying to be normal.' But as Alistair quickly learned, when a loved one is missing there is no such thing as normal. The police and SES searched for Liz, but with no sign of her Alistair joined his family in Canberra. Liz's boyfriend Dave got there as quickly as he could, too. 'It hit home to me then it was real,' Alistair says.

Meanwhile, Anne seemed to be constantly talking to the police but told her children little about the investigation. 'Mum was really struggling and in her mind she was trying to protect us, to not worry us,' Janie says. 'But how could we not worry?'

Janie tried to hold on to hope as her emotions swung back and forth like a pendulum. 'I thought Liz would ring, that there'd be some rational explanation. Even though on some deep level I knew something was deeply wrong, I had to keep it together because if something had happened [and she came back], she'd need me.'

But Liz never did return.

Newspapers often report that police are 're-opening' a cold case, which is a misnomer because all unsolved cases remain open. They may not be in the process of being actively investigated, but if new information comes to light the police are expected to follow it up. What the newspapers usually mean when they announce that cases are being re-opened is that they are being reviewed. This involves detectives digging out the old files and reading them, trying to determine which cases in their jurisdiction are still solvable. Sometimes they will mount a cold case reinvestigation. Depending on the jurisdiction, however, and with resources being limited, only a few historic cases can be actively investigated at a time.

In 2015 Detective Senior Constable Tristan Thexton (now a detective sergeant) from ACT Policing set about doing a review into the disappearance of Liz Herfort. He had been in the job for almost a decade, having been drawn to a career in which he could do good. 'Someone said to me early in my career that sometimes you join the job and think you can make a difference to the world. You can't change the world but you can change someone's world,' he says. With that sentiment in mind, he promised to do all he could to find answers for the Herforts. It would not be a simple task, however, because Tristan's review found there were no new lines of inquiry for police to pursue. This didn't mean the case couldn't be cracked, but Tristan would need the public's help.

Looking back at the old files, he found out that Liz had gone to the ANU bar to meet some friends at around 3 pm on the day she went missing. 'Gradually, the group she was with filtered away and Liz was one of the last in the group there,' Tristan says. It was around 9 pm when Liz and her male friend decided to take the bus home. Tristan says when the friend couldn't find her after going to the toilet he 'proceeded to the bus interchange in the Canberra CBD'. It made sense because it was the nearest bus stop. 'So her friend went walking in that direction but didn't see Liz,' Tristan adds. In fact, he never saw her again.

The police did their best to find the missing young woman but to no avail. Turning to the public for help, they issued a press release. 'Between 16 and 20 June, about four or five witnesses came forward saying they had seen a young woman whose description matched Liz's at the time, attempting to hitchhike,' Tristan says. 'The sightings were at Vernon Circle in the Canberra CBD behind the Canberra Theatre in the southbound lanes.'

One witness went further than that. He said in a statement that he picked her up on Vernon Circle and travelled south over Lake Burley Griffin to the intersection of Commonwealth Avenue and Coronation Drive near the British High Commission. 'That witness had to turn right at that time and the woman had to keep travelling south, so she got out,' Tristan says. 'Police went out again with that new information seeking new public assistance.'

On 28 June another witness, who said he'd been driving south along Commonwealth Avenue between 9.30 and 10 pm, went into the Canberra City Police Station with information. 'He said as Commonwealth Avenue met Coronation Drive, he had to move out of the left-hand lane as a vehicle had stopped in that lane,' Tristan says. The witness said as he drove past the other car he saw a male and female standing on the grass verge at the side of the road beside the rear of the vehicle. The male, he said, was behaving aggressively towards the female. Was it Liz he saw? And who was the man? 'His only distinguishing feature,' Tristan says, 'was that he had a pork pie hat that bookies wear at the racetrack.'

The witness told police he had debated whether or not to stop but decided against it and kept driving. 'Five minutes later he stopped at a set of lights and thought he'd better write down the rego on a piece of paper in his glove box,' Tristan says. After that, he drove home.

By now, detectives had taken over the suspicious case. They identified the owner of the car in question and went to his house. 'The owner of the car agreed the vehicle belonged to him and he agreed he wore what he called a pork pie hat,' Tristan says. He accompanied the detectives to Woden Police Station where he was interviewed. 'Despite the two things he had agreed to, he strenuously denied being at that location on the night of 13 June. He insisted his vehicle had been garaged at home and that no one had had access to it. He denied any involvement in the matter and stated that he had no knowledge of it and did not know Liz. The only explanation he could give was that it had been a mistake or someone was falsely implicating him.'

Nevertheless, the man in the pork pie hat became the police's main suspect. While the detectives spent the next year or so investigating him, other members of the public came forward with information which the police considered too. People speculated that they had stumbled upon shallow graves and items of Liz's clothing, but they were mistaken. 'Police also interviewed all her friends, anyone who'd had recent contact with her, including her boyfriend, who was in Bowen at the time,' Tristan says. 'None of those inquiries resulted in anything of substance.'

Later that year, the main suspect moved interstate, but it did not stop ACT Policing members re-interviewing him. 'He consented to being interviewed on a number of occasions through to 1987,' Tristan says. 'One of his subsequent interviews with police was under hypnosis because he'd been undergoing hypnotherapy of some description. Ultimately, that didn't bear anything of substance either.'

Eventually, the investigation came to a standstill. There was still no sign of Liz and no evidence to say who was involved in her disappearance and possible murder. The case could not go to inquest either because at that time coroners in the ACT were unable to hear matters in which there was no body. In the early 1990s that rule changed, and Janie and Alistair lobbied for an inquest into Liz's disappearance. They were successful and in 1993 the Chief Coroner announced one. It was heartening news and gave police another opportunity to appeal for information.

As it happened, someone did come forward with new information. 'The information they provided raised the prospect of a second suspect unrelated to the first,' Tristan says. The coroner adjourned the inquest to allow police to investigate the fresh information, which took around two years.

The new information had come from a woman whose daughter had separated from her partner shortly before the inquest. 'During her daughter's marriage, she had regularly told her mother that her husband said things to her about being involved in the abduction and murder of Liz,' Tristan says. The mother then saw the police appeals for information in the media. 'So she provided that information and also provided handwritten notes she had made after her daughter had made her disclosures.'

When police spoke to the woman's daughter she confirmed what her mother had said, so the investigators' next step was to interview the ex-husband. Tristan says he admitted saying those things to his wife, but the police read no more into it as the man suffered from mental illness. 'He was extremely ill and it was put down to his illness,' Tristan says. The police were satisfied he was not involved in any way.

So why then had he spoken of Liz Herfort's case? 'He said when he'd been a young teenager in Canberra in the early eighties he'd hung around a slightly older kid in his late teens,' Tristan says. 'He alleged the older teenager had been telling people in the early eighties that he'd been involved in the abduction and murder of Liz.' The mentally ill man took the police to an apartment in Canberra where he said the older teenage had taken him all those years ago. 'The older teenager had allegedly said it was where Liz was killed,' Tristan says.

Police found the man who'd allegedly made those claims years earlier. 'He denied having abducted and killed Liz but conceded he had bragged about having done so to impress the younger friends,' Tristan says. 'He said he was prone to telling stories and tried to shock people.' Police further investigated and ruled out that he could have been involved under the circumstances alleged because the apartment block had not even been built at the time in question. 'So if he was involved it couldn't have been in accordance with the events described and there was nothing else to involve him in the matter.'

The inquest continued in 1995 but was suspended again so police could investigate another new line of inquiry. 'It is sensitive information and cannot be revealed,' Tristan says. 'Suffice it to say, it was another year until the inquest was able to resume.'

So did all this digging uncover the truth about what had happened to Liz? Yes and no. In 1996, the coroner found it was likely that she was deceased as a result of foul play but there was insufficient evidence to lay charges against anyone. The case had reached a dead end. 'And unfortunately,' Tristan says, 'there hasn't been any information of significance since then.'

★

As the years went by, the Liz Herfort case was reviewed several times, the police remaining determined to find out what happened to her. 'We had a small media campaign in 2016 but unfortunately it didn't result in any significant information,' Tristan says. Ivan Milat's name came up several times but even though the notorious serial killer had worked in the ACT, there was no evidence to link him to Liz's disappearance.

Certainly, hitchhikers have been a target for predators ever since there were cars and people in need of a ride, but back in 1980 not everyone recognised the dangers. Today, things are different. 'I am disheartened when I see young people hitchhiking, but on the other hand I am kind of envious of their innocence of the world, that they are so oblivious to the risk they put themselves in,' says Alistair.

And even though Liz had hitched before and someone matching her description had been seen thumbing a ride that night, could police be certain it was Liz? 'The last one hundred per cent confirmed sighting of Liz was between 9 and 9.30 [pm] at the ANU bar,' Tristan reminds us. 'We have a number of unconfirmed sightings thereafter, so it may be another story entirely, we just don't know.' And that is important. 'We would not want to dissuade someone from coming forward with information that doesn't fit with previous theories or information released through the coronial process.'

As you might imagine, Liz's disappearance has permanently shattered her family. You might not pick it at first because they are articulate, well-presented and accomplished. But scratch beneath the surface and you will be hit by their anguish. 'One thing that doesn't make sense to anyone is that, for the first year since Liz's disappearance, getting a word from here to here, my whole throat and neck ached,' Janie says, pointing from her throat to her lips. 'It still feels like my chest is full of concrete and talking about Liz is like chiselling at that concrete.' These days Janie lives with chronic pain which she attributes to the loss of her sister, and throughout our interview she massages her brow and neck. 'If you ask if I'm okay, I'm not,' she says.

Time does not heal: Alistair Herfort at a memorial plaque for Liz
Photo courtesy Jamila Toderas/*Canberra Times*

'For me, it's like from that time when we first learned she was reported missing, time stopped,' Alistair says. 'It's like living the script of a terror movie, like I'm in a dream and waiting to wake up to find that everything is all right, but I never do.' He says it has made him feel separate from others. 'I live in a world that's different from everybody else's world and it's a challenge to function in the other world,' he says. 'I think it's very individual, grief, and how we respond to it. I think it's very isolating. It's very lonely.' And time, he says, does not heal the pain. 'It just gets kind of suppressed by all the other noise of life but it's always there.'

Alistair worries that talking about his experience is challenging for others. 'It's difficult to broach with people other than close family because it makes them uncomfortable,' he says. Being naturally empathetic, like Liz, makes it even harder for him. 'I kind of feel responsible for other people's discomfort,' he says. It has affected his close relationships, too. 'Permanency is an illusion for me. I find I live very much in the now, without a past and with no point in planning for the future, because everything in my life seems so ephemeral.'

Being the father of a daughter has made Alistair hypervigilant. 'Since the birth of my second daughter twenty-two years ago I have lived in constant, possibly irrational, fear for her safety,' he says. He also fears he has burdened her with his grief. 'My daughter never met Liz, but knows of her intimately. She is affected by her father's constant sadness; the inevitable turn of conversation to Liz whenever the family meets for what should otherwise be festive occasions. She has missed out on a normal childhood because of my prejudices of the world and my overprotectiveness.' Yet he cannot help how he feels. 'There is a part of me that is still back there in 1980,' he admits, 'a part of my psyche that is still sixteen years old that has not fully matured or been able to move on.'

In fact, he remembers a bittersweet event around his seventeenth birthday which still haunts him today. His mum had given him Liz's record player and her record collection and, feeling as though it was a gift from Liz herself, Alistair lay down in his room and thought how much it meant to him. Moments later, something strange happened. 'I was facing the wall and I felt something lightly touching my shoulder,' Alistair says. 'I heard Liz's voice saying, "Happy birthday, mate. It's okay, I'm all right."' He then saw what he can only describe as an apparition of Liz, fading against the wall. Stunned, he lay there motionless. 'I'm not a spiritual person so I don't know what I put that down to, but I felt it was a sign from Liz that she wasn't suffering and not to worry,' he says. 'Whether I manifested that thought, who would know? It never happened again.'

In her quiet moments, Janie, a Buddhist, feels like her sister is by her side in spirit. 'The quieter I get, the closer she is,' she says. Janie senses her sister's presence the most when she's in the kitchen. 'She used to bake beautifully and when I bake, she bakes,' Janie says. 'Sometimes, if I get into that quiet space, we bake something really special.'

Sometimes though, Janie wonders if she is wrong and that Liz is still alive. 'A few months back I saw this woman with grey, curly hair out of the corner of my eye,' Janie says. She was driving at the time. 'She had all her stuff in a really beat-up car and I thought she was probably a homeless woman.' Janie didn't stare because she didn't want to shame the other motorist, but something about her – perhaps her untamed hair or her soft features – made Janie wonder if it was Liz, now older and living a nomadic life. 'She might have got amnesia or had an accident, and was living this life in which she was just surviving,' Janie posits.

To provide an added insight into the confusion and emptiness she associates with her sister's disappearance, Janie wrote the following words to Liz, which she wishes to share with readers of this book.

Only in the between-worlds can I explain your absence, the presence of your absence, the reality of missing you, or the feeling that you – who have been with me since birth – live with me still.

I know that I live with the language of absence, and disappear with you, invisible to the world.

To announce your presence may loosen my grip on you further and you may be mistaken for horror. But horror does not belong with you, but with whoever made you disappear.

Maybe I could introduce you as the kindness I sometimes feel towards others or the happiness I feel in another's joy, or the understanding I feel when forgiving those I love.

Yes, this is the you that I'd introduce to a world that listens.

Even though Liz Herfort went missing some four decades ago, Detective Tristan Thexton wants us to hold on for a resolution to what happened to her, and help him if we can. He wants to hear from people who haven't spoken to police before and even people who have. He says that any piece of information, no matter how small, would be welcome. 'Liz was only young, she was eighteen,' he says. 'It's possible that people involved may have been young as well. Or even if those responsible were older, they may still be alive, or people they disclosed their involvement to might still be alive. Allegiances change. People might be looking for an opportunity to unburden their conscience.' If that's the case, he says, that opportunity has arrived.

Alistair could not agree more, and adds, 'About the only certainty we have, apart from the reality that Liz isn't coming home, is that there is someone out there who knows something, or knows someone who knows something. If that is you, we implore you to please come forward to give us the answers we so desperately seek. Or perhaps do it for yourself, so you too may have some peace at last.'

PROFILE

KEITH MOOR

HERALD SUN INSIGHT EDITOR/INVESTIGATIVE JOURNALIST

The Crime Writer

Photo courtesy Andy Dewitt/*Herald Sun*

I came from a working-class family in England. Dad was a bricklayer and Mum stayed at home to look after their four children. I left school at sixteen and got a job as a stores boy for the *Newcastle Journal* where it was my job to fill up cars with petrol and take notebooks to journalists. After six months a junior position came up in the library and I got it. I worked closely with the journalists, helping with their research. Doing so got me interested in journalism but I didn't have the educational qualifications to become a journalist in England. Still, I couldn't help but think, *Gee, I'd love to do that one day.* Thanks to Australia I've been able to do it.

I came out to Western Australia to work in the iron ore mines in 1974, initially as a tradesman's assistant and later as a blast hole driller. There was ▸

the opportunity to make a lot of money. My initial plan was to stay for six months and go back to England but, with the money I saved working in the Koolan and Cockatoo Island mines, I put myself through university as a mature age student. I studied for a journalism degree at the Western Australian Institute of Technology for two years before leaving after being offered a two-year cadetship on the *Perth Daily News* in 1979 at the age of twenty-four. Within weeks of qualifying as a journalist, I returned to England in 1980 and got a job as a reporter on the *Newcastle Journal*. It was very rewarding to work there as a journalist after starting as a stores boy.

I returned to Australia in 1983 and got a job as a reporter with the *Melbourne Herald*. I was based in the media room at Russell Street Police Headquarters as a police roundsman. Back then you could just walk into the Armed Robbery Squad or the Homicide Squad – wherever you liked. I'd start work around 6 am, and once I'd filed my yarns at 10 am for the first edition of the afternoon newspaper I'd drop off forty or fifty copies, hot off the presses, to the detectives. As I gave them their free copy of the *Herald* each day I'd say, 'Anything on the go?' or 'Have you got a story for me?' It was a really good way of getting stories. I really liked doing police rounds and progressed to be the *Herald*'s Chief Police Reporter.

I worked as a political journalist in Canberra during the Hawke and Keating years but still made sure I reported on crime too. I made contacts within the Australian Federal Police, ASIO and the Australian Institute of Criminology, as the headquarters of each were in Canberra, resulting in me filing a number of articles about organised and other crime. I went back to England for a second stint as Industrial Editor of the *Newcastle Journal* ▶

before returning to the *Melbourne Herald* in 1988. I've now clocked up more than thirty years straight at the *Herald* and the *Herald Sun*. I have a particular interest in writing about cold case homicides. I'm fascinated by them and believe the media has an important role to play in helping solve both cold and hot cases.

One cold case that affects me to this day is the murder of six-year-old Kylie Maybury. On the afternoon of Melbourne Cup Day in 1984 her mum sent her to buy a bag of sugar. Kylie walked a hundred yards to the corner shop and never came home.

I heard a 'Code 69' – the code for murder – on the police scanner. I went to the crime scene which had blue tape around it. When the coroner arrived he took the cover off the body. You don't want to look but as a journalist it's your job. Kylie was face down and when they turned her over her little arm flopped onto the kerb like a rag doll. I wrote my stories and went to a press conference at eleven. I didn't think I was affected but when I got home my partner said, 'Did you have to cover the Kylie Maybury murder?' I just broke down and for months afterwards I would wake up after dreaming about her arm flopping onto the kerb. I was determined I wouldn't let that little girl die in vain.

Kylie Maybury's mother Julie did an all-in press interview but allowed me to do a one-on-one interview with her a couple of weeks later. We became friends and I regularly wrote anniversary stories about Kylie's murder. There weren't many new leads but between me and Julie we managed to keep the story going over the years in the hope the publicity would lead to people contacting police with information about the case.

There was a breakthrough after I wrote a long article to commemorate the thirtieth anniversary ▸

of Kylie's murder. I interviewed the then head of the Cold Case Squad at Homicide, Detective Senior Sergeant Boris Buick, and the *Herald Sun* printed a photo of him holding up a picture of Kylie. It prompted a number of calls. One caller said, 'Have a look at Gregory Keith Davies.' As it happened, Davies had sexually offended against other children and had lived near Kylie's family at the time. He was not a particularly strong suspect but some months after the thirtieth anniversary article the police turned up at his house and said they needed a DNA sample from him. He voluntarily gave it, presumably because his wife was with him and it would have looked odd if he'd declined. It matched the DNA Kylie's killer had left at the murder scene. One of the proudest moments of my career was being in court with Julie Maybury in December 2017 to see Davies jailed for life after he pleaded guilty to the 1984 murder of Kylie.

The Bonnie Clarke murder case was another example of the power of the media. In 1999 Homicide Squad detective Ron Iddles was sent to study cold case squads in the United States. We didn't have such a squad in Victoria at the time and Ron established the state's first one after his US trip. I interviewed him about his trip and the new cold case squad. He was not prepared to talk about which cases he was going to reinvestigate because it was early days, so in my story I said something like, 'Among the cold cases that the new squad are expected to look at are this one, that one, and the murder of Bonnie Clarke.' We also printed a photo of six-year-old Bonnie sitting on Santa Claus' knee. It really pulled at your heartstrings and was the page three lead.

The next day a man rang. He said, 'Are you the bloke who wrote the story about Bonnie Clarke?' I said, 'Yes.' He said, 'My girlfriend thinks she knows who killed ▶

Bonnie. She was friends with Bonnie when they were both children and she always thought it was the lodger at Bonnie's house.' I said, 'Ron Iddles really needs to know this.' So I rang Ron and filled him in, then gave him the man's number.

I could have written a story about the new lead straightaway but I'd never knowingly jeopardise an investigation. Instead, I always say to the detectives, 'If this comes to something can you make sure I'm the first to run the story?' I'm much keener on helping solve a case and writing about it then, rather than writing about it and not getting it solved.

Time went by and Ron handed the case to a bloke called Tim Day. It was Tim's first job at Victoria's Homicide Squad as a fresh-faced copper. Ron gave him the files and said, 'It's your job to try and solve that.' One of the first things he did was speak to the woman whose boyfriend had called me. She'd always suspected the lodger but couldn't remember his name. Tim Day eventually narrowed it down to a man named Malcolm Clarke, who was no relation to Bonnie. The police mounted an undercover operation and were able to prove that it was him.

It just goes to show how one paragraph in a story in a newspaper can help solve a crime. Of course, it involved a lot of investigative work for the Homicide Squad, but that one kernel of information gave them what they needed to start gathering evidence.

Another case I have broken many yarns on is the 1980 murder of Thornbury bookshop owner Maria James. I revealed in August 2007 that Father Anthony Bongiorno had emerged as a suspect and that Detective Senior Sergeant Ron Iddles from the Victoria Police Cold Case Squad was undertaking a review of the case.

New information I provided to Ron in 2007 was explosive. It included that a female friend of Maria's, Margaret Quill, had told me of her belief that Maria had confronted Father Bongiorno about her suspicion that the priest was molesting one of her sons. I also told Ron that after I took Margaret to see Maria's son, Mark, he confirmed Bongiorno had tried to entice him into his house with Mars Bars and that he had told his mother about Bongiorno's advances on him. At the time, Mark James told me he was not aware of whether Bongiorno had molested his mentally impaired younger brother, Adam, but that he would ask him. The case against Bongiorno strengthened in 2013 when Mark rang me to say Adam had finally admitted that Bongiorno had sexually molested him and that his mother Maria had found out and had intended to confront Bongiorno about it shortly before she was murdered. I alerted Ron Iddles to the new information and he then took a sworn statement from Adam.

My 2013 article revealing the new information prompted yet another witness to come forward – an electrician who claimed to have seen Bongiorno with blood on him on the day of the murder. At the request of police, I didn't report on the electrician's claim as it might have jeopardised the ongoing investigation into Bongiorno and other suspects. Police had what they thought was the killer's DNA from blood samples left at the Maria James murder scene and they had used it over the years to eliminate a number of suspects. In 2017 Victoria Police discovered that there had been an embarrassing stuff-up and that the DNA sample they'd been using in the Maria James probe was actually obtained from an exhibit from a different case. That discovery by detectives was later revealed by the ABC's *Trace* podcast. ▶

Bongiorno remains a suspect, as do all the suspects who were wrongly eliminated by detectives using the bungled DNA sample.

I also broke the story about how every future murder reward in Victoria would be one million dollars. An article about there being a million-dollar reward in relation to one of the underworld murders prompted Daryl Floyd to call me. Daryl's twelve-year-old brother, Terry, had disappeared in country Victoria in 1975. Daryl asked me how the murder of a dirtbag criminal could attract a million-dollar reward when the reward in his brother's case was only one hundred thousand dollars. I then interviewed the father of missing Melbourne woman Sarah MacDiarmid, who said that while he was glad there was a million-dollar reward in his daughter's case, it angered him there was such inequities with murder rewards, with some attracting a million dollars, others fifty thousand dollars and some no reward at all. He said the community rarely cares about criminals killing criminals.

When the *Herald Sun* ran the story the then Chief Commissioner of Police, Ken Lay, phoned me. He said, 'I just read your story and it makes incredible sense to me. I'm going to order an immediate inquiry into it and I promise I'll reform the system.' Naturally I said, 'And you'll keep me in the loop?' He did, and in December 2014 I was able to break the story about how every murder reward issued from then on would be for one million dollars and that over time all murder cases where rewards had previously been issued would be increased to a million dollars. The reward for information in the Terry Floyd case was also increased to a million.

I'm sure more murders will be solved with one-million-dollar rewards. Not many people would ▸

come forward with information for fifty thousand dollars but if there's the offer of one million dollars and some sort of protection, if needed, a person might come forward. There aren't many murderers who keep their crimes to themselves, and relationships change. So a woman who initially gave her husband an alibi because she loved him might change her story years later when he becomes an arsehole who beats the crap out of her. And that's how million-dollar rewards can work, by enticing that woman to come forward to admit she lied for him and that he wasn't actually with her on the night of the murder. It is a life-changing amount of money.

Some people ask, 'Why don't all cold cases immediately attract one-million-dollar rewards?' It's for a good reason. If it was announced that all cold cases were attracting one-million-dollar rewards, the police would get just one story out of it. But they want every murder to get a lot of publicity, so they announce cold case murder rewards one by one.

I think print media and newspaper websites are the best way for police to get their messages across. If you watch a two-minute crime story on the news you couldn't be expected to remember the spelling of someone's surname or the make of a car that police are looking for. But in print people often go to a second or third reading, and online there is often a link for readers to contact Crime Stoppers.

I think it's important that police, not just homicide squads, recognise that the media is happy to be used. The best way to find a person of interest, a vehicle or other information is to run a story or a picture. I would encourage police to build up a relationship with a journalist they trust because it is a great investigative tool and we're here to be used.

THE SECRET OF SLOPING MAIN

WHO KILLED WOULD-BE ASSASSIN, **REUBEN MATTATHYAHU**?

Mysterious in life and death: Reuben Mattathyahu

Photo courtesy Chris Harris

'I believe I know who has the answers and they have been keeping those secrets for over thirty years. The burden of these secrets must weigh heavily on their consciences.'
Constable Fiona Howard, Tasmania Police

For half an hour the police boat judders across the swell until what looks like a dot on the horizon – a farmhouse – comes into sight. It's lonely out here and the ocean surrounding the property ahead is hundreds, if not thousands, of metres deep. The skipper cuts the engine, and waves lap idly against the boat. Overhead a seagull slows as if it knows why the police have chosen here to stop.

Constable Fiona Howard – a petite, smart-looking detective from Hobart – breaks the silence, saying, 'Reuben could have been dumped in the ocean and no one would ever know.'

Detective Senior Sergeant David Richardson nods, peering at the property through binoculars. 'Whatever happened to him,' he says, 'it started up there.'

Less than half an hour by road to Port Arthur, a nineteenth-century penal colony which later became a twentieth-century killing ground for mass murderer Martin Bryant, this scenic and otherwise peaceful slice of the Tasman Peninsula will always have a whiff of untimely death about it.

In 1982, Reuben Mattathyahu – born Tony Zackary Harris – a woodcutter and self-proclaimed mercenary, came to live here to start a new life. However, he met his premature end around eighteen months later, after telling a friend he wanted to leave.

With no word from Reuben since that day – and no sign of his body – his disappearance is as mysterious as the man himself.

But as the detectives investigating this bizarre cold case know – mysteries, no matter how old, can be solved.

Chris Harris only met his half-brother a few times but Tony still made a big impression on him. Fifteen years Chris' senior, when Tony was twenty-four years old he travelled from England to Australia on an assisted passage and visited his father's family in Mount Gambier. It was a year after the Harrises had left England. Chris says, 'Tony was in the national service, a commando. He was always in fatigues. [When he arrived in Australia] he was carrying two rucksacks and a couple of rifles and a lot of knives. Today you wouldn't get through customs with that sort of stuff, but in those days he travelled like that.'

Before he was Reuben: Tony Harris (right), aged eighteen, after a manoeuvre in the British Army
Photo courtesy Chris Harris

Prior to leaving England, Tony had been living with his mother Elsie who'd been divorced from Tony's dad, Albert, for several years. Albert found love again with a nurse named Brenda and they'd had five children, but they always made sure Tony felt welcome in their home. However, life for the Harris family became less comfortable in 1956 when a credit squeeze hit the UK, leaving many big businesses unable to pay their bills. As Albert's company, which manufactured nuts and bolts, drew its dying breaths, he and Brenda needed to sell the family home to pay off debts. Afterwards they moved to Australia in search of a better life.

When Tony came to visit his father's family in 1958, Chris had something special to show him. Chris and his brothers had built a large underground cubby house in the yard of their government-owned home. It was a glorious, complex structure whose proud engineers were all in short pants. 'We had cross bearers and tube strips – logs that were split to form the roof. It was probably twelve foot by twelve foot, with a trapdoor and dirt on top,' Chris says.

Upon discovering the cubby house, a government official deemed it structurally unsafe and demanded it be demolished. Chris and his brothers didn't want to destroy it, but under Tony's tutelage the demolition turned into a war game. 'There were two of us underground and three outside with water pistols and hoses and we collapsed the thing,' Chris says. At the time no one, not even Tony, gave much thought to how dangerous the demolition process was. 'Tony was like a big kid,' Chris says. 'I don't think he thought at any time the thing could have collapsed with two kids inside.'

Chris fondly remembers playing other games with Tony, including toy soldiers. But his half-brother's action-packed visit was short-lived. 'Tony went as quick as he came,' Chris says. 'After six or eight weeks he decided to go and shoot crocs and buffalo. In those days there was a bounty on their heads.'

It wasn't until a year later, after the Harris family had moved across town, that they heard from Tony again. In the letterbox they discovered a handwritten note on a piece of cardboard, which announced that Tony would be on the next day's train and wanted to be picked up from the station. 'So five kids and Mum and Dad packed into the car, an old Wolseley,' Chris remembers. It was quite a squeeze and would have been even more so with Tony's long legs inside on the way home. But the train came and went with no sign of him. The family paced the platform for an hour but Tony didn't materialise.

By the time the Harrises returned home, however, Tony was sitting on the front porch as if to say, 'Where have you been?'

Looking back, Chris realises Tony must have arrived in Mount Gambier the previous day. 'He's come down, he's written a note and he's gone away again, so he must have been there the day or night before to put the cardboard in the mailbox. He was funny, as in he had a twisted mind.'

After staying with his family in Australia a second time, Tony announced that he was going to Tibet. Chris recalls, 'He never used the word "mercenary" to us but he said he was going to help the Tibetans fight for independence.'

That was the last the Harris family saw of Tony. 'After that he never tried to contact the family again,' Chris says. For all they knew he had been killed in Tibet.

Chris Harris might not have been close to Tony, but they were blood and that mattered.

So in 2000 – half a lifetime and the emergence of the worldwide web later – Chris decided to try and find out what had happened to Tony by posting a message on a missing persons website in England. His hope was that Tony was still alive and living back in the UK. 'Looking for Half-Brother, Tony Harris,' Chris' post read. However, no one responded, so five or six years later Chris renewed his appeal. Again, nothing.

It wasn't until late 2011 that Fiona Howard, a plain clothes constable from Tasmania Police, contacted Chris about his post. Chris remembers her asking him 'an awful lot of questions' to confirm his identity as the half-brother of a man whose missing persons case she'd just been assigned. Fiona wanted to find Tony too.

After reading the original police file about Tony's disappearance, Fiona's first impression was that something suspicious had happened and the case warranted further, more thorough, investigation. 'I felt we were in a better position to do that because of technology and other advances in investigative techniques since 1984 when Tony was reported missing,' Fiona says.

As she began researching Tony's background Fiona learned that unbeknown to his Australian family, Tony had never gone to Tibet at all. Instead, he'd returned to England in 1961 and lived there for a few years before returning to Australia on another assisted passage in 1964.

Three years later he returned to England yet again, where he married Patricia 'Liz' McPherson and they had a son called Adam. In the early 1970s Tony and Liz separated and Tony headed back to Australia. 'In 1972 he worked on the construction of a big telecommunications tower in Western Australia,' Fiona says. 'He also worked for a while in the Northern Territory.'

Chris tells me, 'Fiona was the first person who brought to light that Tony ended up returning to Australia more than once. After Mount Gambier we moved to Sydney but it wouldn't have been hard for Tony to find the family trail.' If Tony had been looking for his family's new address, all he would have had to do was ask Chris' aunt, who, as Tony knew, lived in Kings Cross. 'My aunt knew where we were at any time. I just think he didn't want to be contacted because he had his own life,' says Chris.

Fiona also found out that in 1976, four years after his stint in South Australia, Tony left mainland Australia for Tasmania, where he worked for two years in the timber industry. He then returned to Adelaide from 1978 to 1980, where he found employment as a gardener at the Botanical Gardens before moving back to Tasmania in 1980. His was the life of a freedom-lover, an outdoorsman, an adventurer.

Curiously, by the late 1970s Tony was known by many other names – aliases, some might say. The half-brother who Chris Harris knew as Tony Zackary Harris had changed his name by deed poll to Tony Zackary Harras in England in 1962. Chris assumes the reason Tony changed his surname was 'to get another free passage to Australia, which he did'.

If that name change wasn't strange enough, by the late 1970s Tony, whose family was Anglican, started calling himself Judah

Zachariah Reuben Wolfe Mattathyahu. Some people called him Judah while others referred to him as Zac, Carl or Karl, though the name he seemed to favour was Reuben Mattathyahu, which sounded Jewish. 'The first time I heard the Judah name I thought as far as I knew he wasn't a religious man, why would he change his faith and his name?' Chris says. It was so unlike his birth name – Tony Harris – that one might have wondered if he had reason to hide his true identity.

During his second stint in Tasmania he befriended the owner of the Tradewear Hobart store, John Oldmeadow, and John's staff members, Danny Swan and Paul Minehan. 'From that, Mr Oldmeadow allowed him to use the upstairs flat in his Liverpool Street shop,' Fiona says. 'He also let him leave his property there when he came and went.'

Initially he travelled to and from the Huon Valley, staying in the Hobart digs whenever he was in town. 'He'd always tell Mr Oldmeadow and the other guys when he was leaving and coming back. That's just how he was.'

In 1978, Tony, who I'll now refer to by his preferred name of Reuben, started work barking logs in the Russell River Valley in southern Tasmania, where he made friends with a gentle-natured man named Robert Watson. 'Robert worked in really close proximity to Reuben because they'd be in the forest in camps, and Reuben would tell Robert stories,' Fiona says.

In an interview before he passed away, Robert Watson said, '[Reuben] told me that he was in the British commandos, the Israeli commandos, and he was in the East Timor flare-up when that happened, and he was over there training people for whoever employed him, I don't know who. So he was always in some sort of conflict somewhere.' Reuben also told Robert he'd been a member of the Israeli Defence Force, fighting in the 1967 [Arab–Israeli] Six-Day War and that ASIO had a file on him 'as thick as a phone book'. 'He'd get talking about things and he'd start frothing at the mouth, he was that passionate about it, so, you know, he used to entertain us, I suppose!' Robert recalled.

Reuben told Robert, a Mormon, that he was Jewish, as his adopted names suggested. 'Because we both had religious backgrounds we clicked, so we got on all right that way and I became his friend,' Robert said. 'He indicated to me that he did work for the Jewish people, like chasing war criminals and things like that. He didn't actually say that but he indicated it, cos one time he said he was going to Melbourne for a weekend. They wanted him to come and do some work for them and I just sort of jokingly said to him, "Are you a hitman?" and he just gave me a knowing smile sort of thing, as if to say "yes". He had a colourful life . . . or past.'

On regular bushwalks together, Reuben regaled Robert with his colourful stories as they combed the wilderness looking for sacred Aboriginal sites. Robert also used to take Reuben wherever he needed to go because, despite all his other survival skills, Reuben couldn't drive. Robert also introduced Reuben to his cousin Howard Watson, and they got along well too.

Before he disappeared, Reuben was working for a logger named Ike Kelly who owned a company – like the others Reuben had worked for – which felled and barked trees to sell to factories, passing on a percentage of their profits to the people on whose farms they worked. Reuben was working on one such property at remote Sloping Main near Saltwater River on the Tasman Peninsula when he made the acquaintance of the property's owners, John and Anne Hull, who – in exchange for Reuben doing odd jobs – allowed him to live in an old convict hut on their land. Many of the dwellings in the area had been built by convicts, and huts like the one on the Hulls' property – while earthen-floored and basic – were still functional shelters for farm workers.

Reuben's employment record shows he had long enjoyed the freedom of moving and working whenever and wherever he chose, so living in the hut – even after he'd finished the woodcutting job – probably seemed ideal to him. 'He never drew any social services and so he'd live on the money he'd earned, and when it was running low he'd go off and do some work, build up his bank account and go off and live somewhere,' Fiona says.

During his time at Sloping Main, Reuben's air of mystery magnified. While there, he spoke again of being a 'Nazi hunter'. He also claimed to have travelled with a group of seven men to Africa to destabilise a government, and how when a helicopter arrived to pick them up he was ordered to kill the other men, before being choppered away alone. Reuben frequently led people to believe he was a professional killer and claimed he was the kind of guy who other mercenaries touched for good luck.

Unfortunately, his luck was about to run out.

Fiona believes that Reuben was at the Hulls' farm on the night of Friday, 11 November 1983 when he called Howard Watson to say he was leaving the property. Reuben asked Howard to call Robert – who was presumably not as easy to get hold of by phone – to ask if he could drive to Sloping Main the following day to collect him and take him back to Glen Huon, where the Watsons lived. It was about a two-and-a-half-hour drive. Reuben also asked Howard if he could stay overnight and then be taken to Hobart the next day. He also asked if Robert could make sure there was enough room in the car for his belongings.

Sometime between 9 am and 12 pm the next day, Reuben contacted his friends at the Tradewear shop to say he was coming to Hobart and wanted to retrieve the property from his trunks. 'He told the manager Paul Minehan that he'd had enough down there and had to get out,' Fiona says.

'By four o'clock on the Saturday, Howard had passed Reuben's message about picking him up on to Robert,' Fiona says. At around seven that night, which was the earliest Robert could leave, he began the drive from Glen Huon to Sloping Main. At 8.30 pm, while Robert was on the road, Reuben phoned Howard and asked whether he'd spoken to Robert and if he was coming to get him. 'Howard replied that Robert was on his way and would arrive around nine.' By this time Howard thought Reuben sounded agitated.

Recalling his arrival at Sloping Main, Robert said, 'I got there when it was dark and went inside. His hut door was open and the lights were on and a couple of dogs that he looked after for the Hulls were there [in the yard].'

Robert figured his friend couldn't be too far away and sat on the couch to wait a while. Then he had an unsettling thought. *Reuben never goes away from his hut unless he locks the door. He locks everything!* Robert also knew that Reuben loved the Hulls' dogs so much that he allowed them to sleep inside with him, so it was unusual for them to be outdoors after nightfall. According to evidence he gave years later at an inquest, Robert waited for fifteen minutes and then drove to the Hulls' house at Saltwater River where he asked Anne if she'd seen Reuben. She said she hadn't so Robert went back to the hut and looked for Reuben's personal belongings, which he found in the back room. Reuben was packed and ready to go. But where was he?

Reuben with the Hulls' dogs
Photo courtesy Chris Harris

Next Robert drove to the nearby town of Premaydena to call Howard from a public phone. 'And that's when he told me [Reuben] had rung at about half past eight and was asking if I was still coming,' Robert said.

Robert returned to the hut one more time but with still no sign of Reuben, he went home around midnight, figuring there was a rational explanation for his friend's no-show. 'Because he used to disappear and go off, I thought, *Well, maybe he's gone somewhere,* and so I left a note for him just to give me another call and I'll come back,' Robert said. 'It seemed a bit funny that he wasn't there but he wanted to get out . . . I wasn't thinking of any skulduggery or anything like that. I left there about midnight. Never found him.'

On face value, it might have appeared that Reuben had left Sloping Main of his own accord. After all, he lived a transient lifestyle, his own family didn't know where to find him, and for some unknown reason he had a heck of a lot of aliases. Had Reuben simply moved on? Or had his shadowy past caught up with him?

Initially, Robert Watson didn't report his friend missing. 'He didn't like police and I didn't want to be the one to have police going down there snooping around looking for him if he wasn't missing,' Robert said. 'So I left it a while and I talked to one of the fellas he worked with, who employed him, and they were going to talk to the police about it and that's when we reported him missing.'

Alerted to Reuben's disappearance in March 1984, the police started investigating, collecting statements from people who were associated with him. They also checked Reuben's financial records but discovered he hadn't spent a cent since he was last seen, which didn't bode well.

Looking back at the initial police investigation, which she wasn't involved in, Fiona says, 'They did a huge search of the area, and bearing in mind how remote and vast it was, they did the best they could under the circumstances. They found his property at the shop in Hobart but otherwise didn't mention anything about his other property, which we ended up finding at the hut in 2011. Either the police back then didn't locate it or they didn't think it was important, I'm not sure.'

The original investigation lasted for around three months. After that, Fiona says, 'Reuben was just put down as a missing person.'

In November 2011, when she first read the old files regarding Reuben's disappearance, Fiona was on a six-week secondment to the Cold Case Unit in Tasmania. The first thing she did as part of her investigation into what had happened to Reuben was go back and speak to as many of the original police who'd worked on the case as she could find, as well as anyone who knew Reuben when he was living in Tasmania. 'I also did a lot of checks in the Northern Territory and Adelaide in relation to his wanderings in those areas,' she says. 'I was trying to get a better picture of him.'

With around twenty-seven years having passed since Reuben's disappearance, it wasn't easy for Fiona to track down some people but she ticked as many off her list as could. And when her secondment at the Cold Case Unit ended she took Reuben's file back to Bellerive, where she was stationed. She would not let the case go.

'She drove it. She was unrelenting, dedicated,' says her colleague, Detective Senior Sergeant David Richardson, who became Fiona's go-to whenever she needed guidance.

One of Tasmania Police's most experienced detectives, David started in the job in 1981 and has spent half his career in criminal investigation. He has seen it all and even remembers when Reuben was reported missing. 'I was a detective constable in the 1980s and my senior sergeant was one of the first investigators [looking into Reuben's disappearance],' he says. And though David wasn't involved in the original investigation, his skills as a strategist would be the perfect complement to Fiona Howard's unwavering dedication to the case.

In her quest to speak to everyone associated with Reuben, Fiona contacted the rest of his siblings and found out that they too had been trying to find him. She also tracked down Reuben's former wife Liz and their adult son Adam. 'This will give you an idea of what Fiona is like,' David says. 'She was going on a holiday to the UK and she arranged to meet Reuben's ex-wife while she was over there. She could have just had a holiday but she decided to work on the case while she was there.'

Not only did Fiona visit Liz and Adam in England but she accepted Liz's invitation to stay in her home. Over bottomless cups of tea, Liz told Fiona everything she could remember about her erstwhile husband. Sadly, Adam hadn't known his father, who'd left when Adam was three, but he helped too. 'I managed to get Adam's DNA so I had it on record for future reference,' Fiona says. 'So if ever we found remains which we suspected belonged to Reuben, we could compare them against Adam's DNA.'

During Fiona's visit, Liz quickly put paid to one of her ex-husband's wild stories. 'She didn't believe he'd gone to Israel to become part of the army,' Fiona says. 'She said he'd wanted to and had tried [to] but he'd married her instead.'

It looked to Fiona as though Reuben had travelled to Israel at some stage though, and had possibly lived in a kibbutz there. 'That comes from a bank account which shows he withdrew money in Israel for a short time in '74,' she says.

Once Fiona had found out all she could about the missing man's background it was time to further the investigation. 'We had to consider the various reasons why Reuben might have disappeared,' Fiona says. 'Had he voluntarily gone missing? Had he committed suicide? Had he gotten lost and wandered off? Or was [his disappearance a result of] misadventure by known or unknown persons? We had to go down these various avenues and make sure every possibility was covered.'

Bound for Sloping Main: Detective Senior Sergeant David Richardson and Constable Fiona Howard
Photo courtesy Justine Ford

Fiona and David became convinced Reuben had met with foul play but case sensitivities prevent them from elaborating. 'We felt we could reasonably justify why he wasn't voluntarily missing or hadn't committed suicide,' Fiona says, 'and we came to the conclusion that he was most reasonably murdered by someone known to him.'

Robert Watson paled at the likelihood his friend was murdered, saying, 'If I'd been probably forty minutes earlier I'd probably have got him, or I'd have been in the thick of what happened so . . . it might've been two bodies.'

If it was murder, Fiona and David had to figure out who'd done it, how and why. 'We had to look at who would have had the motive, the means and the opportunity,' Fiona says. But no one could – or would – tell them what happened that night at the isolated property. Perhaps, Fiona thought, there might still be clues in Reuben's hut? She and David decided to take a look.

Entering the dimly lit structure, the investigators noticed that all of Reuben's worldly belongings – aside from those he had left at the flat above the Tradewear store in Hobart – were still there collecting dust, as if waiting for him to collect them. 'We were just flabbergasted,' Fiona says. 'The hut itself was one big main room with a smaller add-on, I suppose you could say. All Reuben's property was there piled up. It nearly took up all of the add-on. We had to take items out one by one and pile them up. There was a huge amount of things and we undid them as we went. There were probably about seventeen bags, all chock-a-block. We were just continually amazed. And it had never been touched. Everything was in its original condition.'

Reuben might have been a nomad but it was clear to the police as they cast their eyes over his home and belongings that he was also a proud man. 'It was rustic but meticulously organised,' David says. 'This was not a hovel.'

As the investigators continued poking through Reuben's belongings they built up an even stronger picture of him as a skilled bushman. 'There were spears, quite a lot of knives, a bark-splitting shovel and axes,' Fiona says. They also found taxation papers, bank books and notebooks, which showed Reuben to be highly organised. A yarmulke in one of the bags further spoke of his religious conversion to Judaism.

The detectives also came across a stash of photo albums in which there were several racy photos of women. Reuben had been quite the snapper. 'We also found black crotchless underpants and a reusable rubber condom,' Fiona adds. The curios told the story of a man who enjoyed single life, but you sure couldn't sell them at a police lost and found auction.

During their search, Fiona and David also came across some letters Reuben had written to his mother in England in 1981. The letters spoke of a son's love for his mother and a rejection of conventional living.

My dearest mum,
Here's a surprise for you, dear, a letter from your prodigal son.
I was just passing thro Peter's place, and I'd thought I would write.
I am still wandering about, always moving, never stop.
I like being independent and free.
At the moment I have a special woman in my life, I'm on my way to meet her now, I've just come out of the desert.
I've read your letters, dear, and thank you for the news.

Words from a wanderer: One of several letters Reuben wrote to his mum in England
Photo courtesy Chris Harris

'My dearest Mum,' one begins. 'I still live in the bush and only come out now and again.' He goes on to explain – in part – his change of name. 'You see when my marriage broke up and I came away I knew I would start a new life completely, and this I have done and do not wish to be reminded of the past. I will never marry again and the girl friends [sic] I have known [sic] this and have to except [sic] it.'

The police also found this poem from Reuben to his former wife, Liz.

I sit here and write of the days that are gone
Of the woman I loved and a small boy, my son.
My Liz and my Adam, I want you to know
You'll always [be] with me wherever I go.
I lost you, my Liz, and I wondered why
One tries to be strong and I knew I should stay,
But I just left our place and wandered away.
I just keep on moving, with no place to go,
And I know I am searching, for what, I don't know.
When we were together, my family and I.
I don't write home now, though I know that I should,
But writing back home don't do me no good.
I know as I write, never again will I see
The people I love, that are so dear to me.

The poem made sense of what Fiona had heard about Reuben's nature. 'When I visited Liz in England she mentioned he couldn't stay in the one place and be committed to family life,' she says. 'He was always going to be wandering.'

Until one day, he wasn't.

In August 2015, with a coronial inquest underway, the police returned to the convict hut where they suspected Reuben had probably realised his time was up. David Richardson arranged for a full forensic examination of the dwelling to be conducted. It meant that more than thirty years after Reuben had disappeared, the property was a crime scene for two days.

'The forensic scientists went over it for a long time looking for blood,' David says. 'They cleared out the hut where he was living and pulled the carpet out but they didn't find anything.' No blood, no evidence and, as expected, no human remains. There was nothing there to prove that Reuben had been killed, let alone to identify who might have killed him. But no one said cold case investigations were easy.

The inquest into Reuben Mattathyahu's disappearance sought to examine the evidence and determine once and for all what had happened to him. Numerous witnesses were called to give evidence and, because of the multitude of names used to refer to Reuben, at times Chris Harris had to remind himself that those in the witness box were talking about his half-brother. 'In the court, everybody knew him by a different name,' he says. 'So when I approached the bench, it was Tony; when Mrs Hull approached the bench, it was Karl or Reuben. When someone else approached the bench, it was Reuben. So it was pretty confusing.'

After considering the evidence, Coroner Simon Cooper stated, 'A good deal of mystery seems to have surrounded Mattathyahu. It is difficult to escape the conclusion that Mattathyahu deliberately fostered that air of mystery.' He noted that there was no evidence that Reuben had fought in the Arab–Israeli Six-Day War or was a member of the Israeli Defence Force.

The coroner also found no evidence to support Reuben's stories about his purported trip to Africa. While accepting that Reuben had told such stories, the coroner said, 'I do not accept that there is a scintilla of truth to any of them.' It was the same with Reuben's stories about being a Nazi hunter.

'None of his accounts of his background are anything other than self-reported,' the coroner said. 'No evidence was uncovered that supports a conclusion that there is any basis for any of the claims – in particular the more outlandish ones of working as a mercenary and as an assassin.'

Chris can only assume his half-brother lied to his family and friends about these adventures 'to build himself up'. But there was no suggestion he'd been killed for merely spinning a yarn. His death, like his life, was shrouded in mystery.

In the end, the coroner found that Reuben was 'most likely the victim of homicide' and that, 'No other conclusion is open on the evidence. There is nothing to suggest that his death was as a result of misadventure, accident or suicide.'

The coroner thanked the legal counsel and those who investigated the case so thoroughly, saying, 'I also acknowledge the professional, competent and detailed investigation conducted by the members of the Tasmania Police Cold Case Unit and in particular Detective Constable [Fiona] Howard after that unit was disbanded.' He concluded by conveying his 'sincere condolences to the family of Mr Mattathyahu'.

In the absence of a body, Chris Harris was surprised that the coroner found his half-brother had been murdered. He still wonders who Reuben had upset enough to kill him. 'It could've been a gambling debt but I don't know if he was a gambler,' Chris says. 'He could have threatened someone, I don't know.'

'It was very rewarding to see Fiona's efforts recognised by the coroner,' David says. 'And for me, it was rewarding to see our processes at work and see people being subject to examination in a judicial setting.'

Fiona was also pleased with the coroner's findings. 'I was really satisfied that he came to the same conclusion as myself and that he agreed we'd done everything we could to resolve [the investigation into Reuben's disappearance] so that gave me some satisfaction,' she says. 'But it's one of those jobs where you may never get a conclusion, unless it's a dying confession.'

After eighteen years in the job, eleven of those in criminal investigation, it was a great loss to Tasmania Police when Fiona retired in January 2019. Not surprisingly, the case she will never forget is the disappearance of Reuben Mattathyahu. 'I feel grateful that I was given the opportunity to work on it. I believe I have done everything that is legally possible to solve the disappearance of Reuben Mattathyahu. There are people who have the answers and they have been keeping those secrets for over thirty years.

The burden of these secrets must weigh heavily on their consciences and maybe one day they will realise that to lift that burden they need to give the answers to his family.'

Fortunately, there is a fine detective still serving in Tasmania Police who won't let go of the case. His hope now is that whoever holds that information will come and see him. 'The door's always open,' he says. 'It's not over until we say it's over.'

HIGH ANXIETY

WHY DID **ATTILA BOGAR** GO MISSING?

Whereabouts unknown: Attila Bogar

Photo courtesy Roza Bogar

'He told me, "They will kill us. They will kill Maryann, they will kill me."'

Roza Bogar, Attila's mother

'Let me tell you a story,' says Anxiety. It's the middle of the night and sleep is elusive. You pull up the covers and block your ears because you know Anxiety has not come with a comforting bedtime story. Instead, Anxiety wires you up, takes a blowtorch to your nerves, and asks, What if your worst fears came true? Anxiety is a demon, a trickster, he is 'It' from the Stephen King novel. He is a master storyteller who commands you to pay attention *or else*.

Attila Bogar was diagnosed with anxiety in 2006. Managing the condition was important to Attila, who was a part-owner in a computer programming company. Intellectually gifted and ambitious, Attila was also kind, affectionate, generous and had a cheeky sense of humour which made him the life of the party.

In October 2014, thirty-five-year-old Attila went missing during an acute episode of anxiety. A week later his silver-grey Audi, with his belongings still inside, was found abandoned on the side of a highway five hundred kilometres from his home in Melbourne. The obvious assumption was that he had wandered into the dense surrounding bushland and committed suicide, but his body was nowhere to be found.

Attila might well have taken his own life, but not everyone is convinced. Some think he might still be alive and that he staged his own disappearance. He certainly had reasons to want to do so. On the other hand, it cannot be ruled out that he became disoriented and, in the increasingly warm weather, perished outside the search radius.

The most disturbing possibility is that Attila Bogar met with foul play because before he disappeared he feared for his life. In his mind at least, he was a marked man.

Born to Hungarian parents, Imre and Roza, Attila and his younger sister Maryann grew up in Avondale Heights, in Melbourne's north-western suburbs. Imre, a meat slicer, and Roza, a part-time factory hand, worked hard to ensure their children had everything they needed. Imre and Roza spoke almost no English, so even as a boy Attila translated for them.

Holding on to hope: Roza Bogar with a photo of her missing son Attila and his sister Maryann
Photo courtesy Carmelo Bazzano/Newspix

'He loved me very much and he loved his father too,' Roza says, her English still halting. 'He was so beautiful. Everybody loved him.'

Traditional Catholics, Attila's parents were surprised when their son came out as gay in 2000, even though all his friends knew his secret. 'We was shocked but a couple of seconds after that we told him, "We love you the same still,"' Roza says. 'He was relieved because it was a long time before he tell us. He told me, "Mum, you don't think I want a normal family with a wife and kids? I can't help it, I'm gay."'

'He was quite heterosexual-acting for a gay guy,' Attila's close friend Matt Wilson* tells me. 'It was very fun to introduce him to friends and family. Everyone would say, "What a great guy!" And he was highly intelligent. He wanted to have banter with other intelligent people about building cars, computers, programming.

But for someone so intelligent, he could talk to anyone.' Attila loved *Star Trek* too and Matt lost count of how many times Attila persuaded him to watch his favourite episodes.

After graduating with a degree in business and computing, Attila – who could create computer programs from scratch – went into business with two others. 'He was very clever but soft,' his mum says. 'If you are a businessman you have to be strong. You are the boss.'

Roza also says Attila was generous to a fault. 'He bought so many things for the office . . . every six months, a new computer, massages for his staff,' she says. 'He had a debt. He owed something for the car and the credit card.'

If Attila felt stressed by his debts, the pressure on him mounted when thieves broke into his office and stole his computers.

Reassuring his mum that a new computer program he was developing would be a success, Attila asked Roza for two loans to keep him afloat. 'He asked me for eight thousand dollars, I give it to him. Another time he asked for five thousand dollars and I give it to him,' she says.

Though Roza's savings dwindled there was nothing she would not do for her son.

Aside from any worries he may have had at work, Attila also found 2014 a tough year emotionally. In his quiet moments he told his friend Matt how devastated he'd be if he was the first in their friendship group to lose his mum and dad. 'The only time he ever cried was about his parents because they were elderly,' Matt says. 'He was really concerned they might die earlier than his other friends' parents, and he'd be the first out of everyone to be alone.'

In April 2014 – six months before Attila went missing – his father Imre did pass away after having a stroke. Matt wonders if Imre's death was the straw that broke the camel's back, because Attila was never quite the same after that. 'It really rocked him,' Matt says.

★

Around midnight on Wednesday, 8 October 2014, Attila called Roza from his home in Moonee Ponds and asked her to come and get him because he'd taken his recently prescribed anti-anxiety medication and did not feel confident driving. Ever the loving mum, Roza said she would collect him in ten minutes.

Roza took Attila home and assumed he was staying the night. 'I gave him a cup of tea and he fell asleep watching the TV,' she says. Yet no sooner had Attila settled in than he was up again, talking on the phone. After finishing the call Attila asked his mother for five hundred dollars for accommodation and to take him back home. When Roza asked what was going on, Attila would not tell her. He just asked her to trust him and gave her his gentle, trademark smile.

'When we arrived at his house, I asked if he wanted me to go inside with him but he said no,' Roza says. When he put his overnight bag in the boot of his car, Roza asked him again what was going on. He replied, 'Mum, I know what I am doing.'

But what *was* he doing?

Later that day – Thursday, 9 October – Roza returned to Moonee Ponds to clean Attila's house, as she often did. She was accompanied by her daughter Maryann. Attila wasn't at home as Roza had expected, so at about 4 pm Maryann called him on his mobile phone. 'He picked up and said he was on the Hume Highway on his way home,' Roza says, adding that she thought, *The Hume Highway? What is he doing there?*

Attila told Roza he'd be home in an hour, at around 5 pm. But something didn't feel right so Roza called him again. This time, Attila said he'd be home at six instead. When Roza asked precisely where he was, Attila told her he was about five hundred kilometres from Melbourne. Roza's mind was swimming. There was no way he'd be home by five! she thought. How could he travel so far when driving made him nervous? And what was the reason for this sudden trip? 'He didn't tell nobody,' she says. 'I wouldn't let him go if I would've known he wanted to go somewhere. I don't understand why he left. I don't understand.'

Roza tried to contact Attila again that evening but his phone was switched off.

To her immense relief, Roza was able to raise Attila on the phone at around 5 pm the next afternoon. He told her he'd wanted to visit their good family friends, Tony and Elizabeth, who lived in Rose Bay in Sydney's east. He said he'd gone to their house but there was something different about it, so he decided not to knock. 'Maybe he didn't take the proper address with him,' Roza says. Still, it was peculiar since Attila was normally so detail-oriented. Attila told his mum he needed to get some medication and something to eat, then he ended the call.

How strange, Roza thought, trying to make sense of her son's behaviour. Had he really driven eight hundred kilometres to Sydney on the spur of the moment to visit their family friends? Had he just wanted a break? That would make sense of why he wanted money for accommodation. Or had he driven across the border for a more troubling reason? His worried mum feared it was possible Attila might have been trying to flee danger because two days before he'd left town he'd alluded to a sinister presence in his life. 'He told me, "They will kill us. They will kill Maryann, they will kill me,"' says Roza.

Who Attila was talking about, Roza had no idea.

Roza's fears for her son escalated when he stopped answering his phone altogether. Mother and son spoke every day so she knew something was wrong. On Sunday, 12 October 2014, Roza did what no mother should have to do – she went to her local police station to report her son missing.

Five days later Roza received a phone call from police in New South Wales to say Attila's car had been found on the side of Picton Road at Cataract near Wollongong. The police believed the car had been there since Monday 13 or Tuesday 14 October. As far as Roza knew, Attila did not know anyone in that area. The police also told her Attila's computer tablet and mobile phone – which he rarely went anywhere without – were inside the car, with his overnight bag. The car was locked as if he'd intended to return to it. Matt Wilson understands that the car's GPS was set to Moonee Ponds – the way home. Yet Attila never made it.

Roza, along with Attila's most recent ex-boyfriend and one of Attila's friends, drove straight to Wollongong to beg the police to find him. They were certainly trying. 'The police search in the bush and the dam. Both side is big bush, big forest,' Roza says. 'A hundred and fifty people walk with the dog. They look but didn't find nothing. They look under the water in the dam and didn't find nothing.'

Weeks, months and years passed with no news. Roza spent every day in tears. 'I lost my husband. I lost my son. I had my own stroke last year. My life is very hard,' she says.

Like many families of missing people, Roza visited psychics. Some said Attila was dead, others said he was still alive. Roza didn't know who to believe.

The day before word got out that Attila was missing, something was bugging Julian Jones. Attila and Julian had been in a relationship which had ended four years earlier. The pair had remained friends but their lives had taken them in different directions. Even though they'd had little contact in recent times, Julian couldn't shake the uneasy feeling that Attila needed him. 'It just kept popping into my head to ring him,' Julian says, describing how he repeatedly picked up the phone but put it down again, thinking it might seem odd to contact his ex-boyfriend out of the blue.

Trying to shake off his unease on what was a picture-perfect spring day, Julian got on with the job of renovating the old army base weatherboard he'd bought in country Victoria two years earlier. At around 5 pm, with a glimpse of daylight left, he decided to start painting the laundry – a giant brick wet room with 1970s patterned tiles and a claw bath.

Julian bent down to cover a roller in paint. As he stood back up to lay the first coat he recalls being confronted by a clear vision of Attila's face on the wall in front of him. 'He had a really tense look in his eyes and he didn't blink. The look said, *You're about to get really bad news*.'

The bizarre vision unnerved Julian. 'It kind of freaked me out,' he says. 'It was like a really high-quality film in front of my face. I couldn't even see the mortar and bricks behind him.' Julian put down the roller and went outside for a cigarette. 'I thought, *You have to put him out of your mind!* So I went back down there and started painting and again, he was there, looking me dead in the eyes. That intimate stare again. I thought, *What are you trying to tell me?*'

Julian is no stranger to the psychic world. 'I've seen ghosts before,' he says. 'I saw a big flash of light when Dad died.' Yet this seemed far more bewildering because Julian had no reason to suspect that Attila was dead, let alone missing.

When Julian found out about his former lover's disappearance he was deeply distressed but sprang into action, putting up missing persons posters with other friends and family, translating a television interview for Roza and supporting her emotionally. It dawned on him that there was another way he could try to find out what had happened to Attila – through the spirit world.

Before Attila disappeared Julian had started a spiritual group of half a dozen like-minded people, all women except for him. They gathered every week to meditate and read tarot cards. Julian had always hated the idea of séances but under the circumstances he felt compelled to call on higher powers for answers. *After all*, Julian thought, *if Attila cast his image on a wall he must want to tell me something*. But what?

In Julian's lounge room, the group set up a homemade ouija board. Julian cut out cardboard letters which he hoped a spirit would form into words. From the kitchen he fetched a glass that was light enough to move across the board without falling over. Once the board was set up, the session began with a prayer for protection. 'May only light come to this table,' Julian said, glancing apprehensively around the circle. Taking part in a séance gave him the creeps but he had to know what had happened to Attila. Breathing deeply, Julian put his questions to the spirit world. 'Is Attila alive or dead? Is he among us? And if he is, could he let us know?'

For a while nothing happened and the group sat in silence. Julian says there was an eerie sense of nothingness until the glass shifted and spelled out a woman's name, 'Ilona'. It happened not once, not twice but three times. 'Then we got [the answer] that Attila was still alive,' Julian says.

Julian told Roza what had happened at the séance and asked if the woman's name meant anything to her. 'She said, "Oh my God, that's Attila's grandmother!"' Incredibly, her name was Ilona. Julian says to me, 'I was a bit gobsmacked by that because the name wasn't common and the spelling was exactly right and had made no sense to us at the time.' Attila's paternal grandmother had died the year before he was born which explained why he'd never mentioned her to Julian while they were dating.

'It was very strange,' Roza says to me. 'Maybe she is looking after him?'

A while later Julian had another unsettling experience which he wished he could explain. Again, he was at home, but this time his mum was staying over in the spare bedroom. 'I thought I heard Attila's voice in my bedroom one night say, "Jules, I'm dead,"' Julian says. Wondering if there was a rational explanation, he sat on the bed and tested the springs. Maybe that was what he'd heard? 'Then I heard it again,' he says. '"Jules, I'm dead."'

Julian's mum said she'd heard a male voice too, but as it was some way down the corridor she'd interpreted it as saying, 'Jules, I'm in bed.' When she told Julian, he felt sure he wasn't hearing things and that Attila was trying to tell him he had passed away. To be sure, Julian asked Attila to give him a clear sign. 'But I haven't heard anything since,' he says.

While Attila's loved ones continued to try and find out what had happened to him, the police investigated his movements. At about six o'clock on the day he drove interstate, Attila made a worrying call to Triple 0. 'I listened to the Triple 0 call and it sounded like he'd breached some sort of security,' Matt says. Attila told the operator he'd made a mistake in accepting a bribe and alleged various organisations had been involved. Police investigated Attila's claim of accepting a bribe but found no evidence whatsoever to support it. 'The police told us he was hallucinating,' Matt says. 'I had never known him to hallucinate but apparently he was.'

Matt says that after a while a different theory emerged. 'The police said he was a divergent: that he left no trace on purpose so he couldn't be found.' Matt hopes they were right because he knows Attila could survive if he started a new life. 'He could disappear anywhere and make good money doing anything for anyone,' he says. 'At first I thought it was foul play but once I started to talk more to his family and friends, I thought, *Maybe he's run away*.'

A week after Attila disappeared, a package containing a new cordless phone with an emergency pendant arrived in the post for Roza. She later found out that Attila had ordered it during that last phone call he made before leaving her house. It made her think Attila had planned to leave Melbourne for good. 'He was always thinking of me, wanting me to be safe,' she says. 'He must have wanted me to have these things before he go.'

If Attila staged his own disappearance, he did so while suffering from escalating anxiety. Around the time he went missing his most recent ex-boyfriend thought Attila was heading towards a breakdown. The police also discovered that the day after he left

Melbourne Attila visited a medical clinic in Wollongong where a doctor gave him a prescription for anti-anxiety medication. Police were unable to find any local pharmacists who had filled the script.

Attila's agitated Triple 0 call, combined with his doctor's appointment to request anti-anxiety medication, painted a troubling picture. Compounding that was Attila's fear – whether real or imagined – that he and his family might be killed. 'I had no idea who would kill him,' Roza says.

It seems no one else knew either. 'He didn't say who was threatening him,' Matt says. 'I think that's what made him crazy.'

So was it suicide . . . misadventure . . . a deliberate disappearance . . . or murder?

By November 2014 the mystery deepened. When Attila's Audi was returned to Melbourne one of his friends found a guest key card to Wollongong's Chifley Apartments under the driver's side floor mat. Chifley's staff told police that the card had been issued at 4.15 am on 10 October 2014 but their records could not identify the user or show when or how the card was used. It was frustrating for Attila's loved ones, who wondered if the mystery surrounding his disappearance might have been solved had the card been found when the car was first located.

In 2017 a coronial inquest shed further light on the circumstances surrounding Attila's mysterious disappearance. Coroner Helen Barry acknowledged Attila's mounting work stresses and loss of revenue. She also noted that he hadn't used his bank account or Medicare card after being reported missing. Nor had he left the country, and no one had come forward to say they had seen him, despite media coverage at the time. 'In short,' Coroner Barry said, 'all available records of Attila appear to end with his disappearance in October 2014.'

Yet to find that a person is dead, the evidence needed to be 'clear, cogent and exact'. Coroner Barry acknowledged there was no clear or cogent evidence that Attila was alive. Then again, she noted, there was no clear or cogent evidence to say he was dead either. 'It would be inconceivable that Attila, who had a close and loving relationship with his mother and sister, would not have attempted to make contact [with them] had he still been alive,' she said.

Coroner Barry acknowledged that though Attila had mental health issues, there had been no indication he was going to take his own life. 'Whilst there has been no contact it is not inconceivable that his mental health issues have directed his behaviour,' she said. 'I am mindful that Attila has been missing for less than three years, and notwithstanding the very thorough and exhaustive investigation by police I am not satisfied that a finding that Attila is deceased can be made at this stage.'

On that note, the coroner found that Attila Bogar was not deceased and handed the case back to the Missing Persons Unit, where it is being treated as non-suspicious. In other words, it is not believed to be a homicide.

If Attila Bogar *is* still alive, it is important that he knows it is not a crime to go missing. His friend Matt has this important message for him: 'Wherever you are, go and tell the police you are all right so they can let your mum know you are okay,' he says, aware that the police need to 'sight' missing people but will not reveal their whereabouts without consent.

Matt keeps in contact with Roza, who leaves a light on for her missing son. If he returns home, Roza will make sure he receives all the help he needs to better manage his anxiety.

'Roza's unbelievable,' Matt says. 'She prays a lot and has faith. She feels in her heart that he is alive. She thinks, as a mother, she'd know.'

* *Name changed*

PROFILE

RACHAEL BROWN

ABC INVESTIGATIVE JOURNALIST, *TRACE* CREATOR

Photo courtesy Andy Taylor

The Podcast Phenomenon

My journalism career began in a paddock. My first taste of the adrenaline hit that comes with chasing a story happened during a Year Ten internship with the *Herald Sun* newspaper. I was shadowing a reporter who'd been tipped off about some malnourished horses. We climbed over fences and through muddy paddocks to find them, destroying my brand-new pinafore and Mary Jane shoes in the process. Soon after we found the horses, their ribs protruding from their lean chests, the reporter got a call saying that the Agriculture Minister was landing at the airport soon and would be holding a doorstop. We raced there. The reporter asked me to park the car but I was sixteen and couldn't drive. So instead he threw me his recorder. I sprinted inside looking for a media pack, and upon finding it I crawled through the reporters' legs and ▶

sat at the minister's feet, holding the recorder above my head. Caked in mud and with my heart racing, I thought, *This might just be the job for me!*

When I began studying journalism at RMIT University two years later, I did as much unpaid work as I could. I did internships at the ABC, Channel Nine and *The Age*. Being out on the road I met reporters who spotted my passion and helped me land stints with Channel Seven – listening to the police scanner with (chief of staff and former crime reporter) Peter Morris – and with Channel Ten, where I worked in its sport department over summer. My first paid journalism job was as an editorial assistant with the *Herald Sun* and I also started filing pieces for the 'Sports Star' column for my local paper, the *Moonee Valley Gazette*. At the Sydney 2000 Olympics I was a waitress in the Athletes' Dining Hall, so I also wrote about that for the local paper. We were taught at uni to 'Write about what you know', so I did. Anything to help bolster my folio for the small number of cadetships up for grabs. I knew how competitive the industry was and desperately wanted to be part of it.

Before graduating in 2001 I applied for two cadetships – one at the ABC, and the other at *The Age*. I got offered cadetships at both . . . on the same day! My folio and the amount of time I'd dedicated working unpaid in the industry must have impressed the interview panels. I asked for the weekend to make this weighty decision but a boss at the ABC said he needed to know that very afternoon. I had about six hours to decide on my professional trajectory. I'd always just assumed I'd go into print. I called that year's ABC cadet to chat about his experience. I was excited by the immediacy of the broadcast environment and the scope of roles at the ▶

ABC so I made my decision with half an hour to spare. Perfect deadline training. In 2002 Nick McKenzie (now an award-winning investigative journalist) and I were ABC Melbourne's newest cadets. It was a stellar year!

For me the magic of journalism lies in those precious glimpses behind usually closed doors, being a voice for people and, hopefully, effecting change. In 2007 I was working as a court reporter when a seemingly innocuous court listing alerted me to a police raid on the Victorian Medical Practitioners Board. I learned two women had made sexual abuse complaints against a dermatologist but had been ignored. A further twelve women were subsequently abused. I sat on this story for a year so as not to jeopardise the women's cases. This exclusive won me the 2008 Walkley Award for Radio Current Affairs. For a twenty-eight-year-old to be up on stage, accepting such a prestigious award was phenomenal. I still get goosebumps thinking about it.

My next proudest moment was landing the ABC's Europe Correspondent posting based in London. Between 2010 and 2013 I got to cover history as it was being written and met friends who will last me a lifetime.

Once I was back home in Australia I followed the medical journey of a promising young sportsman, Jack Vawdrey, who'd dived into a pool and hit his head, leaving him a quadriplegic. I, with the ABC's *7.30* program, filmed an amazing team at the Austin Hospital as they performed nerve transplant surgery to help Jack lead a more independent life. We then followed his progress over the year. The next time I would be a voice for someone suffering it would be through *Trace*.

The US hit *Serial* piqued my interest in podcasts. I thought, *What a fantastic way to present a story*. I also saw ▶

enormous potential for interactivity. Earlier, in 2014, a best mate and ABC colleague, Kerri Ritchie, told me that an electrician had just made an explosive witness statement regarding the cold case of Maria James. The mother-of-two had been stabbed to death in the back of her Thornbury bookshop in Melbourne in 1980. An electrician claimed he'd seen the local priest, Father Anthony Bongiorno, around the time of the murder, covered in blood. Father Bongiorno certainly had a motive: Maria James was about to confront him over the sexual abuse of her eleven-year-old son Adam, who had cerebral palsy and Tourette's. Yet in mid-2015, despite a motive and the electrician's statement, Father Bongiorno was eliminated as a suspect, though Victoria Police wouldn't say why. I couldn't reconcile that and it gnawed away at me.

In early 2016 I was feeling frustrated at work and needed a new challenge. I woke one day at 4 am thinking, *That's it, I should do a podcast on the Maria James cold case*. I thought Victoria Police might welcome a spare pair of hands and the James family might be grateful for someone trying to help them find answers. All these things combined led to *Trace*.

I called Maria's older son, Mark James, and said something wasn't sitting right with me about the police investigation. I asked for his blessing to do a deep-dive into the case. I explained what a podcast was and how it might help and he said he'd love for his mum's case to be revived. I don't think you can, nor should, undertake a project like this without the family's blessing. *Serial*'s Sarah Koenig was accused of leaving that case's victim, Hae Min Lee, glaringly absent (although Koenig did try to reach out to her family). Lee's brother took to Reddit to remind the podcast's listeners, 'To you . . . it's another episode of *CSI* . . . to me it's real life.' ▶

I also asked for the blessing of veteran homicide detective, Ron Iddles. Maria James was his first homicide case as a plucky twenty-five-year-old, and despite a subsequent decorated career, this case would be one he'd never solve. And it still grated. Ron, who was by then running The Police Association of Victoria, said he'd help as long as Victoria Police gave the nod. So I met with Assistant Commissioner Steve Fontana, who graciously said he could see the merit in this project.

The eventual collaboration with Victoria Police wasn't what I'd hoped for. Victoria Police were reluctant to let an outsider in because some journalists had burnt them in the past by releasing information that compromised investigations. And because I'm a journalist, and not a detective, officers might have dismissed my good intentions as meddling. Because it was an open case I knew there'd be sensitivities, but I thought collaborating with Victoria Police would ensure they'd be navigated safely. In the end though I wasn't granted access to any of Maria James' files, nor allowed interviews with any detectives working on the cold case. It made having the eyes and ears of Ron Iddles all the more crucial.

***Trace* uncovered new information and a new person of interest.** The first big revelation was that Adam James had also been abused by a second Thornbury priest, Father Thomas O'Keeffe. I tracked down one of his victims – a man who says Father O'Keeffe made him participate in satanic cult rituals, during which he says he witnessed four murders. While shoring up his claims I found other victims of Father O'Keeffe's torturous abuse and propensity to snap. As one survivor put it, Father O'Keeffe would use 'unreasonable force in reasonable situations'. Given Father O'Keeffe also had the covering ▶

up of his paedophilia as a potential murder motive, this raised the possibility that two priests could have been involved in Maria's murder – Father Bongiorno and/or Father O'Keeffe.

I grew up in a Catholic family so I struggled with what they would think of me telling this story, the darker it got. But I was in too deep, and I had an obligation to Mark and Adam. It scared me, though, the swamp of evil I was wading into.

***Trace* also revealed that a pillow which yielded what police thought was Maria's killer's DNA, was actually from a completely different crime scene.** It meant police had been on a wild-goose chase for sixteen years and now everyone was back in the frame. I was elated by the scoop (that Mark and Ron's suspicions about the killer could still be right) but in the same nanosecond I realised that even if Father Bongiorno *was* the killer it might never be proved if police don't have other DNA samples from the crime scene. It was one of the many times this case reduced me to a crying mess. I'd undertaken this all-consuming project to help give the James brothers answers, and this meant they might never get them.

Even though Father Bongiorno had the strongest motive I could find, others might have had similarly strong motives that I don't know about. Without access to the ten boxes of cold case files about Maria James' murder, which are kept in police storage, there might be crucial pieces of information I'm oblivious to. So I've gone to great pains to stress this and to let listeners make up their own minds. Should criminal charges be laid against someone, I'd hate for a prior focus on any suspect to be seized upon by a defence lawyer as to why their client should walk – either as an exculpatory reason ▸

(if I'd pointed the finger at someone else) or on the grounds their trial is already prejudiced (if I'd asserted their client was guilty).

Through the podcast I was amazed by the incredible power of interactivity. If you can tell a story like we did – being curious and forensic while still remaining compassionate to all those caught in the case's wake – it can foster phenomenal audience investment. I wanted listeners to feel like they were walking through the investigation right beside me, sharing the highs of discoveries and breakthroughs as well as the lows of devastating survivor accounts. This inspired an unprecedented response. Hundreds of emails filtered into *Trace*'s account in the first few weeks; many were fresh leads that I chased down, others were offers of support for the James family like pro-bono legal help or encouraging letters for the brothers. This is one of the things I'm most proud of, that despite the darkness of *Trace* it also brought out the best in humanity as the community rallied.

There's a certain magic about *Trace*. Not only has it been a powerful voice for the forgotten and the abused but it's pioneered audience participation in a realm the ABC has never seen before. I can't reveal any figures as it would be crass to celebrate download records for such a tragic story. But the statistics are a heartening reflection of the audience mobilisation that's possible when listeners are treated as participants, not just consumers, and how we can all change the world in our own little ways if we care enough. Hopefully policing and justice organisations will soon see, and seize, the enormous power of this medium and employ it to their advantage.

THE GIRL WHO MADE NEWS

THE DISAPPEARANCE OF ASPIRING JOURNALIST, **ELISABETH MEMBREY**

Deeply missed: Elisabeth Membrey

Photo courtesy Shannon Morris/AAP Image

'Our loss, our desperation, our anger, and our souls have thundered in our bodies. We are parents of a loved daughter who was mysteriously brutally murdered. Surely anyone with children may be able to imagine how they would, or would not, cope.'

Roger Membrey, Elisabeth's father

In the hours preceding Elisabeth Membrey's disappearance the mercury spiked at forty degrees. Locals in Ringwood, in Melbourne's east, flocked to the Manhattan Hotel after work to escape the dry northerly winds and cool off with a few beers.

Twenty-two-year-old Elisabeth, an arts graduate who hoped to one day make a name for herself in the media, was tending bar that night when her boss asked her to work late. She was happy to help, and besides, she could use the money.

Some time after Elisabeth returned home, however, police believe she was murdered. Australia's best-known homicide detective, Ron Iddles, was called in to work on the case for a short while once it was in full swing. Years later, when Elisabeth's parents called for an inquest into her death, Ron spearheaded a new investigation, examining old leads and looking for new ones. He would spend more than a decade trying to find out who was responsible. Yet despite an all-consuming investigation, no one has been convicted of Elisabeth Membrey's murder and her body has never been found.

★

Elisabeth was the youngest of the three Membrey children, and the only girl. 'We really were thrilled to have Elisabeth because Joy and I really wanted to have a daughter and sister for our two boys,' says Roger Membrey, Elisabeth's father. 'I always felt she was a real privilege to be with. She really was a friendly, nice person to talk to, very caring too. A lot of people gravitated to her on that basis.'

Elisabeth's mother, Joy Membrey, recalls how she and her daughter enjoyed shopping and catch-up lunches. 'Elisabeth was vivacious but she was very deep, so we used to have lots of long chats about interesting topics,' Joy says. 'She was just learning who she was.'

In a stable relationship, Elisabeth and her boyfriend Jason were planning a holiday to Queensland in the new year. Life was good, and her dad believes that before she went missing, Elisabeth – who had long wanted to become a journalist or work in advertising – was also about to receive a major career opportunity. 'I understand Channel Ten were going to offer her a job,' Roger says. A role as a television news reporter would have been a dream come true for Elisabeth, who did end up making the news – though tragically as a missing person.

The countdown to the would-be journalist's demise began at 5 pm on that sweltering Tuesday, 6 December 1994, when Elisabeth started work at the Manhattan Hotel. It was an especially busy night so she agreed to finish her shift at closing time, rather than 8.30 pm as previously planned.

Around 9.30, Elisabeth's boyfriend, Jason, called her and asked if she wanted to go over to his parents' house after work because they had air conditioning. Elisabeth declined, saying she wanted to go straight to bed once she got home. If only she'd accepted Jason's offer she might be alive today.

The following day, Roger and Joy tried to phone their daughter but she didn't answer. By the evening they figured she must have gone out with a friend or been called in to work. But Elisabeth wasn't at the hotel and Jason hadn't been able to reach her either. Thinking it peculiar, Jason arranged to meet Roger and Joy outside Elisabeth's locked unit.

Unable to get in easily, Jason climbed into Elisabeth's apartment through her bedroom window. When he turned on the light he made a frightful discovery: there was a pool of dried blood in the hallway outside her bedroom. After opening the door to let in Elisabeth's parents, Jason alerted them to the thick crimson stains. Her doona was missing too. The anxious trio looked around the rest of the unit, but with no sign of Elisabeth, they called the police. Three days later Victoria Police's Missing Persons Unit determined that Elisabeth had most likely been murdered.

The Homicide Squad investigation into Elisabeth's disappearance was led by Detective Senior Sergeant Roland Legg. Six months into the case, Ron Iddles joined Legg's investigative team. At that time Ron was a detective senior constable making his way back up through the ranks after having left the job for four years.

Grim evidence: blood in Elisabeth's hallway
Photo courtesy Victoria Police/AAP Image

Ron quickly got up to speed with the case. His colleagues had found out that on the morning of Tuesday, 6 December Elisabeth had been at home with Jason, who had spent the night at her Bedford Road flat in Ringwood before heading off to work in Hawthorn.

They'd also learned that Elisabeth's flatmate was away on that Tuesday night and that during the early hours of Wednesday, 7 December 1994 there had been a commotion outside Elisabeth's ground-floor unit. Her neighbour Andrea had been woken by the sound of her dogs barking, which they almost never did, and had gone outside to call them in.

Andrea went back to bed but the dogs woke her again at around 1.30 am. This time they were barking at the front gate. As Andrea went outside to bring them in a second time, she heard a loud bang come from the direction of Elisabeth's unit. Looking through the gaps in the timber fence, Andrea saw a dirty, old white car, similar to a Toyota or a Datsun, parked in her neighbours' driveway. She did not recognise it.

'She said it had four round headlights and "Garden State" number plates,' Ron says, referring to the slogan embossed on Victorian number plates at the time. 'She thought the number plates were new for the type of car; in other words, it had been re-registered.'

It was all rather strange, but then between 7 and 7.30, when Andrea left for work, she noticed Elisabeth's red Mazda 320 parked out the front, along with her flatmate's car. At least that was not unusual.

When the detectives had delved further into Elisabeth's movements in the lead-up to her disappearance, they'd found out that between 11 am and 1 pm on the Tuesday, an old school friend had spotted her in the shallow end of the pool at the Ringwood Aquatic Centre where she was talking and laughing with a fit-looking, sandy-haired man. However, by about 1 pm, a plumber cooling down in the heat witnessed a different scene. 'He later identified Elisabeth as having a heated argument with a man who was in his late twenties, well-built and with broad shoulders. He got the impression the man was very physically fit,' Ron says. 'He was adamant the woman was Elisabeth Membrey.'

The next sighting on the original detectives' timeline came shortly afterwards, around 1.30 that afternoon, when another neighbour saw Elisabeth arguing with a man in the driveway of her unit. 'They were standing near the back of a sky-blue Holden Gemini sedan and the neighbour saw them put some white plastic bags in the boot as they yelled at one another,' Ron says. 'She said the guy was probably in his late twenties and muscular in build.' He sounded like the man at the pool but no one seemed to know who he was.

Between 8 and 8.30 pm, during her break at work, the hotel operations manager saw a man speak to Elisabeth while she was sitting and reading a book. 'It is not known who the man was or if he had anything to do with her disappearance,' Ron says.

At around 11.45 pm Elisabeth left work. The investigators surmised that she probably arrived home a short while later, as she lived only a few minutes' drive away. 'Elisabeth's neighbour Andrea saw lights on in the kitchen that night and we know that around 1.30 the dogs started barking, so it looked like something happened to her around 1.30,' Ron says.

A couple of hours after that, a local milkman saw something suspicious as he drove down Elisabeth's street. 'He came forward and said he saw the lights on at her address at about 3.30 am,' Ron says. 'He also saw a small red car backed up to the front door of the house, which he thought was lit up like a Christmas tree. He recalled thinking, *They must be loading up all their stuff to do a bunk.*'

The investigators believed the car the milkman had seen was Elisabeth's red Mazda 323 so they examined it for clues. What they found inside told them she hadn't been moving out in the middle of the night, but something much more sinister. 'Forensic officers found blood in the back seat. It was established that the blood belonged to a child of Roger and Joy Membrey,' Ron says. The driver's seat was also pushed back as far as it could go, which was unusual because Elisabeth did not keep the seat in that position. 'When it was measured, it was determined the driver would have been six foot or over,' Ron adds. In addition, the forensics team discovered a fine layer of dust beneath the door sills. Had the car been driven on an unsealed road? Circumstantially, it looked to police as though someone had bashed Elisabeth in her home, rolled her up in her doona, put her in the back seat of her own car, and then used her car to drive to somewhere off the beaten track and dispose of her body.

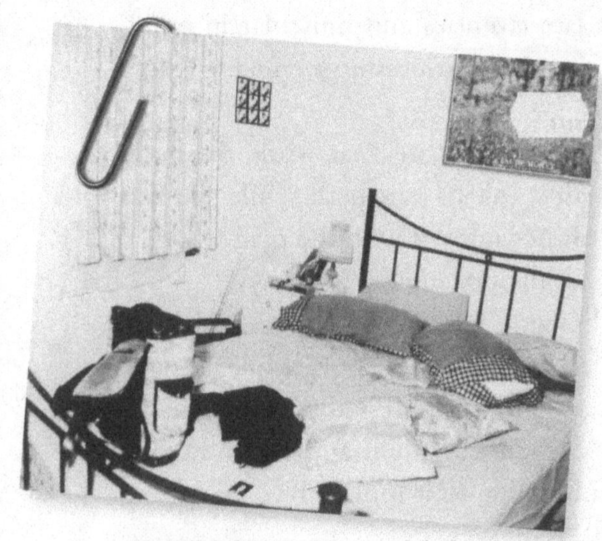

Elisabeth's bedroom: her doona was missing
Photo courtesy Victoria Police/AAP Image

'The other thing that had been established was that there had been an attempt to clean up the blood in the passageway,' Ron says. But there was something curious about that too. 'There was a bucket in the laundry with a wet rag in it but no blood,' he says. 'It was just odd and it was believed it might have had something to do with it.'

The police had also discovered that the blue car near where Elisabeth had been arguing with a man was a Holden Gemini TD model. 'There were 4,100 registered at Vic Roads and they were in the process of checking each of them to ascertain where each vehicle was on 6 December 1994,' Ron says.

Naturally, the homicide team spoke to all of Elisabeth's workmates during the early days of the investigation. Among them was a fellow bartender, Richard Jones*. Richard was friends with Elisabeth, or 'Liz' as he called her. He also knew her boyfriend Jason, who'd once worked at the pub too.

When detectives spoke to Richard's estranged wife, who had first met Richard at the Manhattan Hotel, she dropped a bombshell. Ron recalls, 'She said he was obsessed with Elisabeth and called her his "second wife".'

Immediately Richard Jones became a person of interest and investigators questioned him about what he'd been doing on the night Elisabeth went missing. Richard admitted that on Tuesday, 6 December 1994 he had gone to the Manhattan Hotel with his sister-in-law, who was also his housemate. He told the police he'd been wearing a pair of shorts and a tank top because it was such a hot night, but that he hadn't been allowed in because he wasn't appropriately dressed. Richard said that his sister-in-law had gone in to say hello to someone then came out. They then went home and didn't go out again that night.

The investigators didn't entirely accept Richard's version of events and returned for a follow-up visit. 'Richard then admitted he hadn't been truthful, saying the reason he and his housemate had gone to the pub was to get some smoking dope,' Ron says. 'When he wasn't allowed in because of his clothing his housemate spoke to a guy who allegedly said to go back to his place around 1.30 in the morning and he'd have some smoking dope.'

Richard said he went out at around 1.30 am, bought some marijuana, returned home, smoked a cone and went to bed. His housemate confirmed it.

End of story.

Or was it?

When police questioned the alleged drug dealer from whom Richard claimed to have bought his marijuana, he said that to the best of his knowledge Richard Jones hadn't gone to his house. 'But it was unclear if he was telling the truth or trying to protect himself if he was a drug dealer,' Ron says.

The original investigators couldn't shake their suspicion that Richard Jones was behind Elisabeth's disappearance and Ron says that, 'As a result, certain investigative techniques were deployed to substantiate what they believed.' Ron cannot divulge those techniques as it would expose sensitive police methodology.

Meanwhile, the investigators were still trying to find out who owned the blue Gemini seen in Elisabeth's driveway. In the process they found out that Richard Jones' housemate had once owned a blue Gemini TD model. Some of the detectives thought Richard must have driven her car to Elisabeth's unit that fateful night but there was information to the contrary. According to Ron, 'Richard's housemate made a statement to say that he [Richard] had only driven it once, when he took it to the mechanic's. And that was not on the 6th of December.'

Richard could still not yet be ruled out because he and his housemate had earlier skirted the truth, and the alleged drug dealer had denied that the pair had gone to his house. 'Yet if you accepted that Richard and his housemate were telling the truth, they couldn't have been involved if the timeline was right,' Ron says.

Understandably, the investigators needed to keep digging.

In 1995, Roland Legg asked Ron and Detective Senior Constable Darren Humphries to go through all the information sheets relating to Elisabeth's disappearance and work out which aspects of the case needed further investigation. 'We agreed that police had never positively identified the white car in the driveway around 1.30, which if you accept what Elisabeth's neighbour said, more than likely that had to be the killer's car.'

Ron identified someone else in Elisabeth's life who owned a car of that description, but after taking a statement from him the detectives were reasonably satisfied he hadn't been involved in Elisabeth's disappearance.

Not long after this juncture in the case, Victoria Police needed Ron elsewhere so the other hardworking detectives continued the investigation without him.

It was a gut-wrenching time for Roger and Joy, who had no idea what had happened to their daughter. All they had now were memories of her, which they tried to keep alive in the media. 'The media "adopted" Elisabeth because they (the journalists) were mostly at around a similar age and they liked and respected her image,' Roger says.

In 1996, unable to lay their daughter to rest, Roger and Joy held a moving memorial service for Elisabeth in a theatre where she used to dance. Almost six hundred people attended the service, where a giant image of Elisabeth was projected onto the back of the stage and flowers lined the front. 'Joy said it's got to look like a church,' Roger says, 'so we projected large images of stained-glass windows on each side wall.' A Catholic priest gave a eulogy and a Salvation Army band performed. 'We did that thinking it might give us a bit of finality but it didn't,' Roger adds. 'It did for other people, I suppose.'

Unfortunately, even though there were several 'persons of interest', the investigation did not progress much further, and in late 1999 Roger and Joy complained that an inquest had not been held. In the aftermath of their complaint, Superintendent Dave Sprague from the Crime Department called Ron Iddles and asked him to finish the inquiry and ensure the matter went to an inquest. Ron says he felt awkward taking over a colleague's investigation but he had to comply with the direction. 'It was just about looking at the case with a fresh set of eyes.'

Ron assembled a new team which included Detective Sergeant Tim Peck, with whom Ron would work closely. Ron decided that he and his team would pull apart the whole file and re-canvass people, including the alleged drug dealer. Ron and his new investigative team established that no one had really identified the blue Gemini that had been in the driveway of Elisabeth's unit. They also discovered that Richard Jones hadn't been formally interviewed and decided the first part of the job would be to work on him.

And work on him they did, into the new millennium. 'He was eventually arrested at his home for suspected involvement in Elisabeth's disappearance and her suspected death,' Ron says.

Richard will never forget it. 'It was six o'clock [in the morning], you're in your underwear with hundreds of coppers around your house,' he says. 'Then a big copper [Ron Iddles] put me on the ground and I was officially arrested for murder. If I'd never met him again I'd have said he was seven foot tall and about two hundred kilograms.'

But Richard *did* meet Ron again and so too did his (by now former) housemate. When Ron and a policewoman took the housemate back to the Homicide Squad she immediately wanted legal advice, and as a result of that advice she exercised her right to remain silent.

Richard, on the other hand, agreed to take part in an interview which lasted around four hours. 'He answered every question and denied any involvement in Elisabeth's disappearance,' Ron says. 'He admitted that in the past he had called Elisabeth his "second wife".' But Richard explained he had meant it in the light-hearted way that people sometimes talk about their 'work wife' or their 'work husband'. 'They would talk about personal things and he would say, "That's my second wife," but he didn't have a relationship with her,' Ron says.

What Richard Jones *did* have with Elisabeth was someone in whom he could confide. 'She was a good listener, that's why she was so good,' he says. He valued her as a friend and respected her for keeping her private life to herself, which made her stand out in a bar environment. 'She was a nice girl, working in a pub,' he says.

Richard Jones was released, but not yet exonerated.

Some time later Ron's team received a tip-off from a woman who said that a friend of Richard's ex-housemate had information. Ron says, 'She claimed that Richard's ex-housemate had told her friend that she was Richard's alibi, and that if the police broke her they would break the case open.' It was compelling new information and Ron immediately wanted to know more. The woman also told him Richard's ex-housemate had allegedly said to her friend words like, 'I know there was a bucket of water there but there was no blood in it.' To Ron, this was a very significant statement because police believed at the time that nobody other than the person who cleaned up, or someone connected to the offender, could have known about the bucket of water with no blood in it.

The friend who had reportedly heard this information – as well as Richard's former housemate – were both living in London.

Ron bought a ticket to Heathrow.

After a long-haul flight, Ron hoped the police in London would make his job easier. In Australia, most local officers help overseas police with their inquiries, but Ron discovered this was not the case in England. 'I thought it was the normal course of events that I'd go into the police station around eight in the morning, be introduced to the boss, be driven to the location and given the assistance I needed,' he says. Instead, officers told him where to find the train station, leaving Ron to catch a train an hour and a quarter out of town, before catching a cab to a property where the woman at the centre of the claims was working as a nanny.

Ron says the basis of the woman's statement was that Richard's ex-housemate had told her Richard Jones was a suspect. Ron recalls, 'She'd said the housemate and Richard had been to the Manhattan Hotel that night and that Richard had later gone to get some smoking dope from the alleged drug dealer.' It was the same story the housemate and Richard had told Ron – to a point. 'She also confirmed Richard's ex-housemate had said to her words like, "I'm Richard's alibi. If the police break me, they break the case."' The woman also said Richard's former housemate had told her that someone had cleaned up, and that a bucket with no blood in it had been left behind. 'And that became the crucial thing,' Ron says. 'So I had to ask myself, *Is that statement true? How would the housemate have known those things? Did Richard tell her? Or was she present when the crime scene was cleaned up?*'

Ron's next step was to ask Richard's former housemate for her version of events.

Ron phoned her at work in London, saying, 'It's Ron Iddles from the Homicide Squad. I'm downstairs.'

A few minutes later, the surprised woman met Ron in the foyer of the office building and Ron told her he'd gathered some information which might implicate her as an accessory. 'I also told her I understood she had knowledge of something at the crime scene, that she may have impeded aspects of the investigation and may have been withholding information,' Ron says.

The woman agreed to speak to him after she finished work, but a short time later her solicitor in Melbourne called Ron and said that she would make no further comment. Ron's hopes of breaking the case open that day were dashed. 'At that time I thought she held the key to the investigation and I thought that being in another country she might have felt comfortable opening up and telling me the story,' he says. 'But I had to accept it.'

Ron was especially disappointed because he wanted to get a resolution for Elisabeth's mum and dad, who were counting on him. 'Roger and Joy were on tenterhooks while I was in London,' Ron says. 'I really wanted to give them some answers.'

A few months after her unscheduled meeting with Ron in England, Richard's ex-housemate returned to Australia. Ron charged her with perverting the course of justice but the charges were dropped at the committal hearing. Her legal counsel – for whom Ron has unwavering respect – told him that a charge would not stick because the woman didn't know anything. Ron's gut instinct told him the lawyer was right.

About three months later Ron arranged a meeting with Richard's former housemate and her lawyer, hoping to find out what she did or didn't know once and for all. 'It was done in good faith, in confidence, and without prejudice,' Ron says. 'In other words, if she told me something in that meeting, I couldn't use it against her.'

As it turned out, there was nothing at all to hold against her. 'I came away from that meeting convinced that she'd had no involvement whatsoever, and that her three original statements were true,' Ron says, keeping the details of the meeting to himself as promised. Afterwards he deduced that several people had actually been aware of the bucket's presence at the crime scene and that her knowledge was not even remotely suspicious. 'In the end I put it down to the fact that other people knew about it other than the killer, and the conversation between her and the friend who lived in London was out of context,' he says. 'It was information that had come out in an innocent, not criminal, way.'

At this stage of the investigation Richard Jones remained a suspect, but that would change over the next couple of years, with Ron exhausting numerous investigative processes until he was finally satisfied Richard Jones wasn't a suspect in Elisabeth's murder.

On coming to the conclusion that Richard was finally and fully in the clear, Ron went to Richard's house one day in 2006 to tell him so. 'I can remember sitting on the back porch saying he was eliminated,' Ron says, tears welling in his eyes as he recalls how Richard responded. 'He said something like, "You don't know what you've done. People have publicly accused me of murder." He said, "Wherever I go, to the football or the car racing, quite often people say, "That's the bloke that killed Elisabeth Membrey."'

But Richard had done no such thing.

Having one's name splashed across newspapers as the prime suspect in a murder investigation would have a profound impact on anyone. 'It's destroyed my life,' Richard says. 'I had no job, I couldn't get any work, I had no money.' But there was one thing that kept him going: the knowledge that he was innocent. 'At the end of the day, that's how I got through without necking myself, knowing I didn't do it.'

Ron was impressed with the grace Richard showed when he found out he was no longer a suspect. 'He didn't ask for anything and he didn't ask for an apology,' Ron says, 'but he thanked me for telling him that in the view of the Homicide Squad he had been eliminated.'

The men shook hands and shared a beer. 'I saw the human side [of Richard] from just sitting there chewing the fat, really,' Ron says.

Ron believes the investigation into Richard Jones could have been handled differently at the start, preferably with Richard being formally interviewed in the first year of the investigation instead of six years later. Ron wished he'd been on the case at the very beginning because he thinks he could have eliminated Richard quick-smart. And, while he is not criticising the original investigators, he thinks much can be learned from the way this case was first handled. 'Like how easy it is to pursue someone because you want to make the facts meet your theory,' he says. 'Here was someone who never refused to come to the police station, who never refused to participate in an interview.' He was a man who'd simply worked with Elisabeth Membrey and called her a friend.

So whodunnit?

'Someone rang in and nominated another man,' Ron says. After being tipped off about this new suspect, Ron and his team undertook an extreme overt and covert operation. Ron says the man's alibi checked out and that he passed a polygraph test, and after two years of investigation he was satisfied the man hadn't been involved in Elisabeth's death. He was subsequently eliminated from the investigation.

Eventually, Ron felt he'd done all he could. 'It was coming up to ten years so I said to Roger and Joy, "Well, that's it. The two predominant suspects are now eliminated, and we haven't identified the blue Gemini in the driveway,"' he recalls. 'I said, "If something else does come up, we'll investigate it."'

In the *Herald Sun*, Roger and Joy expressed disappointment that the case had not been solved. In the same article, Ron acknowledged that police had hit a brick wall and were back at square one. Not long after the article appeared, a man called the police to say that several years ago he had nominated a man named Shane Bond to the police as the potential culprit. The caller wanted to know what the police had done about it.

Ron trawled back through the file on Elisabeth Membrey's disappearance, which was thousands of pages long. Eventually he discovered a miscellaneous information report which had been marked as 'complete' by an original crew member. In other words, early investigators had been satisfied that the information contained within the report, after some initial investigation, did not need to be pursued further, so it was never reviewed.

The original investigators had invited Shane to speak with them at Ringwood Police Station. And, while Shane had acknowledged he owned a white Datsun with Garden State number plates, he'd said he didn't know Elisabeth Membrey and that he had no recollection of where he was on the night she disappeared.

Reading through the dismissed information report, Ron discovered why the original detectives had ruled Shane out. 'The woman who'd witnessed the argument between Elisabeth and a man in her driveway did not say the man had a pockmarked face so he was eliminated,' he reveals, adding that Shane Bond had slight pockmarks. But, Ron

Scene of the crime: Elisabeth's flat in Ringwood
Photo courtesy Victoria Police/AAP Image

realised, the witness had seen the argument from a distance of seventy metres, so how could the investigators have expected anyone to see mild pockmarks from that far away? Even if Shane Bond hadn't touched Elisabeth Membrey, Ron thought, he was amazed at the reason he'd been eliminated as a suspect.

As Ron and his sergeant dug deeper, they discovered that Shane had been nominated as a person of interest on six occasions. He says investigators had dismissed another information report, and suspects the man who'd called with information was not taken seriously. Ron made sure the information was finally followed up and set about delving into Shane's past and taking statements from people who knew him. Ultimately Ron charged Shane Bond with murder.

Shane Bond's defence lawyers subpoenaed the entire file of the investigation into Elisabeth Membrey's murder – everything police had done over the previous eighteen years to find out who had murdered her. It meant former suspects would also be asked to take the stand.

'Given Richard Jones had been publicly named, I had to go back to him and say, "Will you go into the witness box and say you were a suspect?"' Ron wished he didn't have to ask that question after all Richard had been through, but Richard agreed to the request straightaway. '[The way I saw it] at the end of the day, my friend went missing, so I'll do whatever I can to help,' Richard says. 'If I could contribute in any way, I wouldn't hesitate.'

Richard was cross-examined, as was the other eliminated suspect. It was the same process for Richard's former housemate who, Ron acknowledges, had been 'put through the wringer by police'. But all three generously gave their time and energy, for which Ron will be forever grateful. 'They came and put themselves out for the benefit of the trial,' he says. 'They could have said,

"You can get stuffed – I've been publicly humiliated, why should I put myself on the stand?" But each of them did.'

In order to prepare for the trial, and because they had given every piece of information they had to the defence, Ron and Tim Peck had to spend six months studying the contents of the file. It involved scrutinising why every other suspect had been eliminated in case they were asked, 'Why isn't the killer one of them?'

The Supreme Court trial ran for ten weeks, and in April 2012, the jury handed down its verdict. 'Shane Bond was found not guilty of any offence,' Ron says. In his whole career, Ron lost only three trials but believed in accepting defeat like a gentleman. 'I went up to the dock, I shook Shane Bond's hand and I wished him all the best,' he says, acknowledging that those accused of murder must always be entitled to the benefit of the doubt.

Walking away from the trial without knowing who had murdered their precious daughter further shattered Roger and Joy Membrey. Still unable to give Elisabeth a proper burial, their grief is as raw today as it was in 1994. Roger says, 'Our loss, our desperation, our anger, and our souls have thundered in our bodies. We are parents of a loved daughter who was mysteriously brutally murdered. Surely anyone with children may be able to imagine how they would, or would not, cope.'

The Membreys try to see something positive in every day – a new flower in the garden, a new book to read, a phone call from a friend – but not a day goes by when they do not feel the fallout from Elisabeth's disappearance. It has been a never-ending roller-coaster ride of anguish. 'The trial and hope and despair, and keeping some sort of equilibrium in between, it's not easy,' Joy says.

Yet, despite their grief and frustration, the Membreys were grateful for the work of those who spent years trying to find answers. 'Vicpol homicide detectives, Ron Iddles and his colleague Tim Peck, worked very hard over a long period to bring about justice for Elisabeth's murder,' Roger says.

But until whoever was responsible is convicted, the murder of Elisabeth Membrey will remain one of Australia's most enduring unsolved cases.

★ *Name suppressed by Supreme Court of Victoria*

There is a one-million-dollar reward for information leading to the conviction of the person or persons responsible for the disappearance of Elisabeth Membrey.

DEATH AT THE DOCKS

A DETECTIVE'S QUEST TO NAME MELBOURNE'S **MYSTERY MAN**

Never giving up:
Detective Senior Constable Allan Creed

Photo courtesy Senior Sergeant Anthoula Moutis, Victoria Police

'Twenty-five years after their loved one went missing there was hope, and so you're walking on eggshells.'
Acting Detective Inspector David Butler, Victoria Police

It was a crisp winter's morning – 13 June 1990, a Wednesday – as the tugboat puttered along the Yarra. There was ample time for the crew of two to enjoy the ride, even to marvel at Melbourne's burgeoning skyline. Of course, there was work ahead once they reached their destination – Victoria Dock on the edge of the CBD – but wending their way there with the breeze on their cheeks sure beat driving to a stuffy office in peak-hour traffic.

When the men arrived at berth four they secured a barge with a rope and winched it in before jumping aboard. The barge would be their workplace for the day – not unusual for these urban salts.

What *was* unusual – for them, at least – was the strange entity they saw bobbing in the water on the starboard side of their boat. *It must be an animal*, they thought, *maybe a dog*. Whatever it was seemed to be demanding their attention because a short while later it floated around the front of the vessel. The men looked once, they looked twice, and then agreed: it was a human body.

Victoria Dock: the area where the body was found, two decades later
Photo courtesy Acting Sergeant Adam West, Victoria Police

After calling the Port Emergency Service, the men used a boat hook to secure the waxy, partly skeletonised corpse and stop it floating downstream. Thankfully, strong-stomached divers soon arrived to fish the body out of the water – or what was left of it, at least, for it had no forearms or legs from the knees down. As the incredulous port workers watched on, the remains were placed inside an enormous plastic bag and taken away on a stretcher.

Perhaps there was something to be said for office work, after all.

Detective Sergeant David Butler, a whip-smart investigation manager, eyeballed his crew. All of them were top investigators. But he decided to hand this job to his newest team member, Detective Senior Constable Allan Creed, who was on secondment to Taskforce Belier from his local cop shop in Melbourne's south-east. The case of the unidentified male at Victoria Dock had gone unsolved for nineteen years, and David had a hunch that Allan was ripe for the challenge.

Belier began as an operation in 2005 and expanded into a full-scale taskforce two years later. The taskforce came in response to coronial inquests which had highlighted inadequacies in the recording of missing persons and unidentified remains. 'When I look back at it now, there were poor communications and data systems,' David says. 'We had an opportunity to clean up what really was a mess.'

Clean it up they did – but what an undertaking! Covering the years between January 1960 and January 2006, the Belier Taskforce was to look at the 579 missing persons files on the books in Victoria, and 221 cases of unidentified remains. Their job was to reconcile the remains with long-term missing people: in other words, to match the missing and the dead, and close as many of these outstanding cases as they could. Fortunately, they now had the tools to do it: a team of crack detectives, the latest investigative methodologies, and a state database furnished with ante-mortem (before death) information about missing people and post-mortem (after death) information about unidentified remains.

For Allan Creed, his secondment to the Belier Taskforce in 2009 began as an opportunity to learn new investigative techniques. 'To me, it was starting from a totally different position to what I'd done in the past,' he says. Allan looked forward to using DNA evidence as a tool as well as working with the Coroners Court of Victoria and scientists from both the Victorian Institute of Forensic Medicine (VIFM) and the Victoria Police Forensic Services Centre (VPFSC). But what started out as a learning curve for Allan Creed ended as an experience he will never forget.

But first things first. When a dead person's name is unknown, they are assigned a case number. The person found at Victoria Dock was known as Coroners Case 2224/1990, and Allan, under the guidance of David Butler, was determined to replace those numbers with a name. The bones of 2224/1990 had once belonged to a living, breathing person – a man, in fact – and Allan and David wanted to afford him dignity in death.

Investigators looking into cold cases naturally need to go back to the original files relating to the dead or missing person to find out what is already known. There was much to digest regarding 2224/1990, so Allan didn't move for hours as he pored over the old documents, including an autopsy report from June 1990. The report said that the unidentified male was about forty years of age or significantly older, and around 173 centimetres tall. He had been dead for at least two to three months when he was found. At some point in his life he'd broken his collarbone and fractured his ribs. Stained teeth and carbon in his lungs indicated he'd been a heavy smoker, and a fibrotic liver suggested he'd also been a heavy drinker. Signs of an unhappy life? Perhaps, but it was impossible to say.

A dental post-mortem had also been conducted on the man which suggested he had probably been to the dentist in the year preceding his death. There was evidence he'd had periodontal disease and while he had some of his natural teeth, others appeared to have been extracted. His mandible was also absent.

Missing jaw, missing forearms, missing lower legs. To the uninitiated, it might suggest something monstrous had put this man in his watery grave, but there is no need to jump to conclusions. When a body has been submerged in water for some time it's not unusual for fish to feed on the remains and for bones to dislocate.

'There was no fresh skeletal trauma or evidence of fresh injury and the cause of death was undetermined,' Allan reveals. As to whether the man's death *could* have been murder, he says, 'It's possible, I guess, but there was no evidence of foul play.'

Back in 1990 it was not unheard of for bodies to turn up at Victoria Dock. 'Sometimes you'd get people who'd jump off the Westgate Bridge, go into the water and get washed around to the docklands,' David Butler says. Fortunately, anti-suicide barriers have since been installed and far fewer people plunge to their deaths from the iconic bridge.

The police at the time of the body's discovery did their best to identify the dead man, hoping his biometric information (his age, height, and the likelihood he'd been a heavy smoker and drinker), would lead to his identification. They contacted the Missing Persons Bureau, the Port Authority Search and Rescue and the Water Police but they could offer no new information. The police also contacted the Royal Australian Navy but the man hadn't jumped ship.

Then came a lead in the original investigation. 'The report about the unidentified male was circulated and it came back with a possible match to a missing person,' Allan says. That missing person had disappeared in April 1990, two months before the unidentified man was found, which was about the same amount of time he'd been immersed in the water. He was about the same age and around the same height. But was that enough to make a match? 'The investigator at the time contacted the missing person's wife who discounted it was him,' Allan says. 'Unlike the unidentified man, her husband was only a light smoker and not a drinker at all. She said her husband was living in Canberra in a Christian religious sect and she wanted him to be left alone.' The police corroborated her story and were satisfied the man was alive. 'So that was really the end of that investigation,' Allan says.

In September 1991, the case went to inquest before Coroner Iain Treloar West, who found that the identity of the deceased, as well as the place, date and cause of death were indeterminable. He was also satisfied by the evidence before him that all possible avenues to determine identity had been explored. A month after the inquest findings, the man was interred at Springvale Cemetery in an area of lawn set aside for paupers and unidentified remains. There was no gravestone to say he would be missed because no one had claimed him.

'It's very sad but I guess the body had to be buried somewhere,' Allan says. 'The area is maintained and kept nice and neat but the general public wouldn't know what's beneath the lawn, and that's how the cemetery likes it, I think.'

Unmarked grave: Allan Creed at Springvale Cemetery where the unidentified man is buried
Photo courtesy Senior Sergeant Anthoula Moutis, Victoria Police

When Allan Creed started looking at the case it was almost two decades after the remains had been discovered, and Taskforce Belier's two modern databases promised to make his job easier. First, Allan compared the ante-mortem information about missing people from one database to the post-mortem information about unidentified remains on the other. He then applied specific filters to narrow down his search. 'The filters that I applied in this case were that the unidentified person was male; aged between forty to sixty – which meant he was born after 1930; his height; and that he was probably Caucasian,' Allan says. Once he pressed enter, the computer spat out nine names worth considering, imbuing the detective with hope.

But as Allan studied the list, his hopes began to diminish. All of the men had something in common with the unidentified male but in most cases it was not enough for a conclusive match. One of the missing men had been a light smoker who did not drink; another was the wrong age and had a full set of false teeth; one had been shot numerous times and was too tall; and another, while around the same height, was also discounted because of his age. Another missing man was ruled out on the basis of his height and full set of dentures; another was believed to have been too old; and one was a prison escapee who police believed had drowned while escaping from McLeod Prison Farm on French Island. There was also a fisherman who had probably drowned after his boat was lost at sea.

But as luck would have it, all was not lost because one man remained, and he could not be ruled out so easily. As Allan uncovered what was known about this missing man – who he calls 'Mr X' – not only was a match possible, it was likely. 'The person who seemed to fit the criteria was born in the 1930s,' Allan says. 'He went missing in 1989. He was 170 centimetres in height. He had natural teeth, some of which were missing. And he was reported to have been a heavy smoker and drinker who'd had a broken collarbone and ribs.' Not only that, but Mr X had been depressed in the past and, as Allan knew, the remains had been found in a known suicide spot. *What were the odds?*

As he examined both cases side by side, Allan dubbed his investigation Operation Solvitude. 'I picked that name because I thought I'd solve it,' he says. The evidence was certainly stacking up.

★

When trying to identify human remains in cases like these, the same methods of comparison are used as in Disaster Victim Identification (DVI) incidents like the 2002 Bali bombings and the 2004 Indian Ocean tsunami. Primary methods of identification are considered first, and only one of these is needed to match against a missing person for it to be considered proof of identity. Fingerprints are one of the methods, but in this case the unidentified man's hands were missing so his fingerprints couldn't be checked. Teeth also provide definitive proof of identity, as does DNA. Unfortunately Mr X's dental records had been destroyed, so DNA was the only primary method of identification left open.

During the autopsy, tissue samples had been taken from the unidentified man and stored at VIFM, but without Mr X's DNA a comparison could not be made. If Allan wanted his DNA he had no choice but to approach Mr X's family. It was not a decision he took lightly but the similarities between the missing man and the unidentified remains were too compelling to ignore.

Still, it was with some apprehension that Allan and another detective from Taskforce Belier arranged to visit Mr X's three sons. 'I didn't know what to expect,' says Allan. 'Their father had been missing for so long they'd probably had little contact with police for decades.' But any anxiety Allan and his colleague felt was quickly put to rest when Mr X's eldest son gave them a warm welcome.

'The family was expectant and hopeful that I might be able to locate their father,' Allan says. Without revealing much about his new investigation, Allan told Mr X's sons he would like to run their dad's DNA through the system to see if a match could be made. Everyone agreed it was a good idea.

The sons had already given police some of their father's belongings, including a wallet in which there were a number of white and brown hairs. From those items, a scientist had extracted a partial nuclear DNA profile. Once that DNA was compared against the DNA from one of Mr X's sons, police would know for sure if they had Mr X's DNA. If they did, Allan hoped it could then be compared to DNA from the unidentified remains, proving the man found dead at the dock was Mr X.

The missing man's sons would have done anything to help and volunteered to provide buccal (cheek) swabs. It was an emotional evening and Allan could see they were counting on him for answers. 'At the end of the day you're doing your job and trying to do that to the best of your ability, but you do feel for the people you're dealing with, particularly in this case. You want an outcome almost as much as they do.'

David, who subsequently visited the family with Allan several times, felt exactly the same way. 'They were a lovely family,' he says. 'The brothers were really accommodating. They were just very friendly people and we wanted to give them a good outcome.' Yet delivering that outcome weighed heavily on both investigators. 'Twenty-five years after their loved one went missing there was hope, and so you're walking on eggshells.'

Luckily, the DNA from the wallet and hairs turned out to belong to Mr X. It gave the investigators one primary method of identification left to explore, and the hope they needed to crack two mysterious cases.

DNA is a technology which, when handled properly, does not lie. And even though Allan had Mr X's DNA, he still needed a DNA profile from the unidentified remains against which to compare it. Allan knew that VIFM had tissue samples from the unidentified male and hoped the scientists could extract his DNA. However, despite their best efforts they were unable to extract either a nuclear or mitochondrial DNA profile.

Though he refused to give up on finding a way to extract the DNA, Allan realised it would be a time-consuming process. In the meantime he decided to explore secondary methods of identification which – though they do not provide incontrovertible proof of identity like fingerprints, teeth or DNA – a coroner might use to rule on a person's identity, if police can prove they are sufficiently compelling.

One such secondary method involves visual identification. If the unidentified male from Victoria Dock had any distinguishing marks, scars or tattoos, it would have been a starting point. However, the level of decomposition was too great to tell if he'd had any such features. And there were no other clues accompanying his body – no clothing, personal belongings or documents to give police his name.

Allan turned to Mr X's medical records in the hope of matching known pathologies but that didn't help, either. He says that after reviewing the records, a pathologist at VIFM said there was nothing specific that could be compared to the autopsy report.

Allan wondered if craniofacial superimposition might hold the key. Using this technique, a forensic odontologist (a specialist forensic dentist) compared photographs of Mr X against the results of the post-mortem on the unidentified remains. Unfortunately, Allan says, 'Several photos of Mr X were located but none of his dental features were visible in them.' In other words, you couldn't see his teeth in the photos. The odontologist also compared the photos against images and radiographs of the unidentified man's skull but concluded that the post-mortem images of the skull were of insufficient quality and incorrectly oriented for a meaningful comparison to be made.

Meanwhile, the quest to extract DNA from the dead man's tissue samples continued. When Victoria Police need extra DNA-profiling grunt they often send samples to a high-tech lab in Texas, so Allan sent them three histology block tissue samples from the unidentified male. Staff from the laboratory told Allan that one of the tissue samples was too degraded to be of use, but the other two could be tested using a different method, which police gave them permission to try. 'Unfortunately,' Allan says, 'this testing didn't occur due to staff changes at the lab, and the samples were ultimately returned to Australia.'

The police had waited so patiently for the DNA results that by the time the samples were returned to Australia, Taskforce Belier had been disbanded and the cases which hadn't been resolved during its operation were sent back to the policing regions from which they'd come for continued investigation.

With the disbandment of Taskforce Belier, Allan accepted a job at the Fraud and Extortion Squad. But, not one to leave an investigation unfinished, Allan asked for – and was granted – permission to take two cases from Taskforce Belier to deal with in his new job. Not surprisingly, one of the cases was that of the unidentified remains from Victoria Dock. 'He was dogged and determined to see it through to the end and get a result one way or the other,' David says. 'I admire him for that.'

With the permission of his new bosses, Allan organised for yet more tissue samples to be sent to the lab in Texas. All three tissue samples were tested but no profile could be obtained due to excessive degradation. That meant there was only one dramatic course of action left: to dig up the body. Allan recalls, 'I requested by affidavit to the coroner that case number 2224/1990 be exhumed as there was no other way of obtaining a DNA profile except from the bones of the skeletal remains. That request was supported by Dr Soren Blau, the senior forensic anthropologist from VIFM and Dr Dadna Hartman, the manager of the Molecular Biology Laboratory.' Allan stated his case to the coroner and hoped for the best.

In the movies, a warrant for an exhumation is granted in a New York minute, but it is not something that is decided upon lightly. 'In coarse terms, you're defiling where someone's been buried,' Allan says. 'The facts pertaining to the case have to be compelling enough for the coroner to grant the exhumation.' It is also costly, but in March 2016 the State Coroner, Sara Hinchey, signed off on the request. Coroners Case 2224/1990 was to be exhumed. It was a triumph for Allan.

After receiving authorisation for the exhumation, Allan contacted everyone involved to arrange a suitable date. For the first time, he and David were able to tell Mr X's sons all about the unidentified body and why it might be their dad. And, though the two investigators implored them not to get their hopes up, Allan says, 'You could see they thought there was a pretty good chance it could be their dad.' He and David invited the family to attend the exhumation, reassuring them that they would not catch sight of the remains. They accepted straightaway because if the man buried in the unmarked grave was their father, they wanted to be there when he was unearthed. They had missed him so much in life that they didn't want him to be alone one more moment in death.

Shortly after sunrise on Wednesday, 8 June 2016, the man's remains were exhumed – at the same time of year as when the dock workers had found him back in 1990. Allan and David attended the exhumation, along with Mr X's family, cemetery officials, gravediggers, Dr Soren Blau and the police chaplain. The area was closed off to avoid attention from nosy passers-by. 'It's a solemn ceremony so we treated it as such and we also arranged for the police chaplain to offer a prayer and conduct a short sermon,' Allan says, adding that there was a moment during the exhumation he will remember forever. 'One thing I found very touching was when the oldest son, whilst he didn't see the remains, patted the new coffin with the remains in case it was his dad.'

The remains were discreetly transferred to a new coffin as the one beneath the ground had deteriorated over the previous quarter of a century. They were then escorted to the mortuary where they were given a new case number. Now, the man found at Victoria Dock was to be known as Coroners Case 2554/2016. The last four numerals – 2016 – reflected that, no matter how many years go by, police like Allan and David never give up.

The next step was for Dr Soren Blau to perform another post-mortem and take a sample of bone from the man's femur, from which Dr Dadna Hartman would extract DNA. Once their work was done, all the police and Mr X's family could do was wait.

Just over a week after Coroners Case 2224/1990 was exhumed, Allan received a call. The preliminary DNA results were in. He drew a deep breath. 'The preliminary results were not good,' he says, as though still smarting from the news. 'It appeared the remains were not that of the missing person I thought it was,' he says. While tests continued on those samples, Allan arranged for further testing of Mr X's hair strands. 'We got a better profile using PP21 – Profile Plus 21 – which gives twenty-one points of identification, many more than before.' The new profile was sent to VIFM for comparison. Yet again Allan could not believe what he heard. 'It was no match.'

Still refusing to accept defeat, Allan waited for the last of the results to come in; confirmation one way or the other of the preliminary results. It all came down to this moment. Yet again, the news was crushing. 'On 22 July 2016, Dr Dadna Hartman informed me that she'd compared the profile from the unidentified remains to the profile of the missing person and confirmed there was no match,' he says. It was hard to fathom because it meant that all the similarities between Mr X and the unidentified remains were just a coincidence.

'I was in a state of shock,' says David, who had been sure the body would be that of Mr X. 'To get that news, I was quite distraught and extremely disappointed for Allan. But because we'd bothered the family of the missing person, that was probably the worst part of all, because we'd told them and it didn't work out.'

Allan and David broke the dismal news to Mr X's family who had to be wondering if they'd ever find out what had happened to their dad. 'It was, I guess, a sombre affair,' Allan says. 'They were very disappointed and there was some emotion. It wasn't easy for us either to see them disappointed.'

'We gave them that hope and it fell away,' David says. 'In circumstances like this, families are likely to be re-traumatised. They're likely to start living a whole lot of emotions again and that's something we've got to be very conscious of. If you're going to knock on someone's door you've got to be really confident you're going somewhere with an investigation, and we thought we were on a winner. So to find out that we were wrong and couldn't give the family the answer they deserved, it puts them back into that emptiness.'

The disappointment felt by Allan and David speaks to their humanity. 'Though you've got to temper that response as investigators, because, at the end of the day, if you get too close to these things they can upset you, and they did upset me,' David says. Yet he believes there were positives to come out of the investigation, in particular, the realisation that Allan was so tenacious. 'The fact that he refused to give up and afterwards he continued on trying to find other possible candidates for the remains – it's just an absolute credit to him.'

The other plus was the immense success of Taskforce Belier overall. The team solved some 150 cases, and were able to put another 200 cases down to suspected drownings. Not only that, but the experience of David Butler – now an Acting Detective Inspector at the Sexual Crimes Squad – at Belier propelled him to successfully lobby with VIFM's Dr Soren Blau for an Australian first: a much-needed national dual-purpose database for disaster victim identification and to help police match the missing and the dead.

The database is called the National Missing Persons Identification System and it has the ability to help solve more missing persons cases than ever. David says, 'It means that ante-mortem data can be uploaded into the system from say, Western Australia, and it's nationally linked.' So, for the first time, information about missing people and unidentified remains can be meaningfully interrogated across state borders. Not only that, but all kinds of ante-mortem information about a missing person can be uploaded if investigators choose; even videos, which can be used to make anatomical comparisons against unidentified remains. Thanks to David and Soren, police now have their best chance yet of being able to give names to the hundreds of unidentified remains lying in morgues and paupers' graves.

But what now for the man found at Victoria Dock, who has once more been buried without a name? Allan is still hoping to identify him, but with no more investigative work left to do, he needs your help. You might have seen or heard something back in 1990, or you might just have a hunch who the mystery man could be. He might have been a Melbourne local, or from the country, interstate or overseas. If you have any idea at all, Allan urges you to contact Crime Stoppers or your local police station. 'I'm hopeful this chapter will jog someone's memory and generate a new avenue of inquiry,' he says.

'We have a chance, don't we?' David adds. 'Do nothing or do something. At least try.'

PROFILE

JAN ROSS

MISSING PERSONS EXPERT, PRIVATE INVESTIGATOR

The Pathfinder

Photo courtesy Freedom Photography

I was a police constable in West Yorkshire, England, when it dawned on me that the way police handled missing persons cases was really quite shabby. It was 1998, and I'd been in the job for eight years when I realised there were two types of officers – those who thought missing persons investigations were a complete waste of time and didn't put their hearts and souls into it, and people like me, who did.

When someone was reported missing the police would scribble down a few details on a one-page form. This form was often lost, misfiled, torn or covered in coffee stains! The police would make very basic inquiries and it would get passed on to someone else, but instead of progressing the case they'd just do what the last person had done. There was never any continuity or direction so ▸

I wrote to the chief and said we badly needed to change things. I submitted my suggestions and heard nothing until seven years later, when a new National Missing Persons Policy was published in line with my recommendations.

The chief said, 'Jan, how would you like to be the MisPer (Missing Persons) Coordinator for your region?' I jumped at the opportunity, and in 2005 I became the first MisPer Coordinator in West Yorkshire. Over a five-year period we had a one hundred per cent success rate in solving current cases, which saved the taxpayer the equivalent of seven million dollars a year.

I believed in treating each case as a potential murder until we knew differently. The first thing we did was grade the priority of each missing person report. A case would be a high priority if the person was a child under ten, someone at risk of harming themselves or others, or someone at risk of death or serious injury. A missing person with Alzheimer's, for example, could easily get hypothermia or break an ankle walking cross-country to a place they remembered from years ago. In a case like that we'd act fast. A low priority case would be the kind in which somebody said, 'I'm trying to trace my uncle who I haven't spoken to in twenty years.' In other words they hadn't actually gone missing, they'd just lost touch. The majority of cases were medium priority.

The critical factor was when the absence was 'out of character'. So if a nineteen-year-old often went out clubbing with his mates or stayed with a girlfriend we didn't need to be too concerned. But the disappearance of a responsible kid like Daniel Morcombe would have raised a red flag for us because the parents were adamant from the outset that something was wrong.

Becoming the 'Single Point of Contact' was vital. I built up a rapport with families, fellow officers, and staff ▶

in children's homes and mental hospitals. They all knew that if new information that upgraded the priority level [of a disappearance] came to light, they could count on me to persuade my supervisors to acquire more resources.

Every day, I produced a summary of what we knew and what we needed to know. I either reassured the sergeant that I could handle the investigation myself or let him know if we needed more staff and expertise. Cases were reviewed after forty-eight hours by the inspector on a weekly basis thereafter, and once a month by the detective inspector. High priority cases were always discussed at the management team meeting. If, at any time, a case looked like it could be a murder, resources such as forensics staff, sniffer dogs, mounted police, CCTV systems, the helicopter and the good ol' 'bobby on the beat' could be called in to locate the victim and offender.

In the past, police would see teenagers who had been missing and say, 'Yeah, they're fit and well,' and close the case. But I'd sit and chat for a while and try and find out why they'd gone missing, who their associates were, how they'd supported themselves and whether they'd become the victims or perpetrators of crime while away from parental supervision. This could give us clues if they went missing again. I'd say, 'It's great that you've come back, but if you feel the need to go missing again or need a place of safety, here's my mobile number, give me a call.' Some colleagues would say, 'That's none of your business, you're not a social worker.'

A lot of missing teenagers are from dysfunctional families. They are at high risk of being groomed for sexual exploitation when they come from homes where there is domestic violence, sexual abuse, drug and alcohol abuse, mental health issues, one or both parents are ▶

in and out of prison or the mother is a prostitute. When a missing person (mainly girls, but some boys too) is about thirteen or fourteen they are often befriended by someone their own age first and then introduced to guys around seventeen to twenty who sympathise with them and say, 'Yeah, your mother's a bitch, but don't worry, I'll look after you,' and give them cigarettes and alcohol. Within a week, they're hooked big-time on vodka and cocaine. The older guys lavish the girls with clothes, makeup, rides in limousines, room service in flash hotels, and treat them like princesses.

Because they've never been treated that way before the girls will do anything for them. It usually starts with a blow job. Then the older male will say, 'You've got to give my mate a blow job too. You know those drugs I gave you? He gave them to me and if I don't pay him back he'll beat me up and it'll be your fault.' At first the girl might object, but the guy will say, 'If you really love me, you'll do it.' Then she gets used to it and realises she can earn money out of it. What she doesn't realise until it's too late is that she is trapped into a vile lifestyle, and some even start self-harming.

The older guys buy the girls mobile phones secretly fitted with GPS trackers so they always know where their assets are. The girls think it's great until the phone vibrates under their pillow at 3 am and the guy says, 'I've got a customer for you. If you don't come here now I'll kill your kid sister.' The girl will sneak out and may have sex with six or seven guys a night. By the time she's allowed back home she's exhausted, stinking, bedraggled and has probably been beaten up. The parents get to their wits' end. They feel like they can't control their kids, so they kick them out on the street, literally. That's why so many young people are homeless and why ▶

we have to take missing person reports seriously from day one.

Not every missing person becomes a prostitute, but every prostitute I came across had been a missing person at some point. In a way I saw my 'social work' as being a crime prevention officer. If someone like me would take the time to prevent these girls from becoming prostitutes, not only would we save them and their families the whole spectrum of fear and physical harm, we could prevent offences being committed against them and by them. For example, most prostitutes get beaten up at some stage or other, either by their customers or pimps, and many murder victims are prostitutes, as was seen in the case of the Yorkshire Ripper. Many prostitutes get involved in shoplifting, deception, drug taking, drug trafficking and robberies. If we could nip all that in the bud, how many police man-hours would that save and how much safer would the community feel?

When someone is missing for some time their loved ones experience 'ambiguous loss'. They are really upset, sleepless and desperate for news. After the first few months they think at least if there was a body they could visit their grave, and then they start to feel guilty that they are wishing their loved one was dead. That's an awful position to be in, but if they know someone has died, at least they can start the grieving process. If people are missing indefinitely that's a whole new ballgame.

I had always been in love with Australia. When I moved here in 2010 people said, 'Why don't you join WAPOL [the Western Australia Police Force]?' At the police academy they told me they only wanted officers with three to five years' service, whereas I had nearly twenty. I can see their point. They just wanted officers with basic training and a little experience who were not ▶

too set in their ways and could quickly learn the Australian way of policing. Still, it was disappointing because I loved being a police officer.

I suggested I be employed as a civilian consultant. They said, 'We don't do things like that!' I explained that besides my experience with missing persons cases I had successfully spearheaded a multi-agency approach to tackling child sexual exploitation. They said, 'It's all right, darl, we don't have a problem with that here.' My eyebrows shot up. Really, *ya think*?

As I often do public speaking I also went to Western Australia's Department for Child Protection and offered to pass on my expertise to their social workers free of charge. They said, 'Uh, yeah, but you don't have a degree in psychology or sociology, so thanks but no thanks.' I thought, *Doesn't experience count for anything here?*

In 2013 I became a private investigator and set up Pathfinder Investigations in Perth. I called it Pathfinder because the art of investigation is finding the path to the truth. Six years later we're still going strong. My bread and butter work is process serving [which involves serving people with court documents such as divorce papers, subpoenas and summons], but finding missing persons is still my passion.

We get all sorts of missing persons cases but one in particular has stuck with me. A guy asked, 'Can you find my son? He went up north in 2004 for work and got in with the wrong crowd. Within a year we lost touch with him and the Salvos spent fifteen months looking for him through their family tracing program but haven't been able to find him.' He'd clearly been through a lot of angst. I said, 'I never give any guarantees that I'll find someone but I'll certainly give it a go.' ►

I found the missing son, now back in Perth, within three weeks. I rocked up to his place with a missing persons poster in my hand and said, 'Is this you?' He said, 'Yeah. How did you get my photograph?' I told him his family was looking for him and asked if it was okay for me to give them his contact details. He was a bit hesitant and said he would have to think about it.

I came up with a strategy for a family reunion. I gave the father the good news but added, 'He's not ready to see you just yet.' I suggested he read a book by a psychologist who writes about healing from family rifts, some of which are so toxic they should be left alone. The dad asked me to send copies to him and his son, which I did. Later I divulged the son's address on one condition: that the whole family didn't all turn up at once. People who have chosen to distance themselves from their families don't need to be bombarded with well-meaning relatives asking, 'Where have you been? Why did you abandon us? What have you been up to?' They can find this overwhelming and run away again, often never to return.

As it happened, when the young man's brother knocked on the door he was welcomed with open arms. The brothers became so engrossed in conversation that the visitor almost missed the birth of his baby! The whole family reunited soon after and a photo of them with beaming smiles was taken to mark the occasion. The found person and his newborn nephew were front and centre, starting a new chapter in the family's history. I keep the photo on my screensaver to remind me why I do what I do.

These days my business covers quite a big area, especially when you consider WA is about a quarter the size of USA! I have thirty-two process ▶

servers covering the Greater Perth area while I do the missing persons or 'skip tracing' inquiries myself. I also have contacts across Australia and around the globe. When I sell the business, I'd like the new owner to be a female ex-cop like me who can show empathy to the clients as well as find the facts. My business is not just about dollars and cents, it's about helping people.

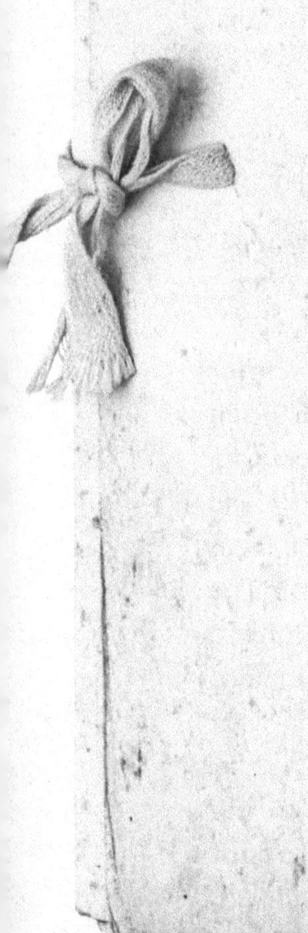

THE MYSTERY OF CALIFORNIA GULLY

WHERE ARE MAUREEN BRADDY AND ALLAN WHYTE?

Missing for more than fifty years: Maureen Braddy and Allan Whyte

Photos courtesy Lyn Ireland and Kevin Whyte

> ***'We thought, where would she go? Why didn't she come home? Nothing made sense that day. It was all really weird.'***
>
> **Lyn Ireland, Maureen's sister**

Deep beneath the earth's surface in a dark, airless, once mossy well, lies the body of Victorian teenager Maureen Braddy. At least that's what her sister Lyn Ireland believes, and while there's no evidence to prove Maureen is down the well, there's no evidence to say she's not. Lyn believes that until Maureen's body is excavated from this fetid hole, her soul cannot rest.

More than fifty years ago, sixteen-year-old Maureen Braddy and seventeen-year-old Allan Whyte went missing on their first date in Bendigo. Their budding romance should have been full of promise and possibility. But some time after leaving a dance, they vanished. It looked to police as though Maureen and Allan had run away, but years later they concluded the teenagers had been victims of foul play. To date, no charges have been laid.

Lyn has her own theories about who murdered Maureen and Allan, as do other locals. Whatever the truth, it's time for it to surface.

Maureen Braddy and Allan Whyte met at the Crystal Egg Company, or 'the egg board' as the locals called it. They worked on the factory line, packing eggs. It was nothing fancy but it was a living, especially for Allan, who was unable to read or write. For Maureen, it meant she could scrimp for new clothes, a welcome change from hand-me-downs. Not that she ever grumbled.

When she wasn't in school uniform, Maureen wore hand-me-downs.
Photo courtesy Lyn Ireland

'She was an outgoing sort of girl. Everyone liked her,' says Lyn. 'She was just a happy-go-lucky sort of a girl.'

Allan's brother Kevin Whyte says he and his siblings were 'brought up hard' and if they weren't at the table in time for tea they'd be sent to bed with rumbling tummies. It was just the way of things for many working-class families in the 1950s and 60s, but Kevin did not feel hard done by. There were plenty of good times too, especially for Kevin and Allan, who, with just over two years between them, were great mates. 'We used to do a lot of fishing and go after rabbits,' Kevin says. Before his brother worked at the egg factory Kevin and Allan also worked as farm labourers. It was hard yakka but they were industrious lads not prone to complaining.

Over at the Braddys', who lived on an oversized hill block in the Bendigo suburb of California Gully, Maureen's dad Stan was also strict but misbehaviour did not necessarily lead to a ban from the dinner table. More often it was met with a 'pants down and a whop on the arse', according to Lyn, who found childhood tough.

Third-born Maureen sought comfort in religion. Stan's mother Charlotte – known as Grandma Braddy – was a devout Jehovah's Witness and encouraged religious education in her grandchildren. 'We used to go to Kingdom Hall when we were kids,' Lyn remembers. As they got older, they continued their studies at home. Lyn enjoyed it and Maureen became devout, regularly visiting Grandma Braddy to talk about the scriptures.

On the morning before the dance, Maureen set off for Grandma Braddy's in the nearby suburb of Golden Square. Whether she took the bush path or caught the tram is unknown; either way it would have taken about ten minutes and she arrived safely. Upon her return, however, Maureen was distraught. Lyn, who was eight at the time, remembers seeing her sister standing in the driveway in tears. 'That was the last time I can really recall seeing her,' she says. 'That really stuck in my mind.'

But Maureen wasn't the only one who was upset that day. Grandma Braddy turned up later and all hell broke loose. 'There was a big argument with Dad and Grandma that day,' Lyn says. Someone else noticed the stoush, too. 'A friend of the family who lived across the road came over cos she knew Maureen. She was a Jehovah's Witness as well. She heard all the screaming and yelling so she didn't bother coming in; she stopped and went home.' So what was it about? 'I couldn't honestly recall the argument,' Lyn says.

Whatever the problem was, it was deeply troubling Maureen. Around lunchtime, a school friend of Maureen's saw her kicking a can around the oval at Long Gully. The friend could see Maureen had been crying and offered her a lift home, but she declined. A moment later, Allan Whyte appeared. Their friendship had been slowly growing and he'd recently plucked up the courage to ask her out. 'As soon as she saw him her mood changed and she picked up,' Lyn says. Perhaps Allan knew why she was so upset?

About a day before the two teenagers disappeared, Maureen had a curious conversation over the fence with her neighbour and close friend, Judith. According to evidence given at a coronial inquest more than forty years later, Maureen, who Judith knew had been unhappy, said something like, 'What would you think if I had run away?' It sounded like she was joking but in light of the events to come it would need to be considered.

It was on Saturday, 23 November 1968, that Allan took Maureen, in a simple but flattering red wool dress, to the dance at the YMCA in Mundy Street, Bendigo. It was the year of 'Jumping Jack Flash' and 'Born to Be Wild', and the dance would have been a fun way for the young townsfolk – many of whom worked hard on the land or in factories like Allan and Maureen – to let their hair down. But Maureen was not allowed to stay out late and Allan, who had never taken a girl on a date before, was intent on respecting that.

Between 8 and 9 pm, Allan and Maureen ran into Kevin Whyte on the steps of the dance hall and he invited them back to his flat 'for a bit of a party'. Allan declined, saying he had to take Maureen home. There was no indication that anything was wrong as Allan and Maureen departed.

The next day, however, there was no sign of either of them. The Whytes figured Allan had simply returned to one of the farms where he'd spent time in the past. 'We thought he'd gone back to this other place to work,' says Kevin, who was twenty at the time.

'We thought, where would she go? Why didn't she come home?' Lyn says. 'Nothing made sense that day. It was all really weird.'

Maureen's sister Rhonda reported her missing that Sunday, 24 November. It's possible that Allan's mother went to report him missing that Sunday afternoon but there is no record of it. Allan was only officially reported missing eleven months later but there is nothing to be read into that; it was simply a reflection of the way some big country families lived. 'We just went our different ways all the time,' Kevin explains. 'That's the trouble.' In hindsight, Kevin believes his brother's disappearance was suspicious. 'He wouldn't have run away, not with the car in the yard. And all his clothes were there and his bank account was never touched.' The fact that Allan hadn't taken his car was the clincher for Kevin. 'If I was going to go missing the first thing I'd take was the car.'

For a while, the police kept in contact with the Whytes. 'I used to have a policeman come around every fortnight and ask if I'd seen or heard from him but no,' Kevin says. 'He did that for a good twelve months or so.'

Lyn says the disappearances were not considered suspicious at the time. 'They [the police] put it down to [them having] run away,' she says. 'They disappeared from the dance, and then there was nothing.'

So *had* the teenagers run away, as Maureen had hinted to her neighbour? Or had something more sinister befallen Allan and Maureen under the cover of night? For decades, these questions would remain unanswered.

In 2001, with the pair still missing and the Victoria Police Crime Department seeking answers, Detective Sergeant Brendon Murphy from Bendigo Criminal Investigation Unit was asked to look at the case with fresh eyes. As Brendon reviewed the original files and interviewed those associated with Maureen and Allan he became convinced their disappearance was indeed suspicious, believing they were not the sort of kids to simply run away. Brendon – an old school country copper who has been involved in countless successful criminal cases including the prosecution of Alistair 'Sandy' MacRae for the murder of three members of the Marafiote family in 1985 – wanted this to be a proper, gold-standard investigation. 'It wasn't until Brendon Murphy took it on that it gelled,' Lyn says. 'We thought, *Brendon Murphy's onto this!*'

The tireless detective devoted thirteen years of his career to the investigation and prepared the brief for the inquest, during which the Homicide Squad was also called in to investigate. For legal reasons, details of the investigations cannot be revealed here, nor can the reason why Lyn Ireland is convinced her sister's body – and perhaps Allan's – ended up down the well at the family home.

In December 2014 Deputy State Coroner Iain West found that the missing teenagers were deceased, having died on or around

23 November 1968, and that foul play was the most likely explanation. On the evidence before him, however, he was unable to ascertain the cause of death or who was responsible.

Still, no one is giving up on finding the truth, and someone reading this book might yet be able to give police the puzzle pieces they need to crack this case once and for all. Lyn, who remains hopeful that one day the well under her old house will be excavated, believes there will ultimately be answers, but in the meantime she does her best to get on with life. 'You just go day by day. You just keep going,' she says. 'I've got grandkids, family, and I'm working. You can't let it drag you down.' Even so, there are times when she can't escape the feeling of being in limbo.

Lyn Ireland and Kevin Whyte in 2017 after the announcement of a one-million-dollar reward
Photo courtesy Eddie Jim/*The Age*

Neither can Kevin Whyte, who says of his long-lost brother, 'I'd like to find him, that's the main thing. Just to give him a decent burial.' For years, Kevin hoped that if he looked long enough at a photo of his brother all would be revealed. 'I'd look at him and say, "Where are you? Where are you?" And you get no answers.' If Allan were still here, Kevin thinks 'he would've had a good life'. He wishes the two could once again go fishing and catching rabbits, like they did as boys. Instead, Allan's unexplained disappearance and death has left him suspended in some kind of cruel eternal youth in which he can no longer come out to play.

Even though there is still much in this case that is unknown, what *is* known is that the families of Maureen Braddy and Allan Whyte still need the public's help because without it the decades-old mystery of California Gully may never be solved. 'Some bugger out there's gotta know where they are,' Kevin says. 'And I wish they'd give us some decent answers. All I want is to find the bodies, and closure.'

There is a one-million-dollar reward for information leading to the conviction of the person or persons responsible for the disappearance of Maureen Braddy and Allan Whyte.

ABSENT WITHOUT LEAVE

THE TRUTH ABOUT MISSING ARMY OFFICER, **SEAN SARGENT**

Making a difference: Sean Sargent in Papua New Guinea in 1998

Photo courtesy Nancy Anderson

'If someone says the words, "This is not normal," you have to think that something has happened.'

Nancy Anderson, Sean's sister

As Sean Sargent's car pulled out of the driveway his sister tore out of the house. Sean, a lieutenant in the Australian Army, had been staying at her place in Mackay in northern Queensland while he was on leave. The siblings were close and had enjoyed a good catch-up, as usual. But the moment Sean's key turned in the ignition an unnerving thought flashed through Nancy Anderson's mind. *What if I never see him again?*

Normally when Sean drove off Nancy stayed inside with her children, but something – a sixth sense? – told her not to let her brother out of her sight. Nancy was a nurse and not generally prone to irrational outbursts, but next thing she knew she was in tears. *This is ridiculous*, she thought. *Sean's not going to war. It's not like he'll go missing in action.*

Yet Sean Sargent *did* go missing – after a party in Brisbane three months later. So, when Sean waved to his sister in the rear-view mirror that day, it was their final goodbye.

Tom Sargent, a factory foreman in New Zealand, had a hankering to call Australia home. One evening, after a couple of beers, he plucked up the courage to call the mayor of Darwin to find out if there were any jobs available in the Northern Territory. Not only did the mayor take Tom's call but she told him there was plenty of work in the Top End and New Zealanders were always welcome.

On the basis of the call, Tom moved his wife Barbara and their children – Nancy, nine; Anthony, six; and Sean, who was four – across the Tasman Sea and into the wilds of the Northern Territory. A welder by trade, Tom says, 'More or less as soon as we got there I got a job. They were building Jabiru at the time.'

Jabiru, in Kakadu National Park, would eventually become a small township servicing the nearby Ranger Uranium Mine, where Tom found work. The Sargent family's new home was a far cry from Gisborne, a scenic wine-producing town on the coast of New Zealand's North Island, where they'd lived in a comfortable three-bedroom home for seven years. Now, they were crammed into an eighteen-foot caravan on a mine site. 'It was a typical 1970s caravan,' Tom says. Think striped upholstery, unyielding bunk beds and orange laminex.

It was an isolated existence, too. There were no old friends to call on, no shops, no medical centre and, for the first year, no radio or newspapers. It was as if the outside world didn't even exist.

It was also a place where there was always danger. 'We moved from a place where nothing could kill you to a place where everything could kill you,' Nancy says, recalling the first time her brothers went swimming in a lagoon unaware until warned that saltwater crocodiles lurked beneath the surface.

The family's new lifestyle wouldn't have been everyone's cup of tea but the Sargents took it in their stride. If anything, they saw it as an adventure, and in those naive years before the 'Slip, Slop, Slap' message, they spent hours every day in the scorching sun. The boys in particular loved exploring the outback and meeting other children. 'Sean had many friends in the Aboriginal and construction communities,' Nancy says. 'He was a gentle and friendly soul who got on with everyone. I can't recall him ever having an argument with anyone.'

After three years the family moved to Western Australia, where Tom worked on the North West Shelf. Two years later it was off to Blair Athol in Queensland to help build a coalmine, then on to

Sarina, half an hour south of Mackay, in 1984. It was the first time since the family had been in Australia that the Sargents had lived in a house. Not that it stopped Sean exploring the great outdoors – sometimes to his own detriment. 'I remember he took a nose dive out of a mango tree and smashed his arm,' Tom says. 'The doctor said he was holding the other one a bit funny so they X-rayed that too and found out he had two broken arms!'

'But he didn't whinge about it,' Nancy continues. 'He didn't even say it was sore!' Such was Sean's way: physical pain was not something to be complained about; it was a challenge to be overcome. And the older he got the more obvious it became that Sean had great strength of mind.

'He was a smart bugger,' Tom says. 'And he was pretty cunning. He'd have you on pretty quick. He was always very academic. He didn't have to spend hours swatting at home – it just stayed in his head.' The combination of Sean's brains and olive-skinned good looks did not go unnoticed by girls from school, either. 'The girls next door used to come over and he'd sort out their homework. Sometimes he'd hide if he'd see them coming!'

Sean was so good at school that the teachers couldn't always keep up with him. 'He was a brainy kid and if he thought they couldn't teach him properly he'd come home and teach himself,' Nancy says.

Sean also excelled on the sports field. 'He was the fastest runner in the school and the fastest swimmer in the school,' Tom says. 'Someone from the school came over one day and pleaded with his mother to convince him to run for the school but he decided he didn't want to be wasting his time swimming and running all the time.'

Lunch was Sean's preferred time to duck off home for an hour, even though it was against school rules. But what were they going to do, expel their brightest and most athletic student for having a toasted sandwich somewhere other than the playground? In any case, school was only a hundred metres from the Sargents' place, so what harm could an hour at home do? Well . . .

'I showed him how to make gunpowder!' says Tom, recalling how he'd passed on his knowledge of explosives to his younger son. One solitary lunchtime Sean decided to try out his newfound knowledge on the front lawn at home where the Sargents had a stone barbecue. It was not his finest moment. 'He blew the barbecue to bits, got shrapnel in his back, and they had to shut the school down,' Tom says. Yet despite having an agonising nugget embedded in his back, Tom recalls that Sean, who had a finely honed sense of the ridiculous, 'laughed like hell about it'.

Then there was the time Sean decided to apply to join the Australian Air Force but found out his application could not progress until he had surgery to fix a sports injury to one of his knees. After the operation, his dad went to the hospital to pick him up. 'He was meant to rest but he wouldn't have a bar of it,' Tom says. 'He went straight to school.'

It wasn't the only time Sean went to school against the advice of doctors. He never took a day off, no matter how sick or injured he was. 'He got viral meningitis so bad he had to have a lumbar puncture,' Nancy says. 'But he went back to school the next day. He refused not to excel.'

While Sean could handle his own pain he couldn't stand to see those he loved suffer, especially his sister Nancy and his mum Barbara, who was a smoker. 'He used to hide her cigarettes,' Tom says. 'He didn't like smoking at all.'

Unfortunately, Barbara had another addiction besides cigarettes. 'She was a really high functioning alcoholic,' says Nancy. 'She wouldn't drink and drive. She used to go to work. But she had an alcohol problem.' Nancy describes her mum as a 'remarkable woman with many facets' who never lost focus on her home and family. 'The house was spotless, dinner was always ready and she had plenty of friends. Other than me and Sean, I don't think anyone else even knew she had a problem with alcohol.'

Quietly concerned for her wellbeing, Sean paid his mum special attention. 'He was a good, good son,' Nancy says. 'He'd always try to help her out. He knew she had issues with alcohol but he didn't try to change her, he just loved her for who she was.' Sean and Barbara had a special ritual. 'He'd come home from school every day and they'd go and lie in her room and he'd watch a video with her.' Barbara, who was from England, struggled with the heat and needed to rest in the afternoons, so Sean seized the opportunity to spend time with her and enjoy their favourite comedies together.

'He was about the closest to her of any of the kids, I think,' Tom says. So it came as an almighty blow when Barbara died when Sean was in Year Twelve. At the time, Tom and the boys had been downstairs firing up the barbecue. Tom remembers it like this: 'Sean, I think it was, came running downstairs and said, "You'd better come and look at Mum."' Barbara had been vomiting and had collapsed, unconscious, onto the floor. She had fallen on her face so hard that her false teeth snapped in two. Straightaway, Tom began CPR. 'Sean said, "You don't know what you're doing," and took over,' Tom recalls.

Barbara left the family home in an ambulance, never to return. 'She'd had a massive coronary so there was no bringing her back,' Nancy says. 'She was forty-six. Sean was sixteen at the time. There's nothing worse than losing your mum early, and he was so close to her.'

Having left home to get married a few months before her mother died, Nancy says the male Sargents 'lost the plot for a while'. Pregnant with her second child and grieving herself, Nancy did what she could to support her father and brothers. She could see Sean was devastated but he had his own unique coping mechanism. 'Sean's way of dealing with his grief was to make sure everything he did was a tribute to Mum,' she says. 'It was like he decided, *I'll be the best I can be.*'

If Sean had pursued excellence before his mother's death, now it obsessed him, and when he graduated from high school he was named dual dux. 'Because he wouldn't run and jump and play silly buggers for the school they wouldn't give the whole thing to him,' Tom says with an eye roll.

Such was Sean's academic prowess that he could have studied medicine. 'He wanted to be a doctor but he didn't think it was okay to ask Dad to pay for it,' Nancy says. 'He didn't want to be a burden.'

So instead Sean joined the air force, receiving funding from the RAAF to study engineering at the Australian Defence Force Academy (ADFA). After a while he decided to transfer to the army. 'He said he couldn't do what he wanted to do in the air force,' Tom says. 'I don't know what it was. He might've wanted to get into the SAS. He wanted to get out there and get blisters. He wasn't keen on being an engineer.'

Sean took to army life right away. 'He was pretty green,' Tom says. 'He liked the army. He liked the uniform.'

After completing his studies at ADFA, Sean was promoted to the rank of lieutenant. As a junior officer he was respected by both his peers and superiors, who agreed that he coped well under pressure and was well organised, confident and relaxed. He also made firm friends and enjoyed the camaraderie.

The army gave Sean the opportunity to pursue physical excellence as well. 'He went to ADFA this weedy little boy and came back built like a brick shithouse!' Nancy says with a laugh. Whenever he visited her he'd guzzle unappetising protein shakes and exercise like there was no tomorrow. 'He said if he didn't work out he'd lose two kilos a day, so he ate and did lots of workouts to keep that muscle mass. He never really sat still.'

Sean completed his officer training at Duntroon and was posted to Enoggera Army Barracks in Brisbane where he was a troop commander in charge of up to fifty other soldiers. His specialty was communications – ciphers, frequencies and other secret squirrel activities. Ever ambitious and keen to improve on his knowledge, midway through 1998 Sean asked the army if he could be posted to the United States to learn more about satellite communications.

Green through and through: Sean in the jungle in Papua New Guinea
Photo courtesy Nancy Anderson

His career manager said no because he was too junior in rank. He'd have to be patient; he was up for promotion at the end of the following year, so anything was possible.

In October 1998, however, Sean's squeaky-clean record was tarnished when he was charged with assaulting a bouncer after reportedly stepping in to defend a mate at a nightclub in Townsville. Sean took out a loan and paid the bouncer four thousand dollars in compensation. The charge was subsequently dropped and the army placed Sean on additional duties, warning him not to get involved in any further incidents or they might take more serious disciplinary action.

Around that time Sean, who had previously only drunk on weekends, would occasionally drink until he blacked out. As someone who was normally so disciplined, this troubled him, even though it wasn't something he did regularly. 'Sometimes he'd think he shouldn't drink because he was such a healthy dude,' Nancy says. 'It was just an odd time and he wondered if [alcoholism] ran in the family. But his friends didn't think he had a problem.'

Four months after the incident at the nightclub Sean enrolled in a Masters of Business Information Technology degree. By now twenty-four, his life appeared to be back on track and he started dating Rachel Kayrooz, a twenty-one-year-old secretary he'd met in a nightclub and driven home. 'We sat outside in Sean's car until the sun came up,' Rachel remembers. 'It was such a romantic night.' After inviting Sean in for coffee, she says they spent the rest of the day together. 'From that moment I think we were basically inseparable.'

Rachel glows when she remembers her first dinner date with Sean at the Novotel in Spring Hill. 'He opened the door, pulled the seat out, he was a real sweetheart,' she says. 'He set the gold standard in how to be respectful and chivalrous with women. God broke the mould with him.' As the young couple shared their feelings, they quickly became close. 'It was out of the ordinary and it was very special, and it was all those things a young girl dreams about,' Rachel adds.

Also aware how much Sean loved the army, Rachel says, 'He was a dedicated soldier. He would have given his life for this country.' And he always made an impression, especially one day when he went into Rachel's office to escort her to lunch. Rachel remembers the excitement in the receptionist's voice when she called to say he'd arrived. 'Oh, Rachel,' she said, 'there's this gorgeous man in uniform here to take you to lunch!' The secretarial pool was all aflutter. 'The other girls were dipping their heads round the corner to see who he was!' It was like a scene from *An Officer and a Gentleman* and Rachel was Debra Winger.

Yet, just as the relationship was taking off, Sean, who had seemed just as smitten as Rachel, ended it unexpectedly. 'I just remember we were at my place in bed together,' Rachel says. 'It had been very intimate, romantic and lovely.' But afterwards Sean appeared out of sorts so Rachel asked him what was wrong. He climbed out of bed, growing increasingly troubled. 'He said, "I don't want to do this, I don't want to do this,"' Rachel recalls. Naturally, she asked what he didn't want to do but he wouldn't tell her. 'He said, "I can't, I can't."' Sitting on the floor next to the bed, Sean began to cry. 'He said, "I don't want to break up with you but I have to. There's something I have to do and I don't want to do it."'

Sean would not explain himself any further. Rachel wondered if he was going to be deployed. He'd been to Papua New Guinea in 1998 so she knew that another posting overseas (albeit not to the United States just yet), was a possibility. She'd told him on a previous occasion that if he were to be stationed elsewhere she would wait for him. 'He saw my loyalty in that moment, that I would do that for him,' she says.

Tragically, Rachel never did find out what Sean had to do because the following month, the only man she truly loved went missing.

On Friday, 19 March 1999, Sean went to a party in the Brisbane suburb of St Lucia, a university precinct surrounded by the Brisbane River, six kilometres from the CBD. Witness accounts from a coronial inquest many years later would illuminate the events of that night.

The party was hosted by an old school friend of Sean's called Ben, who'd invited around fifteen to twenty people. Sean arrived with a bottle of vodka and some cola but no one considered him particularly drunk. Rather, he was 'the life of the party', regaling the group with entertaining stories.

Around eleven o'clock Sean, Ben, Ben's girlfriend and his mate Adam went to another party nearby. Adam drove as he hadn't been drinking. It was a much bigger event, with about one hundred guests. It's understood that after disturbing a heavy statue of a lion on the host's front porch – and refusing to put it back where it belonged – Sean started a fight with a headbutt. The altercation was quickly broken up but Sean and his companions decided the best thing to do was leave. So after just fifteen minutes at the second party Sean went back to Ben's place with his friends and they drank water on the balcony. Sean seemed down in the dumps and was troubled about the fight. By this time he had drunk at least half his bottle of vodka, if not more.

An hour later Adam left Ben's place and was about to drive home when Sean walked past his car. Adam told Sean, who was still worried about the fight, to forget about it, saying, 'These things happen.' He also warned Sean not to drink and drive. Sean gave Adam an undertaking that he wouldn't drive and would sleep it off in his car. Adam didn't see Sean's car but had no reason to suspect Sean planned to do anything other than what he'd said.

But some time after Adam drove away that night both Sean and his car disappeared, and no one seemed to know how or why. He didn't return to his share house that weekend, and while it wasn't unusual for him to spend the weekend away, he always returned on Sunday evening to get his uniform ready for the week ahead.

At the start of the working week the army realised something was wrong when Sean failed to turn up for duty. Nancy, who was listed as Sean's next-of-kin, was the first to hear about it. 'I got rung by someone in the army at about nine-thirty on the Monday morning and they said that Sean hadn't turned up for work,' she recalls. 'They said, "We've spoken to his flatmate and he hasn't seen him since Friday. Have you seen him?"'

Nancy's stomach churned as she recalled the niggling fear she'd had the last time she saw her brother. It had seemed irrational at the time but now . . .? It was like she'd had a premonition. 'That morning I knew Sean was dead because he did not miss a single day of work in the army and I hadn't heard from him since earlier that week, which was unusual because we talked so often,' she says. 'I knew that immediate moment that he wasn't on the planet but I had to find his body. I felt absolute panic. I knew that it wasn't all right or okay.'

Nancy rang their father immediately and asked him to talk to the police. 'I let Dad do that because he needed something to do,' she says. 'He needed something to focus on otherwise he wouldn't survive it.'

From that day on, Tom hounded the authorities to find his son. 'He never stopped calling the police or the army. He just pushed and pushed and pushed.' Yet no matter how much he pressed them for answers, no one could tell him where to find Sean.

A few days before Sean went missing he'd asked Rachel if he could see her and she'd said yes. He'd said he would call again during the week to make arrangements for the weekend but never did. Instead, Rachel received a call from one of Sean's close mates who told her he'd gone missing. Days went by and no one heard a peep. Rachel recalls, 'It was like, is this real? Surely he's going to turn up.' She chastises herself now for not calling Sean when she hadn't heard from him. 'What if I'd called him on the Friday night and said, "Hey, what's going on? Let's catch up." Maybe he wouldn't have gone missing. That's torn me up for years.'

Just two weeks after Sean was last seen Nancy learned she was expecting her fourth child. Her pregnancy – coupled with Sean's disappearance – made her vomit all day, every day. 'I was trying to keep it all together,' she says. 'I even lost my relationship with Dad, which has really only got back on track in the last six years.'

Nancy speaks of her father's tireless crusade for answers about Sean's disappearance with great admiration. 'It was definitely all-consuming for him,' she says. 'He would have done anything to find out what happened to Sean.'

'I didn't know what the hell was going on,' Tom says. In the beginning he felt like the army was leaving him in the dark. 'You couldn't get much sense out of them. If you ask me, it was hare-brained.' Thankfully, after three months or so, the army appointed a highly skilled and dedicated investigator, Sergeant Tom Bere, with whom the family became good friends. In hindsight, the Sargents believe the course of the investigation might have gone down a different path had Tom been appointed on day one and been given accurate information on which to base his inquiries.

So what had happened to Sean? 'First of all, there was the theory that he was gay,' Nancy says. 'He did used to go to gay clubs but he had a girlfriend who went with him. I'm sure as shit that he would've told me [if he was gay] because he wouldn't have seen that as a bad thing. The theory was that he'd run off to be gay because he couldn't be gay where he was. I'd take it [that theory] because it sounded like fun and it meant that he wasn't dead.'

He was living the high life, according to another rumour. 'There was a theory that he'd joined a gang of underground, high-faluting gay lawyers in Sydney,' Nancy says. *What are 'underground' lawyers*, she remembers thinking, *and why would they hang out in a gang?* The whole thing seemed absurd but Nancy thought if Sean was out boogying the night away with a group of gay lawyers, all power to him.

'The army were trying to change his character,' Tom says. 'They were trying to tell me he was gay and I knew he wasn't.' A photo of Sean on a bed with another man seemed to be at the heart of the theory, but more on that later.

There was also talk that Sean had joined the French Foreign Legion. 'He was interested in it so he could have run off to join,' Nancy says. He had already asked to be stationed overseas and, with his intellectual giftedness, ciphering skills and physical ability, he might have been an attractive prospect to the elite French infantry corps.

It was also suggested that he'd slipped under the radar so he could work for ASIO. 'At first the army wouldn't classify him as AWOL,' Nancy says. So did that mean they knew something Sean's family did not? Was Sean on a clandestine assignment for one of the nation's intelligence organisations? These were questions to which the Sargents wanted answers.

What made the possibility of Sean being sent on a classified mission seem feasible was that Tom and his second wife Ruth started receiving mysterious phone calls from Australia and abroad at all times of the day and night. It had never happened before. 'I just couldn't make head nor tail of it,' Tom says. 'The police were tracing these calls. They were coming from all sorts of places. It was just odd.' Sometimes, the caller just listened to Tom's voice asking over and over, 'Is that you, Sean?'

For a while, the phone calls gave the Sargents hope. 'It was something to hold on to,' says Nancy, who also received a number of strange calls. And even though she'd thought Sean was dead when she'd learned of his disappearance, she couldn't stop the theories buzzing around in her head like fireflies. Still, it was out of character for Sean to make a major life change without telling her. The siblings were 'like peas in a pod' according to their father. Sean simply adored Nancy. He was also a doting uncle to her three daughters – all the more reason to think he would not vanish on purpose.

The theories kept coming, though, the most outlandish of which was that Sean was part of a Satanic cult. 'That was put in a paper,' Nancy says. She thinks the only reason Beelzebub got a mention was because Sean enjoyed playing video games and 'back in the day if you played computer games you killed people'. And disappeared into the flames of Hell, apparently.

'Another option was that he'd killed himself,' Nancy says. 'I don't think he would have done that because he knew how badly death affected a family and would have thought that would have been cruel.'

Sean had also been one of a group who'd found another soldier dead after hanging himself at the barracks. While it is not Nancy's opinion, she said Sean considered suicide 'the coward's way out'.

Another theory was that, under the influence of alcohol, the young officer had accidentally driven his car into the Brisbane River and drowned. There were no witnesses but nor were there any barriers to his car rolling into the water in the dimly lit street. 'There were no guard rails and no foliage that could have been wrecked,' Nancy says. 'If the river had been dragged within a week we'd probably know.' The river *was* dragged – numerous times – but not in the immediate aftermath of Sean's disappearance.

So then, where does that leave the last and most chilling theory – that Sean Sargent was murdered? 'I had people say he'd been attacked,' Tom says, but he did not believe his son would have been killed because 'he could fight like a thrashing machine'.

Yet there was this: 'Someone tried to use his ATM card about a month after he disappeared,' Nancy says. The identity of the person who tried to use the card was never established but Nancy couldn't help but wonder if it was someone who knew her brother was dead. His killer?

The disappearance of Lieutenant Sean Sargent became the subject of a report on the crime-fighting television series *Australia's Most Wanted* which, between 1997 and 1999, was responsible for results in around eight hundred cases. It was a program that offered hope to families of the murdered and the missing so Tom seized on the opportunity to use it to appeal for information. As a result of the report – and other media coverage – several people came forward claiming to have seen Sean.

One man said he spoke to Sean for about two and a half hours in a pub at Spring Hill in Brisbane two weeks after his disappearance. He told the military police that he'd remembered Sean's first name because it was the same as his. The man, who was homosexual, said that Sean had disclosed he was gay and that it was difficult being gay in the army. He said that Sean had also claimed to be a binge drinker, a trait that ran in his family.

A ranger in northern New South Wales also suspected he'd met Sean and contacted the Queensland Police Missing Persons Bureau to report it. The ranger, who'd once been in the police force and in the Army Reserve, said he'd encountered a man meeting Sean's description camping illegally out the back of a caravan park in Byron Bay. When he approached the camper and saw his campsite he wondered if the young man had been in the army because of the ordered way in which his campsite was set up. He'd also been clean-shaven and respectful.

A truck driver also came forward, telling police he'd met two men at a road stop between Warren and Gilgandra in central western New South Wales and that he believed one of the men was Sean.

The sightings sounded promising – but if one those men was Sean, why was he hiding from his family?

The mystery deepened around two months after Sean's disappearance when a package turned up in the mail. It contained Sean's army files and was marked 'Top Secret'. Sections of the documents had been redacted but Nancy could clearly read the letters MIA – 'Missing in Action'. Did that mean the army had indeed posted Sean somewhere he was not allowed to reveal and that he'd gone missing during active duty? Nancy's heart leapt. 'Sean would have volunteered for something like that,' she maintains. 'If it was secret and special and would have helped other people, he would have done that. He loved that secret stuff.'

That wasn't all Nancy saw. 'There was a form saying "Potential for Bad Publicity",' she says. When she alerted the army to the files she was alarmed at their response. 'They said, "You should not have that. If you do anything with it we'll prosecute you."' Nancy responded in the only way one sensibly could. 'But you sent it to *me*!' She returned the files, as requested, but felt like a criminal.

Years later Tom would try to get back the files through Freedom of Information. Nancy says, 'First, they told him they'd been destroyed in a flood, then a fire, and that everything to do with Sean was lost.' Eventually, however, the family received some files and discovered that Sean had been classified as 'Absent without Leave' a year after he went missing. He was ultimately discharged. There was nothing to shed any light on his disappearance.

At least the mysterious phone calls were eventually explained. It's thought that some of them were early scam calls – the kind everyone is so used to today. Others, however, were made by someone the Sargents knew, extinguishing the family's slim hope that Sean had been on the other end of the line. The Sargents were gutted. 'But trolls have always been there,' Nancy says. 'Sociopaths have always been there.'

Years passed and the Sargents were none the wiser about Sean's whereabouts. It wasn't until 2016 that Nancy received a phone call from a Queensland Police detective who told her Sean's case was being looked at again in preparation for an inquest into his disappearance. Nancy says the new investigator formed the view that Sean was indeed gay and leading a new life somewhere. *If he thought it too, it must be right*, Nancy figured. 'Our generation was brought up to trust police,' she says. So she trusted that the information was correct – that the brother she knew so well really was gay – and he had chosen to abandon his family. That meant he had abandoned *her*. It flicked through Nancy's mind that maybe she didn't know him so well, after all.

But at the inquest, everything the Sargents had been led to believe about Sean – all the rumour and innuendo – finally unravelled, and the truth about Sean Sargent finally emerged.

The inquest began in December 2016, but Queensland Police asked that it be adjourned so they could launch a fresh investigation, apparently due to concerns about deficiencies in past investigations. Operation Paper Jupiter, as it became known, was led by Detective Senior Sergeant Malcolm Gundry, who had worked on the successful investigation into the murder of Brisbane woman, Allison Baden-Clay. His team was made up of detectives from Indooroopilly, Brisbane and the Queensland Police Homicide Squad. An intelligence officer completed the team of six.

Over four months, the investigators reviewed witness statements and took some thirty-five more witness statements from around Australia; they conducted proof of life, traffic and weapons checks; carried out further searches of the Brisbane River; arranged for an exhaustive historical review of the river's sidescan data (sonar images depicting the state of the river floor) by the Brisbane Port Authority; obtained old photographs of The Esplanade at St Lucia; requested information from ASIO, the French consulate and the French Foreign Legion; tried to obtain Sean's DNA profile; organised a re-examination of his computer's hard drive; and looked into the possibility of an air search over Mount Superbus, the highest peak in southern Queensland.

The results of the investigation were mixed. The proof of life checks gave no indication that Sean was alive. The police also learned that the chances of finding him in the river now were next to nil and a search of Mount Superbus would be pointless as it was too dense a location in which to find a car or a body. ASIO said they could not help because the request from police was not terror-related. Sean's DNA could not be obtained as it wasn't possible to get a sample from his electric shaver. As for Sean's hard drive – it contained a few pornographic images but they were of a heterosexual nature: nothing at all to suggest he was attracted to men.

Detective Senior Sergeant Malcolm Gundry did not believe Sean had committed suicide. There were several reasons for this: Sean had been progressing well in the army; he'd recently paid for his university textbooks; he'd seemed normal to Nancy the last time she'd seen him; the alleged assault matter in Townsville had been finalised; a witness who spoke to Sean on the night of the party at St Lucia had said he was happy; and Sean had shown himself to be of resilient character after his mother's death.

As for the French Foreign Legion, Coroner John Hutton noted in his inquest report in October 2017: 'Detective Senior Sergeant Gundry is not of the opinion that Sean purposely disappeared to join the French Foreign Legion. This is because if Sean had joined the French Foreign Legion under an assumed identity and had fulfilled his five-year contract, he would have had continued contact with his family, particularly with his sister, with whom he had a very close relationship.'

Significantly, Malcolm Gundry found no evidence that Sean had met with foul play.

As for the possibility Sean was gay and leading a double life, something happened during proceedings which clarified the situation. 'If things happen because of fate, that moment restored my faith in humanity,' Nancy says. 'In the courtroom they were talking

The photo behind the gay rumour: Sean and a mate on holiday in England in 1997
Photo courtesy Nancy Anderson

about Sean being gay and running off. There was that photo of Sean and a friend on a bed in a hotel room. I heard someone behind me lean over and say, "I took that photo."' Nancy turned around and spoke to the young man, an army officer named Ben (not the Ben whose party Sean had attended). The officer named Ben, Sean and the other man in the photo had travelled to England together in 1997. Both Sean and the other man were just sitting, fully clothed on the bed. End of story. 'Ben said, "He'd be really surprised to find out he was gay,"' Nancy adds.

Ben was sworn in and spent around two hours giving evidence about the Sean he knew. It was the Sean the Sargents knew too. They couldn't believe it. Other army friends also gave evidence. 'I've never heard such a bunch of eloquent men,' Nancy says. 'It was hard to watch because Sean would have been like that. It was really cool to see.'

'Ben said no one had ever spoken to them [the officers],' Nancy says. The Sargents were devastated to hear that, because before he'd disappeared Sean had spent most of his time with these men and they'd known him very well. Had Sean been gay or planning to desert the army and his family, surely one of them would have known about it.

Among the special things Ben said about his mate Sean was something Nancy will never forget. 'Ben said he'd excuse himself from social occasions to call his sister,' she says, breaking down. 'He said, "He loved his sister."'

Nancy's immense love for her brother emanates from the core of her being and the inquest reminded her who Sean really was and how important his family was to him. 'I thought I'd skewered everything in my brain,' she says. 'But Ben stood up and he was beautiful. He said, "I know Sean, he was my best friend."'

In his findings Coroner Hutton accepted Detective Senior Sergeant Gundy's conclusion about the most likely cause of Sean's disappearance, which he'd earlier explained in his report thus: 'Detective Senior Sergeant Gundry is of the opinion that Sean, affected by alcohol, and unaware of his surroundings, drove his vehicle into the Brisbane River in the vicinity where The Esplanade connects with Upland Road, St Lucia.'

He also said, 'Given the time that passed between Sean's disappearance and the searches of the river and riverbanks, as well as the limited scan technology available at the time, it is likely that Sean's vehicle was missed. Unfortunately, because of the 2011 and 2013 floods, and the effects of salt water on vehicles, even with modern day technology, Sean's vehicle and body may never be found.'

Tom says, 'I have to accept what the coroner's come up with but there's not a sign saying, "This is what happened. It's the most likely thing to have happened." I always thought he'd gone over a bank or something but I didn't want to admit it.' Yet for Tom all the bizarre theories had served a purpose, in the beginning at least. 'You'd grab at any straw that came past.'

So if Sean died in the Brisbane River, how did that explain the attempted use of his ATM card and the sightings after his disappearance?

The coroner expressed the view in his report that the man who said he met Sean in a pub was 'not a credible or reliable witness'. Among the reasons he cited for this conclusion were that the man's recollection of what Sean looked like came from a television show; that the police had never shown him a photo board; and that he'd drunk between twenty to thirty rum and Cokes at the pub in an evening.

The coroner considered the park ranger who thought he'd possibly spoken to Sean to be a credible witness, but again the police had never showed him a photo board. The ranger was also a 'reasonable distance away' and speaking through a mosquito net when he met the camper. There was also a shadow over the man's face which, as he had been reclining, was at the farthest distance from the ranger. It was the view of the coroner that there was 'nothing necessarily unique about the campsite' to suggest it was inhabited by Sean or anyone else from the army and 'there were inconsistencies in key pieces of information' provided by the ranger.

As for the truckie's alleged sighting of Sean, the coroner found there were too many inconsistencies in his evidence for it to be relied upon.

After years of media interviews the Sargents were exhausted, and who could blame them? Yet Nancy agreed to speak to me to set the record straight about her brother. Nancy was 'deeply devastated' by the misinformation she received about her brother over the years and says, 'I thought my memory of my brother was not who he was.'

The inquest cleared it all up, which was some relief. 'I wanted people to know the truth,' Nancy says. 'I hated hearing some of the shit things that were said about Sean. I would like Sean's memory not to be whitewashed by bullshit.'

While Nancy feels terminally disappointed that it took so long for the truth to come out, she is grateful to former army investigator Tom Bere and former Queensland Police Missing Persons Bureau Sergeant Jim Hayes, who she says never let her down. She says if the original investigation had treated Sean's disappearance with the gravity it deserved, at the very least his body might have been recovered from the river. It would have hurt like hell but the family could have been spared decades of anguish. Echoing the view of missing persons expert Jan Ross, who is profiled in this book, Nancy says, 'If someone says the words, "This is not normal," you have to think that something has happened.'

These days, Sean's loved ones try their best to get on with their lives but each copes differently with Sean's long-term disappearance. Now approaching eighty, Tom can do no more to find his son and suspects he'll never be able to give him the military burial he deserves. 'You get used to anything,' he says grimly. 'If you cut your leg off you'll walk on the other one. You'll get used to anything after a while.'

Though cool and calm on the outside, Nancy battles crippling anxiety and is scared to let her children out of her sight in case they too go missing. Sean's disappearance has changed her forever. 'Something like that destroys you,' she says. Sometimes, her mind plays tricks on her and tells her that everyone's safety and well-being is up to her. She knows these thoughts are not logical but they aren't easy to control. 'I think if I just do the right thing, everyone will be okay.'

Sean's former girlfriend, Rachel – who has survived violence in other relationships – is now a leading domestic violence advocate and keynote speaker who will never forget how Sean showed her what a good relationship can be like with the right person. Even though she and Sean were only together for around five weeks, their bond was deep and no one has measured up since. 'They just

Before the breakup: Rachel Kayrooz when she was dating Sean
Photo courtesy Rachel Kayrooz

don't make them like that anymore,' she says. 'You meet someone like that just once in a lifetime. Sean was one of those special angels in life who just restore your faith in humanity. I think I've held a candle for him for a long time. Sometimes it's like, *Am I in love with a ghost?*'

Even though Sean's loved ones believe it's unlikely they'll see him again, without irrefutable proof that he drowned in the river there will always be a skerrick of hope. So for now they must cling to their memories of a gifted, kind, intelligent, funny, warm and chivalrous man who touched the lives of many.

Nancy says, 'I would like the world not to forget that Sean cared, he loved people and everything he did was to make the world a better place.'

Lieutenant Sean Sargent, we see you as you *really* were. Exceptional.

PROFILE

DR XANTHÉ MALLETT

FORENSIC ANTHROPOLOGIST / CRIMINOLOGIST / TV PRESENTER

Photo courtesy Jo Bursill

The Puzzle Solver

Something awful happened to me when I was twenty but it changed my life in an incredible way. I was doing my A-levels in the UK when I was very badly injured in a serious car accident. I was hoping to become a PE teacher and work with disabled kids but the accident left my knee a mess and I needed multiple operations. A sports career was no longer possible so I had to find a new direction.

Archaeological Science sounded interesting so I enrolled at the University of Bradford in England. I knew I didn't want to be an archaeologist though. I wanted to do something with a contemporary application, so after completing my Bachelor of Science degree I went on to do a Masters in Biological Anthropology at the University of Cambridge. By then I knew I wanted to work in a ▸

forensic context so that I could do something to help people, something that had utility. I'd always liked sticking my nose into things and I enjoyed solving puzzles, so finishing my formal education with a PhD in forensic science seemed the most natural course for me. I also have a strong stomach and poor sense of smell, which help!

Anthropology is the study of man. You can be a cultural or social anthropologist or, like me, a physical anthropologist. My area of speciality is biological anthropology focusing on bones and soft tissues to help identify people – alive or dead. Bones can tell you loads – sex, age, approximate height and ancestral origin. In some cases you can tell if someone had a disease, if they did something habitually with one hand or if they'd had an injury.

While I was studying I saw lots of skulls. I spent a year looking at how the head and face adapt to extreme environments on a population level. I learned that Inuits' noses and sinuses, for example, have changed shape and adapted over time so that they can breathe in super-cold air.

I loved learning. In my PhD I looked at facial recognition technologies to see how they could be improved. Basically, a team of us analysed over three thousand faces by highlighting specific anatomical facial landmarks by adding dots to faces in the photographs. We then compared all the faces in the database using an advanced algorithm looking for the 'average' face, which we didn't find because faces are so variable. It was about seeing which points on the face help us identify people and how that kind of technology can best help police identify suspects. The aim was to be able to reduce faces to a series of key landmarks and be able to use computers to scan faces in crowds quickly to identify persons of interest or track people – security technology which is widely applied today. ▶

I got involved with some interesting case work at the University of Dundee, where I accepted a lectureship at the Centre for Anatomical and Human Identification. The police asked us to help identify alleged sex offenders who had photos on their computers of children being sexually abused. Whoever took the photos was touching a child at the time so you couldn't see the offender's face but you could see other body parts such as their hands. We were trying to find out if there was any way of determining if the images had been downloaded from the internet, or if the person in possession of the material had committed the act themselves. There was a way, and it was by comparing the body parts in the photos against photos of the suspect's own body.

In one case, a suspect had images of Asian children being abused. The police didn't know if the suspect was actually travelling to Asia to offend, or if he had downloaded the images from the internet. The suspect was red-headed and freckled and had a scar on one hand. In the photos the man's hands also had freckles and a scar, but it's important to stay objective and give someone the presumption of innocence until you've carried out a detailed comparison. At the end of the process we were able to provide significant evidence that the suspect and offender could be the same person. When presented with our report he confessed that the photos were of him. That was a very satisfying moment in my career. I later worked on similar cases in Australia, too.

Once I helped identify an offender by his penis! There was a guy who police suspected of offending against his stepdaughter, who was disabled. The girl's mother had found a video in which you could see the girl being abused, and you could see a penis. In order to do an anatomical comparison of a penis it must be erect so ▶

that you can study the vein pattern. The suspect's penis matched the penis in the video. He pled innocent but he was found guilty. I was like, 'Yeah, gotcha!'

The paedophiles had networks through which they distributed photos online. I thought, *How are they finding these other guys? How do criminals pick each other out?* I learned that they did it by putting out subtle feelers in online chatrooms and seeing what responses they got. The little comments they made were almost like dating techniques. It's changed now, with a lot of the interaction taking place on the dark web.

For me, I consider paedophilia – which is an attraction to pre-pubescent children – is a sexual inclination, not a choice. After later writing about paedophilia, a number of men reached out to me and said it was an inclination they did not wish to have but that they would never act on it. They hid their feelings from their families and friends who would have shunned them if they had known [about their inclinations]. I think we need to help and understand people like that. Child sex offenders, on the other hand, are predators who act on their impulses; often victimising children not because they are preferentially attracted to them but because they seek out vulnerable targets to prey on. Helping the police to identify child sex offenders and seeing them found guilty is very rewarding as it reduces their ability to hurt anyone else.

I became increasingly interested in criminal behaviour. Some practitioners think that's strange for a forensic scientist because most are interested in either hard science or social science, not both. But to adequately interpret a crime scene you need to understand the people who created it. It's about more than interpreting blood spatter, for example, it's also about working out how the ▶

people interacted to cause that pattern. The behavioural and the physical go together.

I was writing papers about paedophiles' networks and how they connected online when I applied for a job teaching criminology at the University of New England in Australia. Most criminologists in their forties have come to criminology from law, social sciences, history or, like me, forensic backgrounds. There never used to be degrees in criminology, like there are now. I got the job and moved to Australia in 2012. I already knew that I loved inspiring young minds and now I could bring the forensic science together with the criminological interpretation. I said to my students, 'I don't want to tell you what to think, I just want you to think for yourselves.' Now I'm lecturing at the University of Newcastle where I have another opportunity to give students the confidence to have their own opinions and watch them grow.

I'm involved in research at the first Australian human body farm on the outskirts of Sydney in New South Wales where we're studying decomposition. Time-lapse cameras record the decomposition of cadavers – which are put in large cages to protect them from scavengers – for up to a year. The research will be of great use to scientists and police who can learn exactly how humans decompose under certain conditions, helping us determine how long unidentified people found in Australia have been dead – which, in the end, will help us identify them.

The body can move an astonishing amount after death. We saw a dead person's arm move loads due to the foreshortening of the tendons. If you hadn't watched it on time-lapse you'd think someone had come along and moved it. At the start the arm was by the cadaver's side but it ended up at a forty-five-degree angle from the torso.

If a police officer saw a cadaver in this position with a syringe nearby they might conclude that someone else had injected a fatal dose, when in fact the person may have injected themselves and their arm may have moved away from the needle by itself.

In particular bush environments, bodies don't tend to fully decompose; they mummify. I would have expected mummification in winter, but in summer I would have expected the remains to have been fully skeletonised. Also, there are a lot more ants here than in the UK and the US. I'd always thought that flies were the first to arrive but it was ants. Within a couple of hours after a cadaver has been positioned for study the ants are there.

I am also involved in DNA phenotyping, which is using DNA to produce a facial likeness of a deceased person or a person of interest in an investigation. As long as DNA is available we can get an idea of what an unidentified body or a possible perpetrator of a crime looked like. Once the police have the likeness they still have to investigate their case using all the normal channels, but to be able to recreate a likeness based on DNA alone is amazing. It's a tool that should be more widely used.

It concerns me that sometimes people are imprisoned when evidence, in my opinion, is lacking. I question the verdict in the case of Kathleen Folbigg who was found guilty in 2003 of the manslaughter of one of her babies and the murder of her three others, even though there was a medical reason for each child's death. She may have killed those children, but in SIDS (Sudden Infant Death Syndrome) cases a mother is more likely to lose another child than in families where there is no history of SIDS. That research was available at the time of the trial. ▶

The conviction of Keli Lane also troubles me. In 2010 Keli was found guilty of murdering her newborn baby Tegan in 1996. People ask me why I am on Keli Lane's side, but I am not on anyone's side. I am on the side of justice and want to see the system work properly. When someone is convicted in the absence of a body, forensic evidence, eyewitnesses, or a decent motive, it means anyone can end up in prison. If there's evidence, let's see it.

I've been a presenter on a number of TV shows and the reason I enjoy that is because it can help solve crime. When people ask me what I'm going to do next, I say, 'I still don't know what I want to do when I grow up!' My career has been interesting and rewarding so whatever I do has to involve looking at cases – often cold cases – and trying to move them forward. So long as it helps people I'll be happy. I'll always be solving puzzles!

THE BELLE OF BELLES

WHO KILLED **BRONWYNNE RICHARDSON** ON THE NIGHT OF THE BALL?

Buried in her best dress: Bronwynne Richardson

Photo courtesy Fiona Hume

'Sometimes people don't tell because they don't want to get into trouble . . . If you're one of those people, you need to speak up for the sake of the victim.'

Detective Superintendent Scott Cook, New South Wales Police Homicide Squad

The seasoned country-town doctor regarded his patient over horn-rimmed glasses. Days earlier, Noelle Richardson had been rushed to hospital in Melbourne with a ruptured ovarian cyst and internal bleeding. Her situation was so grave that without urgent surgery and a blood transfusion she would not have survived another day. A fast-acting medical team saved her life but her GP didn't want her taking any risks, warning Noelle, 'Under no circumstances should you have any more children.' The message was clear: one more pregnancy could be the death of her.

Sometimes, though, there's no stopping Mother Nature, and a few years later Noelle found herself pregnant with baby number six. *The doctor can hold his fire*, she thought, and waited until her first trimester was over before riding her pushbike to his surgery to break the news.

The doctor chastised the wilful thirty-year-old but softened when he realised how determined she was to have the baby. He had delivered all of Noelle's children so far and figured she might yet have the physical strength to bear another. She certainly had the resolve. 'Oh, well,' he sighed. 'You never know if you'll lose a child, so it looks like you're having this one.'

Those words must have travelled straight from the doctor's mouth to the devil's ears because four years later, Noelle *did* lose a child. It was her fourth-born, Bronwynne, and she was murdered.

Some girls wait for life to happen to them, but not Bronwynne Richardson. As a teenager she had tonnes of energy and community spirit to boot. 'She was always looking to help somebody,' Noelle says. 'She used to babysit for one of the local policemen and she loved raising money for charities – St Vinnies, the Salvos and St Johns.'

Fiona Hume, Bronwynne's younger sister and Noelle's miracle sixth child, echoes her mother's sentiments, saying, 'During those formative years, she was developing her sense of self and who she wanted to be, and she was an extremely kind individual. She was thirteen when I was born so by the time she was sixteen or seventeen and going out on dates she took me with her. Even though I was only little she was happy to take me anywhere she'd go.'

Some of Bronwynne's dates turned into steady boyfriends but, understandably, she felt too young for a serious commitment. A healthy and well-adjusted young woman, she was content to enjoy the novelty of dating and romance.

It was a simple country life for the Richardsons in the small New South Wales border town of Corowa, where Noelle and her husband Stan ran the local bus company and drove taxis. 'It was very happy times in those days,' Noelle says, recalling how, to the amusement of the rest of the family, Bronwynne and her dad used to waltz around the living room together. 'She was very fun-loving. Her father was a dance instructor in his young days and he used to teach her to dance and she loved it.' Bronwynne played piano too, although she wasn't crazy about her teachers – nuns at the local Catholic convent – who were strict, to say the least. Still, they knew how to tinkle the ivories and Bronwynne soon picked up the basics.

Taking centre-stage came naturally to the poised teenager who entered – and won – several beauty contests. At twelve she won Miss Rowing, at fourteen she became Miss Moodemere, at sixteen she was named Miss Rutherglen Show, and at seventeen – impeccably presented in a navy and white pinafore and donning a fashionable, wide-brimmed hat – she was crowned Miss Corowa Show Beauty Queen. 'She was very elated,' Noelle says. 'We were very proud of her, that she'd taken this interest. She was going to go far.'

'She was a bit like Sandra Dee,' Fiona says. 'She knew she was a pretty young girl and I guess she didn't mind that other people saw her like that. She had a strong image of how she wanted to present herself and that was glamorous – the hair, the makeup, the shoes, the shopping and the rest of it.'

Sometimes Bronwynne even wore stylish wigs in the pageants. 'At that time wigs were a sensation so she could just pull a hairstyle on,' Noelle says.

But with middling grades and yearning to be independent, Bronwynne left school at sixteen. In those days it was more common than not for students to leave school before the Higher School Certificate, but Stan and Noelle felt Bronwynne was too young to leave home. Fiona overheard the arguments between her parents and Bronwynne. 'I think she was a strong-willed teenager,' Fiona says. 'She had this plan to move out and hadn't counted on the word "no".'

Despite her parents' opposition, during the summer of 1972 Bronwynne moved to Albury, about sixty kilometres from Corowa. The only comfort to Noelle and Stan was that their daughter boarded with her responsible big brothers – first Robert, then Garrie, who lived with his girlfriend Julie, who was good friends with Bronwynne. She found work as a secretary and later as a cashier at Coles but her dream was to move to the bright lights of Melbourne. 'I think if she'd made it to Melbourne she would have continued along the pageant path,' Fiona says. 'A cousin was a Miss Australia entrant and I think she would have mirrored that.'

She was just seventeen: Bronwynne before she died
Photo courtesy Fiona Hume

But it was not to be because Bronwynne Richardson never even reached adulthood. A killer – or killers – stole her beautiful life three months before she turned eighteen.

The Richardson family's nightmare began on Friday, 12 October 1973. It was a still night – or at least it felt like one – as Stan drove Noelle and Fiona to a relative's birthday party in Albury. On their way, they drove past Horseshoe Lagoon, a daytime swimming hole on the Murray River, where they noticed a car with its headlights on. The scrubby nature reserve would otherwise have been pitch-black. 'Somebody's fishing late tonight,' Stan remarked, and kept driving.

Once at the party, the Richardson trio put the odd sighting behind them and happily greeted their family and friends. But no sooner were the celebrations in full swing than the phone rang. It was a policeman wanting to speak to Stan. After putting the phone to his ear, Stan's eyes began darting around the room. It turned out that someone had handed in Bronwynne's handbag and it was down at the police station.

It might have seemed to the police like a simple case of a lost and found handbag, but the Richardsons had a strange feeling about it. Bronwynne always took such good care of her belongings and hadn't been known to lose or misplace anything before, especially in the street. The last time Stan and Noelle had seen Bronwynne was when they'd caught up with her for a quick bite to eat earlier in the day while she was on her lunch break from Coles. 'She was lovely, excited and nervous about going to the

Belle of Belles Ball,' Noelle says. 'She had a new frock to wear. It was pink, water-weight taffeta. It was beautiful.'

The Belle of Belles Ball – to be held in nearby Coreen that night – promised to be Bronwynne's grandest pageant yet. She was to compete against other winners for a coveted regional title. With kitten heels, frosted lips and beneath a mist of Cedel, each girl would take her place on the stage, proudly representing her hometown. Bronwynne longed to win, but even if she didn't, she planned to enjoy the company of the other girls, the music and the dancing. They were innocent times and innocent country girls.

Unable to enjoy the party after the perplexing phone call, the Richardsons left straightaway. 'Stan, myself and Fiona went to the police station,' Noelle remembers. 'We said who we were and they said the handbag had been handed in at the Smollett Street Catholic Church.' A woman had found the bag in the driveway of the presbytery and, after playing bingo in the church hall with her friends, handed it in to the police. The Richardsons took the bag and headed home, planning to give it back to Bronwynne when they next saw her. Still, they felt uneasy.

Back in Corowa, the Richardsons tried to work out how Bronwynne might have lost her handbag near the church, which was opposite the Coles supermarket where she worked. It was pointless phoning her landline because no one would be home; Bronwynne could well be up on stage at the ball and Garrie and Julie had gone to Myrtleford in Victoria. 'We were upset and mystified,' Noelle says. 'We didn't sleep.'

By one o'clock the next day, when Noelle had not heard from Bronwynne, she started to panic. Surely Bronwynne would have rung to let her know if she'd been crowned the Belle of Belles? No one else had heard from her either. 'It was unusual because she always kept us informed where she was at all times,' Noelle says. The worried mum phoned Bronwynne's boyfriend who said she hadn't turned up at the ball. The Richardsons rushed to their local police station to report her missing but were told – erroneously – that they should make the report at Albury Police Station instead.

From that moment on, every passing moment seemed critical. For all Noelle and Stan knew, their daughter's life was hanging in the balance and there was no time to lose. They had to get to Albury Police Station fast – but what if something happened to Bronwynne in the forty-five minutes it took to get there?

Her head pounding, Noelle called her son Robert and asked him to go around to Bronwynne's while they drove to Albury. Robert raced over to his sister's place but she wasn't there. Then he made a worrying discovery that suggested she hadn't even made it home after work to prepare for the ball. 'Her dress was still hanging on the back of the door,' Noelle says grimly. It was in pristine condition and had not been worn.

The Richardson family filed the missing persons report at Albury, as directed. 'That's when the police got fair dinkum about looking for her,' Noelle says.

In the meantime, Stan was doing his own detective work. His first stop was the church presbytery where his daughter's bag had been found. He didn't have to search for long before he made a disturbing find – a black corduroy shoe belonging to Bronwynne. There was also a copy of *Dolly* – Bronwynne's favourite magazine – strewn on the ground at the scene. It was probably hers too.

Already petrified by now, Stan then spotted something even more ominous in the form of scrape marks along the footpath. Examining them more closely, it looked to Stan as though someone had been dragged from the footpath onto the road. In that moment he felt certain his daughter had been abducted, and from that very spot. Could he and Noelle find her, or was it too late?

'I don't know if we were on automatic, I don't know,' Noelle says. 'It's very scatty, that part of looking for her, not knowing where to go, what to do. I wasn't the nervous type, I took things in my stride, but it was unbelievable.'

What happened next was even harder for the Richardsons to fathom. The following morning, on returning to the police station in Albury, they received the news they'd been dreading. Bronwynne was dead; her bruised and ravaged body had been found dumped like illegal garbage in the Murray River. The policeman whose children Bronwynne babysat had identified her body.

'All I remember was the screaming. I was screaming, Stan was screaming,' Noelle says. 'And from that day on it's been sort of like living in Hell.'

When her body was found, Bronwynne was wearing only a purple jumper. A section of her pantyhose was tied around her left ankle, perhaps to restrain her. Her vagina appeared to have been bleeding, suggesting sexual assault. It was clear that what happened to her was no accident.

Making the appalling situation worse for the Richardsons was being told *where* Bronwynne's body had been found: Horseshoe Lagoon. They felt sick when they realised that the car they'd seen there with its headlights on may not have belonged to a fisherman after all. More likely, Noelle thought, it belonged to someone involved in her daughter's murder. 'We didn't know at the time, but we were probably driving past Bronwynne . . .'

Noelle, the daughter of a World War One soldier who fought in the trenches of Passchendaele, had always considered herself part of the 'stiff upper lip generation', but not anymore. 'We cried all our tears,' she says. 'We had no more tears to give.' Their faithful family doctor did what he could to help. 'We were doped to the hilt. It was the doctor's way of protecting us.'

Two post-mortems, which clarified Bronwynne's injuries, illustrated the brutality of the fatal attack on her. She had cuts and bruises on her face, body and limbs as well as haemorrhages in her eyes, neck and tongue. Her hymen was bruised and torn, confirming she had been raped. The pathologist found the cause of death to be the result of 'pressure on the neck and drowning'.

It is Noelle's understanding that her daughter put up a fight, clinging onto a willow tree in the lagoon for dear life. 'She was badly marked from that,' Noelle says, hoping Bronwynne would not have been aware when she was submerged in the water. 'She was unconscious because of the markings on her neck.'

Later, when Fiona was given a copy of the forensics report, she feared other unimaginable details within. 'To this day, I've never opened it,' Fiona says. And why would she? The whole family had already imagined – in vivid detail – the violent events that led to Bronwynne's death. Stan in particular did not need more information about his daughter's injuries because from the day he found out she was murdered he was never quite the same. 'When Bronwynne died my father went grey, literally overnight,' Fiona says. 'It really hit him bad.'

Homicide detectives, from what was then known as the New South Wales Special Crime Squad, were despatched from Sydney to Albury to lead the investigation into Bronwynne's murder and work with local police. They combed over the crime scenes, made an appeal for information from the public in the local paper and spoke to locals. They figured someone must know something.

They found out that on Friday, 12 October Bronwynne finished work at Coles around 5.45 pm. A friend of her boyfriend had agreed to pick her up but was late after making a simple mistake: he'd thought he was meant to collect Bronwynne from home, not work. Bronwynne had waited in the supermarket car park with other staff members but after a while she became agitated that her lift had not turned up. This was, after all, her big night – the Belle of Belles Ball!

Tired of waiting, Bronwynne crossed from the northern side of Smollett Street to the southern side near the church.

A witness told police she saw a young blonde woman in Smollett Street on the evening of Bronwynne's disappearance and had a feeling from God that she was in grave danger. She recalled seeing two cars and said she'd watched the young woman run onto the road and appear to talk to someone. Was it Bronwynne? And if so, who had she been talking to?

There were numerous other witness accounts, but the most chilling came from a man who actually saw the abduction, which he said had occurred at about five past seven, based on what had been on television when he'd left his house. He said that as he drove down Smollett Street he saw a group of people who appeared to be scuffling near a car, which was angle-parked. He then saw someone being bundled into the car. At the time he'd figured the group was just mucking around. Later it appeared likely he had witnessed the prelude to Bronwynne Richardson's murder.

Believing the man to be a truthful witness, the police circulated his description of the car allegedly involved in the abduction – a green FB Holden – in the media. The detectives at the time did not find who owned it but Fiona, at just four years old, sensed it was important. From that time on, whenever she went on family trips in the car she peered out the window in the back seat looking for clues. 'I knew there was a car involved so I wrote down the number plates of all the cars that we passed,' she says. After every trip Fiona ended up with a 'big long list of number plates'. Maybe one of the drivers was the person who'd taken her sister away, she thought. Her junior detective work didn't amount to anything but it gave her something to cling to: hope.

As the police continued investigating Bronwynne's murder, around two thousand people – most of her hometown, really – attended her funeral. Some knew her and were there to grieve and support the family but Noelle felt that others were just 'stickybeaks' who turned up out of morbid curiosity.

Bronwynne was buried in her white satin debutante dress, the most beautiful gown in her wardrobe, and her favourite. 'We thought it was the right thing to do,' Noelle says. The town busybody had different ideas and chased Noelle into the supermarket the next day, cursing her over and over. 'It's a wicked waste,' she snarled, 'burying her in that frock!' Noelle screamed until the supermarket manager came to her rescue and took her home. 'After that I couldn't go down the street,' she says.

Bronwynne's younger sister was targeted too. 'I was ostracised when Bronwynne died,' says Fiona, who started school in 1973, aged five. 'My little group of friends wouldn't let me play unless I described absolutely everything that had happened to her. It obviously came from their parents but because I wouldn't do it I couldn't play. So I'd just leave school at recess and go home.'

Incredibly, some adults seemed to get a kick out of the Richardsons' plight. As time passed with no arrest the family received countless prank phone calls from strangers who claimed to know who had killed Bronwynne. 'It just about drove us around the bend,' Noelle says. 'Looking back on it now, I don't know how we coped. We never went out publicly for at least twelve months. We just couldn't handle it, I don't think.'

'There hadn't been a significant murder [in Albury] since the Pyjama Girl,' Fiona points out, referring to Linda Agostini, whose body was found in 1934 in a culvert in Splitters Creek near Albury.

But nothing could excuse the bad behaviour of those who victimised the Richardsons. 'Today the way people treated us would be described as troll behaviour but they did it in their own overt way,' Fiona says.

In an effort to escape their tormentors, the Richardsons moved across town. 'We thought things would be different but it didn't happen,' Noelle says. 'The nightmares got worse and the phone calls got more insistent. It was unbelievable in the first two years.'

When the nasty phone calls became too much to bear, the Richardsons moved out of Corowa altogether and settled in

Canberra. 'We were whipped out of a town we loved and where we had a business,' Noelle says. Yet despite the turmoil, Stan and Noelle shielded their remaining children as best they could. 'We didn't let it interfere with the upbringing of the kids left behind.'

Fiona remembers her parents presenting a united front. They refused to let Bronwynne's murder tear them apart, as often happens to families of the murdered or missing. Stan and Noelle knew their children were traumatised and cried their own tears behind closed doors. 'I don't remember walking in on them when they were frozen in grief or unable to operate or function, but that would be because I was sheltered from it,' Fiona says. Looking back, she knows they were shattered.

On top of everything, the Richardsons struggled to read the confronting 'Murder of a Beauty Queen' headlines. All the while they wondered, where was the outrage from the community at large? 'It's the injustice of the time,' Fiona says. 'If you compared it with the outrage that happened in the eighties with Anita Cobby, or if you look at the outrage over what happened to Jill Meagher, the thing that has been so difficult to come to terms with is the absolute lack of support we received. If it happened today there would be a different outcry.'

When police investigate homicides they must hold their cards close to their chest, but in those early days Stan and Noelle felt like outsiders in their own daughter's murder investigation. 'We weren't told much at all,' Noelle says. 'We were informed every now and again.' And of course there was little or no counselling in those days.

At an inquest in Albury in 1975 the coroner delivered an open finding. He confirmed that Bronwynne had been murdered, having died, as the pathologist had earlier observed, as a result of being strangled and drowned. Who did it remained a mystery and the cold case turned positively freezing.

The pages of the calendar kept turning without the Richardsons getting any answers about who had killed Bronwynne. It wasn't until October 1989 – sixteen years after she was murdered – that charges were laid. The night before the anniversary of her murder, the justice-seeking Derryn Hinch speculated on his current affairs TV show that Mr Stinky – aka the notorious double murderer and rapist Raymond Edmunds – might have been involved in Bronwynne's murder. He was worth considering, at least.

A Victorian dairy farmer, Raymond Edmunds had been convicted of a number of rapes in the 1970s and 1980s, as well as the 1966 murders of teenagers Garry Heywood and Abina Madill near Shepparton. He had shot eighteen-year-old Garry through the head and bludgeoned sixteen-year-old Abina to death after raping her.

The day after the *Hinch* program went to air, a man anonymously phoned Murray Bridge Police Station in South Australia. According to police, the caller seemed to know a reasonable amount about Bronwynne's murder and said that Edmunds hadn't been there. The policeman asked how he knew that. The man said it was because he was there, but not involved. He gave police three other names – one of whom was a former boyfriend of Bronwynne's, though not the boyfriend who was supposed to accompany her to the ball. The switched-on police officer on the other end of the phone took copious notes.

A short while later the anonymous man called again. He gave more detail and talked about a green FB Holden, which was the make and model police believed was involved in Bronwynne's abduction. The policeman put the information in a tray for detectives in Albury to progress but somehow it was overlooked, and for a while nothing happened.

Sometime later, an eager new detective at Albury Police Station was looking for something to do and went through the tray, identifying a man who might have made the call. The man in question was interviewed and admitted he was the caller but would not sign a statement. He gave police a version of events involving the three other men, two of whom, he alleged, had been involved in Bronwynne's abduction, rape and murder. Police spoke to the other man who'd been named but who was said not to have been involved in the crime. They say his account was similar but with a few discrepancies.

Bronwynne's ex-boyfriend was subsequently charged with her murder.

The case went to a committal hearing where the two informants refused to adhere to the information they had given. As a result the charges against Bronwynne's ex-boyfriend were dismissed. The informants were subsequently charged with misprision of felony – which would now be known as the crime of concealing a serious offence – and the matter went to trial. Both were discharged by direction of the trial judge.

In 2004, thirty-one years after Bronwynne's murder, New South Wales Police formed an Unsolved Homicide Team to review and investigate cold case murders. Times had changed and investigators now had new technology – including DNA testing – at their disposal. Regardless of these technological advances, investigating cold cases is challenging. Often leads have turned cold, witnesses are hard to find or have died, and evidence – even when it once existed – can be hard to locate in police storage facilities.

In 2008, the Southern Region Unsolved Homicide Team – under the leadership of Detective Sergeant Steve Morgan – turned its attention to Bronwynne's case. It would end up being the most exhaustive – and exhausting – investigation into Bronwynne's murder to date.

Steve Morgan remembers seeing the original brief about Bronwynne's murder when he was a young uniformed constable in Albury back in 1987. The older, world-weary uniformed police didn't want to take the new kid on the block out in the car with them so Steve ventured into the detectives' office and asked if they could give him something to do. 'Have a look at that, Sonny,' the boss said, pushing a box of files towards him. Steve picked up the box and paused a moment: this was the first time he'd seen anything to do with a murder. And while Steve didn't work on the case at the time, he would never forget the statements he read or the photos he saw, nor would he forget how he felt: that Bronwynne Richardson deserved justice. He had no way of knowing that decades later he would be the one trying to get it.

Thirty-five years after Bronwynne was killed, Steve was a veteran investigator who could see that, with a bit of work, the case might be cracked. It had already been reviewed and was considered of 'medium solvability'. It helped that some witnesses were still alive, that various relationships had broken down – increasing the chances that people might now tell police what they knew – and that there were exhibits on file.

Aiming to advance the case to another inquest, Steve and his team looked at the original persons of interest, tested witness statements, re-canvassed areas of significance, re-examined evidence, and conducted scientific testing, which included re-analysing Bronwynne's clothes. The problem was that the garments had spent up to thirty-six hours in the Murray River so any DNA had been washed away.

'Nothing has been successful in identifying evidence against a known suspect [in the Bronwynne Richardson murder],' says Detective Superintendent Scott Cook, who has been the commander of the New South Wales Police Homicide Squad since December 2017, after years overseeing several of the state's other formidable criminal investigation squads.

Steve Morgan could not do enough to try and find answers for Stan and Noelle. 'He was a beacon,' Fiona says. 'He nurtured them. I think it was because he lost his own mum, he had this want, almost like a son to a mother, to make it better for them and solve it for them.'

Scott Cook says Bronwynne's murder is the kind that hits close to home for many police. 'It's horrific,' he tells me as he turns the pages of the Police Facts Sheet regarding her murder and digesting the horror within. 'As a father of two daughters, this is my worst nightmare. I really feel for her and the family.'

During their reinvestigation, Steve and his team were able to interview most of the people associated with the original investigation. Though some were frail or suffering from Alzheimer's, others were able to give police fresh statements which enabled them to garner more evidence – though it was unclear if it would be enough to crack the case.

Complicating matters was the fact that the investigators were receiving snippets of false information. Some people – no matter how well intentioned – said they'd seen things they couldn't have seen. It seemed that some people had imagined certain events and, as time had gone by, their imaginings had evolved. Eliminating false information is time-consuming but the detectives did it, all the while wearing down more shoe leather in their search for the truth.

In 2010, with the help of Bronwynne's family, New South Wales Police announced that the reward for information about Bronwynne's murder had been increased from fifty thousand dollars to two hundred thousand dollars. They hoped the increased reward might encourage someone with knowledge of the crime to creep out of the woodwork.

In 2011 a second inquest into Bronwynne's murder took place in Albury where, much to the investigators' surprise, fresh information turned the case on its head. The name of Bronwynne's second cousin was introduced into the investigation. At the end of proceedings Coroner Carmel Forbes said the evidence did not allow her to make a finding about the circumstances surrounding Bronwynne's death and referred the case back to police for further investigation. Addressing the reason for her finding, the coroner stated, 'I decline to make any comments on the material I have heard so far on the basis it may affect the future investigation.'

The New South Wales Unsolved Homicide Team were champing at the bit to investigate the new lead. 'They said we have this information we want to test,' Scott says. As a result, the detectives conducted extensive inquiries, some of which were covert.

Upon learning the identity of the new person of interest, the Richardsons were gobsmacked, though Noelle says, 'We didn't have much to do with that side of the family.'

In July 2014, after a highly sensitive investigation, the Unsolved Homicide Team – who were alleging it was actually Bronwynne's relative who'd called police from Murray Bridge in 1989 and not the man they'd previously spoken to – charged him with her abduction, rape and murder. But prosecutors dropped the charges in November 2015 before the matter went to a committal hearing. 'We were left dangling,' Noelle says.

The fact that yet again the case would not make it to trial left Stan, in particular, desolate. He had recently survived radical surgery for stomach cancer, but when the charges were dropped he felt it was back to square one. 'The will to live left him and he just didn't care about eating or anything and just went downhill from there,' Fiona says. He died in October 2016 not knowing who had murdered his darling Bronwynne.

'Our promise is that this case will not be forgotten,' Detective Superintendent Scott Cook says. 'The only time I can see this coming off our books is when everyone involved is a hundred and twenty years old. Until that point it will keep getting looked at.'

Even though Bronwynne was murdered as long ago as 1973, Scott is convinced whoever did it is still out there. 'Why should they be free after what they've done to Bronwynne? Why should they be free?! They need to answer for what they did to her for the community's sake, for the family's sake.' One thing's for sure, Scott believes if anyone can still solve it, the New South Wales Unsolved Homicide Team can. 'They're absolutely meticulous.

They are so involved in the cases that they want to see every single case through to finality. Sometimes I have to drag them off matters to investigate others. They are like dogs with bones. They are one hundred per cent committed, to their own detriment.'

But realistically, can the murder of Bronwynne Richardson be solved after so many years? 'I'm hopeful,' Scott says. 'As long as there's opportunity, there's hope.' He hopes someone might still come forward with information and he doesn't care how inconsequential it might seem; he just wants the team to be given the opportunity to investigate it. He also hopes the passage of time will work in his favour. 'Sometimes people don't tell because they don't want to get into trouble, because they're in fear. Over time, perhaps some of the fear is gone. If you're one of those people, you need to speak up for the sake of the victim.'

Despite the setback, Steve Morgan vows to keep doing everything in his power to solve the case for Bronwynne's family, especially her mum Noelle. 'He rings Mum at least once a month and she'll always send him a birthday card like he's one of the kids,' Fiona says. 'He's just connected.' Steve's connection is tangible. Talk to him about the Bronwynne Richardson case and his eyes glisten. He doesn't want this to be the case that haunts him in retirement.

Longing for answers: Fiona Hume (left) and Noelle Richardson
Photo courtesy Fiona Hume

Meanwhile, Bronwynne's family will continue in their quest for justice, but it's been almost fifty years and Noelle is getting tired. If she doesn't see the case solved in her lifetime she asks us to do something for her. She wants us to bear witness to the short but important life of her late daughter: the caring, spirited, lovely Bronwynne Richardson. The eternal Belle of Belles.

There is a $200,000 reward for information leading to the arrest and conviction of the person or persons responsible for the murder of Bronwynne Richardson.

KILLER IN THE HOME

THE MURDER OF HOUSEPROUD WIDOW, **MILICA TRAILOVIC**

Milica Trailovic: her body's still missing

Photo courtesy Victoria Police/AAP Image

'From looking at the scene, the blood spatter expert was able to tell us Milica had been hit with something while standing, while kneeling, and then while she was on the ground.'

Narelle Fraser, former detective, Victoria Police Homicide Squad Missing Persons Unit

At first glance, nothing looked out of place in the modest brick veneer home.

The owner is houseproud, thought Senior Detective Narelle Fraser as she cast well-trained eyes around the combined living and dining room. There was a neat fabric lounge, a tasteful wooden dining table with matching chairs, and framed photos which told the story of loved ones overseas.

Sixty-one-year-old widow Milica Trailovic lived in the well-kept house – or had – until she went missing on Boxing Day in 2003. The Victorian Homicide Squad Missing Persons Unit had been called in to investigate her disappearance because it looked suspicious. Milica had never gone missing before and no one had heard from her in weeks.

Narelle Fraser's instincts, honed over years in the job, told her Milica had met with foul play – and that she was never coming back to the home she so clearly loved.

Serbian-born Milica Trailovic was looking forward to the new year. She had bought tickets to a neighbourhood celebration in the suburb of Keysborough and was planning to attend a traditional Serbian New Year's Eve function two weeks later. She intended to take her partner, Apolonio 'Tony' Serrano, to both events.

Tony and Milica had been together for three years but, with Milica widowed and Tony divorced, marriage was not at the top of their to-do list. Instead they lived ten minutes' drive from each other in Melbourne's south-eastern suburbs; Milica in verdant Endeavour Hills, and Tony in a unit in Hallam. To some, they seemed an odd couple – Milica was plus-sized and towered over Tony, who was short and wiry.

In late December 2003 Milica's friends and neighbours realised they hadn't seen her for a few days. When someone asked Tony where Milica was, he explained he'd dropped her at a bus stop in Dandenong as she was travelling to Queensland for a holiday. He said Milica had insisted he leave the bus stop before she departed. It seemed peculiar. Around the same time, Tony told others that Milica had gone to Queensland for a Jehovah's Witness conference. Perhaps she was holidaying *and* praying?

By early January 2004, with no word from Milica, Tony reported her missing to Dandenong Police. He told them he had not seen or heard from her since farewelling her at the bus stop. The police started to investigate and grew increasingly concerned about her welfare.

One morning a few weeks later, Narelle Fraser was sitting at her desk at the old Victoria Police Headquarters on St Kilda Road, drinking her second mug of government-issue instant coffee. She drank four mugs a day and suspected it was four too many, but she liked her mind sharp.

That morning, as the detectives from the Missing Persons Unit reviewed the state's suspicious missing persons reports, Narelle found herself drawn to the Milica Trailovic case. From what she could tell, Milica was not the kind of person to leave town indefinitely, if at all. It suggested to her that someone else had been involved in Milica's disappearance. 'The Dandenong Police had also smelled a rat,' Narelle says. 'They did the basic investigation and contacted us because they thought something wasn't right. So we took over in March 2004 from the divisional detectives.'

Narelle learned that Milica's partner Tony was staying at her house, perhaps waiting for her to return home. 'The first thing we did was go to her house and have a chat with him,' Narelle says. 'We sat on the couch, got the history of Milica and the history of their relationship.'

Even though Narelle suspected Milica had met with foul play, she didn't assume Tony had anything to do it. 'I went in with an open mind,' she says. 'At Detective Training School they teach you the mind is like a parachute, it only works when it's open.'

Sitting across from Tony, Narelle could see he looked after himself. 'He was small, well-built and quite handsome,' she says. 'He kept himself well. He had grey hair, was clean-shaven and very well-dressed. He had on good quality clothes and shoes.'

Narelle learned that sixty-four-year-old Tony, who spoke with a strong accent, was born in Spain. After losing his parents he had grown up in an orphanage. It was a joyless environment where misdemeanours attracted harsh punishment.

As an adult, Tony had worked as a cabinet maker and a metal worker and was qualified to drive a heavy truck and operate an excavator. At the time of Milica's disappearance he was on a disability support pension and was working casually for a rental car company. Apart from a couple of minor scrapes with the law there was little in Tony's background to set off alarm bells.

Still, it bugged Narelle that he had given Milica's friends differing accounts of her trip away, including, as it turned out, that she had left him for another man. Narelle says, 'He told Dandenong Police the same thing then changed his tune to say he dropped her at the bus stop at Dandenong so she could go to Queensland to a Jehovah's Witness conference, which he said she'd booked.' After that Tony stuck to the Jehovah's Witness story. 'He never mentioned an affair again,' Narelle recalls.

It is common knowledge that when someone goes missing under suspicious circumstances, or they are murdered, police investigate those closest to the victim first. The reason for this is simple: the majority of homicide victims are known to their killers. Milica had no family in Australia so that ruled them out. She was closest to her partner Tony so the investigators had to look into his background.

What Narelle found out about him at the start was strange but not necessarily sinister. 'He was besotted with money,' she says. 'When Milica stayed at his house he asked her for money for the electricity, for the shower, for water.' Eventually, Milica decided such payments should work both ways and asked Tony for money to cover electricity and water when he stayed with her, too.

Neighbours, who last saw Milica on Boxing Day, told Narelle of hearing a loud argument at her place. 'It was either on Christmas night or the following day, and they heard Tony's car leave late at night which was very unusual,' Narelle says. 'We were now starting to get a bit of a picture. He was all about power. I think he had little man syndrome. Milica was a big woman. She was a matronly woman, at least six foot and probably a size twenty-two. They were like chalk and cheese.'

Milica regularly spoke on the phone to her sister in Serbia and had talked about her relationship with Tony. It wasn't all roses. 'Her sister knew that she was arguing with him,' Narelle says. 'She didn't trust him.'

Yet there was no evidence to indicate that Tony and Milica's arguments were anything more than tiffs and there had been no suggestion of violence in the past. The only way to find out exactly what happened to Milica was through old-fashioned detective work. As two investigators took a statement from Tony, another searched his bank records, Medicare and phone accounts and two others prepared a warrant for a meticulous search of Milica's house. In the meantime, two other detectives conducted a fresh doorknock.

'Dandenong Police had already done a doorknock,' says Narelle, 'but we asked different, more involved questions because we had more time.' The fresh doorknock yielded more information. 'We found out that Milica hadn't gone to a dance as planned about two nights after Christmas.' The detectives also confirmed that Milica had not been seen since around Boxing Day.

The investigation started hotting up when the detectives found out that after Milica went missing Tony had visited a doctor with a broken finger, which he said he'd caught in a door. Narelle recalls thinking, *Either he's telling the truth or Tony injured himself another way – perhaps assaulting Milica?*

Narelle's interest in Tony as a suspect heightened when detectives discovered that, between Christmas and New Year, Tony, a man of independent means, had been trying to find out if he was a beneficiary to Milica's will. First, armed with a copy of the will, Tony visited the woman who had witnessed it. He then met with the solicitor who had prepared it. Lastly, he asked to see a lawyer at the Serbian Welfare Association, saying he was trying to find out where the will was located, which was strange, considering he had a copy.

A day or two into their investigation, the Homicide Squad Missing Persons Unit was granted a warrant to search Milica's house. What they found was straight out of a horror movie.

Despite appearing immaculate to the human eye, when sprayed with Luminol the combined lounge and dining room was spattered with blood. 'There was blood on the walls and smear marks where it had been cleaned,' Narelle says with a shudder. 'There was blood on a cushion and on an armrest of the couch where we'd been talking to Tony. From looking at the scene, the blood spatter expert was able to tell us Milica had been hit with something while standing, while kneeling, and then while she was on the ground.'

In the light of this new knowledge, the investigators started looking for a weapon. 'We noticed there were three chairs at the dining table,' Narelle says. 'Normally there are four or six and we believed one was missing from the table.' They did not have to go far for an explanation. Behind the garden shed they found two broken chair legs which were the same as those at the dining room table. One of the chair legs was flecked with blood. They also found a pair of smashed reading glasses – probably Milica's.

Back inside the house the investigators observed that a piece of carpet in the living room was missing and covered with a mat. It looked innocent enough, but it led the crime scene investigators to the discovery of a human tooth wedged in between the skirting board and the carpet in the living room. 'I felt a bit ill when I saw the tooth,' Narelle says. 'You'd have to be belted senseless to be missing a tooth. It was a really awful feeling.'

The turning point in the investigation came when the police could not establish that anyone other than Tony had been in Milica's house around the time she went missing. 'That's when everything changed and Tony Serrano became a suspect,' Narelle says.

Tony was formally interviewed at Victoria Police Headquarters in St Kilda Road. For a few minutes Narelle was left alone with Tony in an interview room while fellow crew members fetched him some water. Looking back, Narelle suspects her colleagues left her alone with him because she had a knack of getting suspects to spill. 'I was thinking, *Oh my God, I'm in a room with someone who I'm pretty sure belted a woman senseless*,' Narelle says. 'It was a bit uncomfortable. Obviously you keep a chair or table in between you. It was only fleeting but I thought, *God, what am I doing here?*'

By that time Narelle knew the Jehovah's Witness gathering in Queensland was made up. 'The conference that Tony said Milica was going to never happened,' she says. And as for Milica having an affair, based on what she'd learned about the missing woman, Narelle did not believe it was Milica's style. 'Her sister knew she wouldn't have gone off with anyone else.'

During the interview with Tony, Narelle was rattled by his behaviour. 'He was uptight, nervous and aggressive,' she says. 'He would turn the interview around and was so argumentative and bombastic that you'd ask him a question and he'd say, "Why would you ask me a question like that?" In the end it was like he was trying to take control of the interview. He was a control freak and a very angry man.'

Narelle wondered what growing up in a postwar orphanage had done to Tony Serrano. 'I think he was intimidated by women – and women in power in particular.' Still, that did not mean she felt sorry for him. 'I didn't like him and he didn't like me,' she says. 'He was a sly little prick.'

It was rare for Narelle to play the bad cop; her whole career had been built on being the good cop and making genuine connections with people. Neither approach was going to work with Tony Serrano because he was making no admissions no matter how much she asked for his side of the story. 'If we didn't give him that opportunity it could have been criticised in court and thrown out,' she says.

Circumstantially, it looked like the hostile suspect was responsible for Milica's disappearance, but Tony Serrano raised a fair point. 'In his interview he said he couldn't lift her,' Narelle says. 'And he had a hernia.' So if he'd killed Milica, how had he removed her from the house and disposed of her body? The detectives needed more evidence if a murder charge were to stick. 'We had a lot [of information] but we needed another piece of evidence to charge him,' says Narelle.

When Milica's neighbours told police that Tony was frequently going out and not coming home until late at night, the detectives hatched a plan. Hoping his late-night outings might lead them to Milica's body, the detectives put a tracking device on his car. 'The other reason we decided to use the tracking device was because he'd got a speeding fine up Newborough, Moe, Morwell way and we couldn't establish why he'd been there,' Narelle says. The area in which he'd been clocked speeding was in Victoria's La Trobe Valley, a regional area more than an hour's drive from Endeavour Hills.

The tracking device showed Tony's car returning to Newborough and stopping for two minutes in a secluded area off a bush track. Narelle knew it was the kind of place where a killer might dump a body. Straightaway the police assembled a search party and headed to the scene. Within a few hours they made an incriminating discovery: a pile of badly burnt plus-sized clothing and a pair of women's shoes. 'The clothes were a size twenty-two, and the shoes a size eleven,' Narelle says. They were Milica's style and size and had been there a while. It looked to the investigators like Tony had come here to, at the very least, dispose of her clothes.

Even though there was no sign of Milica's body, the police now had enough evidence to charge Tony Serrano with Milica's murder. 'Looking back, I'm pretty sure the tracking device and the discovery of the clothes was the clincher,' Narelle says. Statements from Milica's neighbours compounded the case against him. 'But still, he never ever admitted it.'

The detectives prepared a brief of evidence. In order to prove that the DNA at Milica's house was hers, they needed to compare it against the DNA of a relative. The detectives asked to go to Serbia to get a sample from Milica's sister but their request was denied as it was too expensive so the team came up with an alternative plan. 'We had a DNA kit sent by registered post to a doctor in Serbia and he went to see Milica's sister,' Narelle says. 'It was enough for us to say it was her DNA.' The blood on the chair leg was Milica's too, which suggested it had been the weapon used to bash her.

In any murder investigation – especially one in which the victim's whereabouts are unknown – there is no room for error. 'We had to be one hundred and ten per cent pedantic, so we dotted every i and crossed every t,' Narelle says. 'And fair enough because we had to inculpate or exculpate our suspect.'

★

After a committal hearing, the trial was set down in the Victorian Supreme Court for June 2007. But Tony Serrano wasn't sticking around to learn if he'd be found innocent or guilty. Before the trial ended he hired a van, turned off the fridge in his unit, grabbed some clothes and went on the run.

'It didn't surprise me,' Narelle says. 'I thought if anyone was going to do that it'd be him. I think he couldn't handle being caught because he thought he was smarter than we were.'

A warrant was issued for Tony's arrest and police and the media were alerted nationwide. Yet despite the accused killer's disappearance – and his legal counsel's subsequent decision to withdraw – Justice Stephen Kaye ruled that the trial should continue.

During the trial the court heard that the last reliable sighting of Milica Trailovic was on Boxing Day 2003, and that after that Tony Serrano gave various accounts of her plans. The blood spatter in Milica's living room, the blood-stained chair leg and the discovery of clothes matching Milica's added weight to the Crown's case. The accused's interest in Milica's will was also raised.

On Friday, 15 June 2007, after deliberating for a day and a half, the jury found Apolonio (Tony) Serrano guilty of murder in a unanimous decision. 'I felt relieved he was found guilty because without a body you need a bloody strong case with lots of corroborating evidence,' Narelle says. 'We went down every burrow known to man and it was painstaking but it was all worth it in the end.'

In sentencing, Justice Kaye said, 'In my view, the jury was entitled to be well satisfied, beyond reasonable doubt, that the prisoner had murdered Milica Trailovic in her lounge-dining room in the circumstances alleged.'

He said it would never be clear exactly what happened to Milica Trailovic, nor why Serrano murdered her. 'A number of possible motives may be suggested from parts of the evidence, but there is, in my view, insufficient evidence to enable me to infer beyond reasonable doubt that the murder occurred other than in circumstances involving a spontaneous eruption of violence by the prisoner,' he said. 'Forensic evidence establishes beyond reasonable doubt that the prisoner struck Ms Trailovic a number of blows. He struck her at least two blows while she was standing near the dining room window, at least one further blow while she was either sitting, staggering or bending by the table, and another blow while she was lower down near the couch. I am satisfied that those blows were struck either with a dining room chair, or with a leg from the dining room chair. Clearly the jury was satisfied that the prisoner inflicted those blows with the intention of either killing Ms Trailovic or causing her really serious injury.'

His Honour outlined how the gravity of Serrano's conduct was aggravated by his behaviour after Milica's murder. He cited, among other factors, Serrano's removal and hiding of Milica's body; the false accounts about her whereabouts that he gave to friends, neighbours and the police; and the approaches he made about Milica's will after her murder. 'In my view,' the judge said, 'the only reasonable inference from that conduct of the prisoner is that, having murdered Ms Trailovic, he perceived an opportunity to take advantage of her disappearance and death by benefiting from her estate.'

But Serrano would not be receiving any money from Milica's will. He was not even a beneficiary. What might surprise some was that he was still receiving Centrelink benefits while on the lam. Despite entreaties from police, Centrelink would not stop the convicted killer's payments.

Serrano was sentenced to a maximum seventeen years' jail with a minimum of thirteen years. It was not until a tip-off the following month, however, that he was found at a hotel in Cairns. When the police arrested him, the sixty-seven-year-old went without a fuss. It was over.

To this day, Narelle mulls over how Serrano could have removed Milica from her house and disposed of her body. 'She would have been a dead weight. She would have been very heavy,' Narelle says. 'I wonder if he cut her up and used his skills as an excavator to bury her.'

Over the years, Narelle successfully investigated scores of missing persons cases, murders and other violent crimes. As you've already read, it's the kind of work that can come at great personal expense when police struggle to shake off violent images. For Narelle, the Milica Trailovic case is yet another terrible crime that sticks in her mind. 'It's because of the tooth,' she says. 'And I thought it was very sad that it happened in Milica's own house at the hand of someone she trusted. Seeing the blood everywhere with the Luminol, I thought, *That poor woman. What must she have gone through?*'

And even though justice has been done, one piece of the puzzle is still missing.

'Tony Serrano is now in Her Majesty's Prison,' Narelle says, 'but where is Milica?'

PROFILE

TIM WATSON-MUNRO
CRIMINAL PSYCHOLOGIST

The Shrink in the Clink

Photo courtesy Piers Laverty

I still remember the first time I walked through the gates at Parramatta Jail. I was struck by the smells, the movement and the sound of bells ringing. It was like hopping out of the Tardis into another universe, but I was exhilarated by it. I'd recently finished a master's degree in psychology and was offered the job of prison psychologist. I was twenty-five. A lot of my friends counselled me against accepting the job because I played classical guitar and was a sensitive kid, yet I was drawn to the gates of Hell. But I adjusted well and saw it as a challenge.

Some of the prisoners wanted to offer a 'Day in Jail' program to deter juvenile offenders from a life of crime. I thought it was a good idea so I oversaw the group and gave them some basic training in counselling techniques to help them mentor the young toughs. It was a ▶

great success and turned around the lives of countless boys who left Parramatta Jail quivering in terror, never wanting to see the inside of a prison again. The program received widespread media attention and I went from being a kid in shorts to having a high-profile role in a very tough jail.

At twenty-seven I was offered another life-changing opportunity. I met the prominent Welsh forensic psychiatrist Dr David Sime who said, 'You should come and work with me in Melbourne.' I lived in Balmain in Sydney but the offer was too good to decline so I moved to Melbourne in 1981. Most of my work involved assessing prisoners who were facing trial or had been found guilty. David was a great mentor and friend and I worked with him for twenty years until he died.

Forensic psychology in Australia has evolved over the past forty years. Psychologists working in prisons and the criminal justice system decided to call ourselves forensic psychologists as a subgroup of the Australian Psychological Society. At the time there were probably fifteen to twenty forensic psychologists in New South Wales, two in Victoria and one in Adelaide. Fast-forward to today and now there are professional doctorates in Forensic Psychology and we are also known as criminal psychologists. Over my career my work has predominantly involved assessing people accused of crimes, writing reports and going to court to give expert opinion. I have been involved in more than twenty thousand cases.

My breakthrough case involved Julian Knight, who murdered seven people and injured many others in Hoddle Street, Clifton Hill, in August 1987. When I heard about it on the news I thought, *This is horrendous.* The case was hitting world headlines and Julian was referred to me. I didn't know what to expect. ▶

I thought, *Am I going to be dealing with a psychopathic monster who'll kick me out of the room in sixty seconds flat?* On my way to meet him the prison officers kept saying, 'He's a low rat, he won't survive in here.' What I encountered was a bewildered teenager, a kid who was overwhelmed by what he had done. He was in his pyjamas in a rubber room [padded cell]. I found him to be incredibly respectful and it was hard to reconcile that with what he'd done. I wondered if he would have a defence of temporary insanity, but no. Without trivialising it, he'd just had a very bad Sunday night.

One of the issues was that he'd had ready access to firearms. Julian retrieved his weapons – a .22 semi-automatic Ruger rifle, an M14 Carbine and a twelve-gauge shotgun – from beneath his mother's bed at home while she was watching television downstairs, totally unaware of his movements. If he hadn't had such ready access, he might have just slept it off.

On the day of the Hoddle Street Massacre Julian Knight did evil deeds. It was the worst crime in the country at the time. But I've met far worse people over the years in terms of the way they view others, including serial killers and people who rape and murder children. What Knight did was an intense outpouring of rage, murder and terrible behaviour but I don't think that percolates in him. Other people I've met are actually evil and spend time thinking about their next rape or murder or revenge. I do think evil exists.

I am still in contact with Julian Knight who, for the first time, told me he was sorry for what he did. It was his first expression of remorse. He says it happened out of frustration and not an explosion of rage. To me that's nonsense. To shoot all those people, it was an act of rage.

My next big case was Alan Bond. In 1993, after a stint in prison the previous year, Alan Bond was facing new criminal charges. He was having trouble with his memory and his lawyers couldn't make sense of his instructions. I assessed him and concluded he was suffering from cognitive impairment. He'd had open heart surgery and was not the first such patient to experience temporary memory loss. When I was called into the witness box to give evidence about his mental health and more particularly, his cognitive functioning at the time, I said, 'I'm telling you that today, he couldn't run a corner store.' Even as it was coming out of my mouth, I knew it would end up on the front page, but it was true!

I assessed many famous underworld figures during the Melbourne gangland war. One of them was Alphonse Gangitano, who'd been accused of the 1995 murder of Greg Workman in St Kilda. Gangitano had such a menacing presence, not towards me but towards the prison officers, who were terrified of him and treated him with great deference. What struck me was that he was a charismatic bloke who was highly intelligent. He liked reading Oscar Wilde. After the charges against him were dropped I thought I'd seen the last of him but he came back for consultations because he felt he could talk to me. He said to me, 'You're the only person I've ever met who insists that I pay them.' I said, 'But I like being paid.'

Jason Moran was another client. I was under no delusions about him; I knew he was an extremely violent criminal. But he had a great sense of humour. Often in that context the person you meet is very different from their public persona. And he paid his bills.

I saw a number of sexual abuse victims of the Christian Brothers in Western Australia. That was heartbreaking stuff. I saw maybe twenty-five or thirty of ▶

these broken men. They'd been sent to Australia [from the UK] as children to escape war-torn Europe and had been told their parents were dead. Their parents had also been told their children were dead.

For a time, working as a criminal psychologist changed me dramatically. I couldn't get over the Hoddle Street massacre, I think because of the sheer horror of it. In the crime scene photos I'd seen people with their stomachs blown out and I'd seen a lady whose head was blown off. She had a baby seat in the back of her car. I paid a huge price because of what I did.

I developed features of post-traumatic stress like sleep disturbance and depression. At that time I had a hell of a lot of ego and arrogance. I was getting a lot of work, making a lot of money, I was on TV three times a week. I thought I was bulletproof. I was an out-of-control workaholic doing one hundred hours a week. I was drinking a lot and had developed an expensive cocaine habit. Most telling was that I lost my creativity and became cynical, not trusting people. It had a big impact on my mental health and it blew up publicly. For nearly three-and-a-half years I was banned from practice. But, looking back, if that hadn't happened I'd probably be dead through overwork or being reckless. It made me a better practitioner and psychologist. My humanity's come back and my arrogance has gone.

I've had an amazing life, really. I've learned so much about the human condition, including my own. It was a case of no pain, no gain to get to where I am now. I can look back on that period and what I could have done without opprobrium and without drugs. I regret that part of my life but I don't regret the career I've had. Although it's confronting it's fantastic. I've never had a bored day in the office. ▶

I've written two books. My first book, *Dancing with Demons*, is a memoir. It's about how I became a forensic psychologist, some of the high-profile cases I was involved in and the toll they took on me, my family and my career. It's about the demons I danced with at work and in my personal life.

My second book, *Shrink in the Clink*, is about the psychology of crime and the different sorts of crime. It looks at Australian serial killers, contract killers, sexual deviants and bikies. The reality is they're mostly bad and not mad. It's a serious quasi-academic account without being a textbook and it includes case studies and some funny moments too.

People are more fascinated than ever by the way criminals' minds work. Figures suggest there has been a twenty per cent increase in true crime book sales over the past twelve to eighteen months and, interestingly, women account for a high percentage of readers and crime series viewers. The reasons behind this are multi-factorial and include basic voyeurism at a safe distance; requited desires for closure and retribution; to obtain a better understanding of the criminal mind, both theoretically and in terms of personal survival; as well as solid adrenaline-inducing entertainment. All this from the secure comfort of your lounge room!

THERE'S SOMETHING ABOUT MARTYN

THE SEARCH FOR FREE SPIRIT, **MARTYN TANN**

Martyn Tann: taken by a shark? Living rough? Or on a spiritual journey?

Photo courtesy Colin and Maree Tann

'A lot can happen in five years . . . You have to stay positive. But the longer it goes, the harder it gets.'

Maree Tann, Martyn's mother

Upon hearing that a man had gone missing from Perth's Mullaloo Beach, some people figured a shark had taken him. It sounded like a reasonable assumption because Perth – in fact all of the Western Australian coastline – is no stranger to shark attacks. Their incidence has risen so sharply over the past decade that you might think twice before dipping your toes in the water.

But just because someone goes missing from a Western Australian beach does not necessarily mean a shark is to blame. In the case of missing twenty-four-year-old Martyn Tann, it's just one possibility. Naturally, his parents, Colin and Maree, and his older siblings, Andrew and Gemma, want to hold on to the hope that Martyn is still alive. And when you see Martyn through their eyes you'll see why they think he's still out there.

From the age of six months, living on windswept Flinders Island in Bass Strait, Martyn Tann was fascinated by the ocean and the wonders of the natural world. His mum, Maree, says, 'We'd go down to the beach and he'd be mucking around in rock pools.' Martyn's love of nature grew when the family moved to the outskirts of Narrabri, a historical agricultural centre on the Namoi River in north-western New South Wales. The Tanns often took their children camping after the move, continually nurturing their love of the environment. The family also had a menagerie of pets, including cats, dogs, fish, chickens, pythons and rats. Martyn looked after them all.

A cheeky youngster, Martyn enjoyed teasing his teachers with made-up stories. Once he said there'd been a massive flood beneath the family home after his dad Colin, in pursuit of a snake, accidentally hit the pipes. When Martyn's teacher next spoke to Maree and expressed her alarm, Maree said, 'No, that didn't happen. That was a Martyn story!' But Maree didn't mind her son telling the occasional tall tale; she was pleased he liked to stretch his imagination. 'He was smart and would push the boundaries. He would allow you to think everything was hunky-dory and then he'd go out and do his own thing.'

'I think he benefitted from being in a country area,' Colin says, recalling how as Martyn got older he explored the countryside on foot and spent countless hours abseiling and kayaking. 'Being the youngest child, he probably had the most freedom,' Colin adds.

Yet Martyn was no loner. By the time he hit his teenage years he could talk to anyone. 'He's very gregarious and gets on well with his peers,' his dad says, speaking in the present tense about the son he has not seen for some years.

Martyn was popular with the opposite sex too and had his first steady girlfriend at sixteen or seventeen. 'He'd hop on my small two-stroke motorbike and visit her at 3 am,' Maree says. Once, a local police officer who knew Maree called to ask if her bike had been stolen as he'd spotted it hidden in bushes across town. But Maree was wise to her son's late-night outings and explained to the policeman that Martyn had taken her bike to sneak over to his girlfriend's house. Not that he mentioned it when he got home. 'He'd come back and be all innocent in the morning!' Maree says with a laugh.

After graduating from high school Martyn took a gap year. When he heard there was a job opening at a liquor store he decided to apply for it. Maree had always instilled in her children the need to present themselves well at interviews, but Martyn had his own style. 'He rocked up in bare feet or thongs and with dreadlocks, and they said, "Yeah, you've got the job!"' Maree says. It was not unusual for people to respond to Martyn with such enthusiasm, and he was a popular staff member at the liquor store from day one. As his mum explains, 'He's got a bit of an aura.'

After saving his pennies during his gap year, Martyn went to university in Canberra where he started two degrees before settling on environmental science. 'Interestingly, he didn't do any science at school,' says Colin, a retired senior experimental officer at the CSIRO. 'His big brother gave him a crash course in chemistry.' It helped that Andrew was a science teacher and that Martyn was able to pick up the fundamentals quickly. But after two years Martyn, who loved the sea and its treasures more than ever, realised he wanted to train as a marine biologist and transferred to marine science in Townsville. 'When he got to James Cook University he never looked back,' Colin says. 'He loved it.'

Maree remembers driving Martyn to his new campus in Townsville for the first time and how he reacted when they arrived. 'He said, "Oh, this is so good. I don't know anybody!" I was going, "*What?*" But he said, "I want to see who I make friends with and how this all pans out." It was like a challenge. He didn't like the comfort zone.'

Nothing illustrates that more than Martyn's choice of accommodation once his university dormitory shut down at the end of his first semester. He set up camp on a dry creek bed out the back of the university grounds, where he wove palm fronds into a makeshift shelter. He was proud of his handiwork but Maree could

Living rough: Martyn at home on a dry creek bed
Photo courtesy Colin and Maree Tann

not understand why he was calling a campsite home, even temporarily. 'He took me down there and I said, "Why are you living here?" Because he didn't have to. He had friends he could stay with. He could even have slept in the back of his four-wheel drive, but he chose to sleep in a dry creek bed instead.'

Martyn explained that he enjoyed the challenge of sleeping rough. 'He'd scrounged up some pots and pans and made a fire,' Maree says. He'd even worked out how to maintain his personal hygiene. From his campsite he'd look up at the dormitory bathroom, and if there was an open window he'd climb up the drainpipe, hoist himself inside, and take a hot shower. 'That is the sort of shit Martyn would do,' his mum explains. 'It's that independence. That sense of, *I'm going to do things my way*.'

Yet, in doing things his way, Martyn never overlooked the needs of others. He always had a ready ear for his friends. 'When he was at university we used to call him the counsellor,' Colin says. 'People used to come to him with their problems and he'd listen without being judgemental.'

'He was respectful,' Maree adds. 'He'd walk the girls home after a party, or when they were upset he'd jump into bed with them. It was nothing sexual but it was to make them feel better.'

At one stage Martyn was offered a dormitory room in what his mum describes as a 'lovely garden setting' but he was too much of a people person for that. 'He wanted to be on the second or third floor in amongst everything – the noise and the parties – so he shifted up there,' Maree says. He just loved the company of others and a good conversation. 'Not in the way you'd talk a glass eye to sleep, but he was interested in people.'

In March 2013, Colin's younger brother Trevor, who lives in Perth, was getting married in the Margaret River region of Western Australia. Having just completed a professional divers' course in Honduras, Martyn flew to Perth especially for the wedding.

After his parents picked him up from the airport, Martyn and his sister Gemma hired a car to make the four-and-a-half-hour trip together to the town of Denmark.

As the siblings drove into the country Gemma remarked on how many landmarks she recognised from the book she was reading, *A Fortunate Life* by A. B. Facey. Gazing out the passenger window, Martyn made a curious comment. 'He said it'd be interesting to live off the grid and disappear for about five years,' Gemma says. 'I thought he was talking crap so I didn't pursue it.'

The wedding was beautiful and the family stayed in cabins at a resort. 'Everyone was together and Martyn was fooling around and entertaining a few people,' Maree says. Martyn was in excellent spirits and enjoying the company of his close, happy family.

The look of love: Martyn lets his mum Maree adjust his tie at the wedding
Photo courtesy Colin and Maree Tann

After the celebrations Colin and Maree returned home to Narrabri. Trevor and his wife were not going on their honeymoon straightaway, but returning to Perth for a while instead. Martyn – who'd made plans to travel north – stayed on at their home for another week. 'So Martyn wasn't alone and there was no indication he was in a dark space,' Colin says.

Colin remembers the last phone conversation he had with his son, which was the day before he disappeared. 'He wanted to get out of Perth,' Colin says. 'He doesn't like cities.' Martyn had been hoping to travel to Broome to pursue work as a pearl diver. Even though he hadn't worked on a pearl boat before, if anyone could do it, Martyn could. The course in Honduras was just one of many difficult diving courses in which he'd gained accreditation. He had been a diver on his university's research team and had dived – and thrived – in the kinds of conditions that often overwhelm others.

So, hoping for a new challenge, Martyn had contacted the owner of a pearl diving company in Broome. There was no position available, but Martyn had emailed to say he would be in Broome on 2 April. He thought if he showed the boss his qualifications, he'd be in with a chance.

Martyn found a lift to Broome – almost twenty-four hours' drive away – on the Gumtree website. Unfortunately, the offer fell through at the last minute when the driver emailed Martyn to say she had cut her foot open and was waiting for the all-clear before she could get going. Martyn spoke of his disappointment during the phone call with his dad. 'He was very frustrated,' Colin says. 'He wanted to get moving again.' After Martyn went missing some twenty-four hours later, this final conversation would churn around Colin's head like a monster wave.

It was after lunch on Tuesday, 2 April 2013, when Martyn, with a small backpack slung over his shoulder, asked his cousins if they wanted to go to the beach for a swim. 'They declined,' says Colin, who feels deeply sorry for his nieces, who later regretted not saying yes.

So Martyn, who was a strong and confident swimmer, went alone to the beach at Mullaloo, as he had done many times before. Exactly what happened after that is unclear, but later that afternoon a kite surfer spotted Martyn's bag, which appeared to have been abandoned. When the kite surfer got out of the water some time later and saw that the bag was still there, he looked inside and discovered a mobile phone in which he found the number of Martyn's parents. He called to tell them of his discovery, which left Maree and Colin scratching their heads. As they were back in Narrabri there was little they could do right away except call Trevor, who hadn't seen Martyn since he'd left for the beach. When Martyn still hadn't turned up later that night, Trevor grew increasingly worried and called the police because for Martyn not to return was out of character.

From that moment on, every effort was made to locate Martyn Tann. Search and rescue specialists started looking for him that night. 'They used some sort of technology that could pick up heat,' Maree says. 'Then it was a full-on search the next day in the light.' Surely there was a simple explanation for Martyn's no-show? 'I was thinking, he'll just turn up, he'll just surface.'

When Martyn hadn't been found by the end of the day, Colin and Maree packed their bags and began the arduous trek to Perth. It was a seven-hour drive to the airport in Sydney, followed by a four-hour flight. They arrived on the second day of the search to find divers in the ocean, and police and quad bikes combing the foreshore. They immediately joined the search, covering kilometres of coastline. 'Then the next day there were mounted police and dogs on the shoreline,' Maree says. 'The Water Police ran the search. We went to their headquarters and they were very good to us.'

'The search was very, very thorough,' Colin adds. 'There were searches from the air, the sea and the land. The police were fantastic.'

Search officials told the Tanns about the conditions on the day their son disappeared. The sea had been calm and there was no rip current. Nevertheless, says Colin, 'Martyn does tend to swim out a bit and there were reports that people saw him swimming and not coming out of the water.' But if Martyn had drowned, the searchers said his body would probably have floated back towards the shoreline because the undercurrent was moving towards the shore in the days surrounding Martyn's disappearance. Similarly, if Martyn had been taken by a shark, 'something' would probably have washed up.

'We were all pretty cut up, thinking of different scenarios,' Colin says. 'You can sit on a rock and imagine a shark taking Martyn out to sea. It does happen but we sort of discounted that. People have been attacked by sharks there but the number of people going in the water there has increased. You can't make a deduction unless you have evidence that such a thing has happened.'

The Tanns did have to steel themselves, however, when it emerged that a man's ripped shirt had been found on the beach. 'It was a collared white on blue shirt with buttons,' Colin says. 'Would he have worn something like that? No, I'm ninety-nine per cent sure he wouldn't have worn a collared shirt. He wore nothing to the beach or a singlet. That shirt wasn't him.' It was some comfort.

With no sign of Martyn after four days, the search was called off. 'I can imagine how much that search would have cost – in the millions,' Maree says. She wonders if Martyn had gone for a walk without his backpack, then, upon realising there was a full-scale search for him, felt too embarrassed to return. 'You'd be feeling pretty ashamed for what had gone on,' she says. 'I don't know what decision you'd make.'

The Tanns were heartened when they remembered that Martyn had walked away from his belongings before, and that it had been accidental. 'He could be forgetful and a bit careless with leaving his stuff around,' Maree says. 'When he was overseas he had lost a bag, so there was precedent.'

In the wake of Martyn's disappearance the Tanns did what many families of the missing do: they put up posters, talked to anyone who might have encountered their loved one, started a Facebook page, and turned up anywhere he may have visited. In Martyn's case, Colin and Maree thought it prudent to speak to the staff of Perth diving stores and, even though Martyn was not known to have mental health issues, they also contacted mental health facilities. Their inquiries drew a blank.

One of Martyn's friends, Louis, who lived in England, was so devastated to learn he had gone missing that he set up a GoFundMe page to raise money to come to Australia and mount his own search. Louis had only known Martyn since meeting him overseas in 2012, but Martyn had made a big impression, as usual. 'It was a pretty amazing thing to do,' Colin says, 'so he was pretty upset that he didn't get a result.'

As time passed without answers, the scientifically minded Tanns did something they never thought they would do. They spoke to three psychics in different states to find out what they thought had happened to Martyn. 'None of them have said he's deceased and one was seeing him walking along but in a different mindset,' Colin says. 'There also seemed to be a common thread about him being in a remote Aboriginal community, which is possible.' If that were the case, how would the Tanns ever find out? 'You'd have to know someone to infiltrate,' Colin says, adding that two friends who slept in Martyn's old bedroom in Narrabri prompted him to further consider the theory. 'They both had a dream that he was involved in an Aboriginal community,' he says. It also fit with Martyn's comment to his sister that it would be good to live off the grid for around five years.

While Maree is sceptical about accepting a psychic's word that Martyn went to live in an Aboriginal community, she admits it would appeal to his sense of minimalism and love of the bush. Maree recalls running the notion past the first detective on the case. 'He said a white person's not going to just walk into an Aboriginal community and be accepted, but we said, "You don't know Martyn! He's friendly and would walk in there and be accepted."'

Wherever he might have gone, Martyn's mum does not believe he'd be alone. 'He's not someone who'd want to disappear into the ether,' she says. 'Wherever he goes he makes not just friends but very strong connections.'

Colin understands his son's free spirit and how it might have influenced him. 'Just going off for an adventure, I can see myself

In his happy place: Martyn at the beach
Photo courtesy Colin and Maree Tann

doing that too,' he says. 'In fact, I did that before I got married. I used to go camping by myself and taking in nature.'

But Martyn always told his family where he was going. 'I suggest if he's around that he's caught in some environment where they won't let him out,' Colin says. 'If he's been through certain initiations, he may not be permitted to leave.'

The other question that has to be asked – and the police have – is whether Martyn used drugs. If so, then perhaps that had something to do with his disappearance. The Tanns told the police Martyn had dabbled in marijuana but they could not rule out that he had also used other substances. 'He did like to experiment,' Maree says. Fortunately, their relationship was so close that she could talk openly with him about taking drugs. Maree recalls, 'I'd say, "Well, what about this crazy stuff like ice?" and he'd say, "I wouldn't be so stupid."' That, at least, was reassuring.

There was something else that might have contributed to Martyn's disappearance – of all things, his spirituality. Colin has long enjoyed yoga and meditation and some years before he'd given each of his children a book about it. 'I thought it was a good start for them but Martyn was the only one who used it,' he says. 'He could see that he needed to pursue this. He was very inquisitive. I wasn't able to answer a lot of his questions but I was able to give him some direction.'

In 2012, Martyn even did an arduous Vipassana meditation retreat in Canada. The retreat involved long hours of meditation and days of not speaking a word – not an easy undertaking for someone as outgoing as Martyn. 'It was very difficult for him but he embraced it and understood what was happening when he embraced stillness,' Colin says. 'He got out of it what he should have gotten out of it.'

Afterwards, Colin and Martyn enjoyed many more deep conversations about religion and spirituality. 'I have my own religion and it's based on my own beliefs,' Colin says. 'We talked about it and he was inquiring about that too.' Church was not a place Colin encouraged his son to go, however, so he does not expect to find him drawn to a traditional setting. 'I warned him against going down the religious track. Religion's fascinating to study and they've all got a common ground, but organised religion is about power and control and I tended to warn against that.'

Colin did encourage his son to explore Eastern philosophies, however. 'I said maybe you should visit an ashram or [Buddhist] monastery one day and he thought that was a pretty good idea,' Colin says. 'The funny thing is, Buddhist monasteries and ashrams are two places where he'd be very comfortable. Martyn keeps things to a minimum – he doesn't wear shoes. He's minimal to the point where he'd refuse to take a towel to the beach.' So could it be that Martyn has gone somewhere to further explore his spiritual side? 'I actually did contact a lot of Buddhist monasteries around Australia,' Colin says, 'but they wouldn't divulge anything.'

While most people who go missing are found within a week, it is not unheard of for people to disappear for days, weeks, months, even years, before turning up. I can remember at least three cases while I was working on the television series *Missing Persons Unit*, in which people reappeared after being missing for several weeks and their families had thought they'd never see them again. Two of these cases involved men who wanted time out and left home without telling anyone where they were going or what they were doing. As a result of the program, they contacted their loved ones to let them know they were safe and well and were ultimately reunited.

In another case, a young woman had been missing from the New South Wales north coast for five years. A member of the public saw her photo on the program and told police they had recently seen her dancing with friends in Bali and had a photo to prove it. The police flew to Indonesia where they positively identified the missing woman. Not only did it highlight the power of the media to help solve such cases, but it gave a desperate mother the answers she'd longed for. When mother and daughter were reunited, the daughter confessed that she'd been embarrassed to return home because so much time had passed without contact. Her mother didn't care; all she wanted was her daughter back.

In 2017, news reports told the story of a woman named Sandie Gillette, whose partner Russell Jenkin left the family home in Werribee in Victoria in 2006 and did not return. In January 2017 – just over ten years later – Sandie revealed to news.com.au that she'd seen Russell outside a shopping centre on Queensland's Sunshine Coast. She did not speak to him but later wished she had.

Then there is the case of Sydney man Gabriel Nagy, documented in the first *Unsolved Australia*. After failing to return home one night, Gabriel's burnt-out car was found by the side of the road the next day. Two weeks later, he purchased camping supplies in Newcastle, after which no one heard from him for twenty-three years.

In 2010, a meticulous policewoman who was preparing Gabriel's case for the coroner discovered he had a Medicare card. From there, she tracked him down and learned that he had severe memory loss after the car crash all those years ago. He had only just remembered his name, which is why he'd applied for the Medicare card. And while things would never be the same, he was reunited with the family who had missed him for more than two decades.

And so it will be if Martyn returns home. Years may have passed but he will not be scolded for his absence; he will be met with open arms even if he disappeared on purpose, as he'd alluded to. 'He'll be very welcome,' Maree says. She acknowledges that aspects of Martyn's life may have changed, but that is all right too. 'A lot can happen in five years. He may not have dreadlocks. He may be a different person, it depends on where he's been. You have to stay positive. But the longer it goes, the harder it gets.'

Aside from feelings of ambiguous loss, the Tanns have had to deal with practical issues too, like Martyn's superannuation and his car registration, official bits and pieces which they have kept up to date. 'We don't have power of attorney, which makes things difficult,' Maree says. 'There are other things that we've had to take care of too, such as jury duty and fines for not voting.'

As time continues to pass, the Tanns consider new theories about where their son might be or what he might be involved in. If the ocean or a predator beneath it did not take their son, then he is out there somewhere and the Tanns want us to keep a look-out for him. 'Anything that can help, so be it. That's what gives us hope,' Colin says. 'You just keep positive, don't you? And that's where our strength lies. We know how resourceful, independent and free-spirited Martyn is. And fearless. The possibilities of where he is and what he is doing are limited only by your imagination.'

If you have any information about any of the cases featured in this book, contact Crime Stoppers on 1800 333 000

Need help?
In the case of an emergency contact 000.
If someone you know is missing, contact police immediately. You do not have to wait. The sooner police know, the sooner they can investigate.

For help with mental illness, contact your trusted healthcare professional. Other organisations can help too.
Lifeline 13 11 14 Crisis Support and Suicide Prevention
Beyond Blue 1300 22 4636

For more information about the Missing Persons Advocacy Network, go to mpan.com.au or email info@mpan.com.au
For MPAN's tips on what to do when someone goes missing: www.missingpersonsguide.com

ACKNOWLEDGEMENTS

My sincere gratitude goes to the families, friends and associates of the missing persons and homicide victims featured in this book, who have so generously shared their time and insights. Thank you to: Nancy Anderson, Maryann Bogar, Roza Bogar, Brent Cilia, Chris Harris, Alistair Herfort, Fran Hodgetts, Fiona Hume, Lyn Ireland, Julian Jones, Richard Jones*, Rachel Kayrooz, Catherine McDougall, Jim McDougall, Janie McGough, Barry McIntosh, Joy Membrey, Roger Membrey, Noelle Richardson, Tom Sargent, Barry Sharpe, Colin Tann, Maree Tann, the late Robert Watson, Kevin Whyte, Allen Yardley, June Yardley and Gemma Younger.

This book was produced with the kind cooperation of ACT Policing, New South Wales Police, Northern Territory Police, Tasmania Police and Victoria Police. I would like to especially thank the following exceptional investigators: Detective Sergeant Matt Allen, Detective Senior Sergeant David Butler, Detective Superintendent Scott Cook, Detective Senior Constable Allan Creed, Constable Fiona Howard, Detective Superintendent Scott Moller, Detective Senior Sergeant David Richardson, Detective Sergeant Tristan Thexton and Detective Sergeant Dave Turner. I also wish to acknowledge Detective Sergeant Steve Morgan from New South Wales Police and Detective Sergeant Brendon Murphy from Victoria Police who, while not interviewed, went above and beyond to try to solve cases in this book.

Many thanks to the dedicated media liaison and police public affairs managers who have facilitated police involvement in this project and understood its value. They include: Jemma Ball from Tasmania Police, Ainslie Blackstone from New South Wales Police, Jason Gates from Northern Territory Police, Senior Sergeant Anthoula Moutis from Victoria Police, Kate Prestt from ACT Policing, Lisa Stingel from Tasmania Police, and the super-heroically-named Acting Sergeant Adam West from Victoria Police. I am also grateful to those who assisted me from Supreme Courts and Coroners Courts around Australia.

Thank you to former homicide investigator Ron Iddles who, along with being interviewed in one of the chapters, kindly wrote the foreword to this book and has always believed in the value of the media as an investigative tool.

To the humble crusading professionals I profiled – thanks to Rachael Brown, Narelle Fraser, Xanthé Mallett, Keith Moor, Jan Ross and Tim Watson-Munro.

To my brilliant agent, John Timlin, thank you for your unwavering support, compelling case suggestions and friendship.

Producing a book is a team effort so I'd like to thank everyone at Pan Macmillan who worked hard to make this book possible, including my terrific publisher, Angus Fontaine, who has supported me as a writer, guided the work and believes in publishing books with community benefit.

Many thanks to Pan Macmillan's Director of Non-Fiction, Ingrid Ohlsson, for making these books possible. Your expertise and enthusiasm inspire me to keep writing.

To my outstanding editor, Brianne Collins, thank you for your hard work and thoroughness, which reflects on every page.

Thanks also to my copy-editor, Louise Thurtell, a legend in Australian publishing. I hope we work together again.

And thanks to Georgia Webb for the editorial support, photo research and importantly, the tea!

Gino Campagnaro – you did it again! What an artist, what a cover.

To the wonderful booksellers who recommend my books – I am grateful for your ongoing support.

I'd also like to express my appreciation to the producer of Australian True Crime podcast, Monica Masters, for your kind assistance.

As always, enormous gratitude goes to my family and friends. Your support has allowed me to do the work that is dear to my heart.

And to you, dear readers, a huge thank you for your loyalty and support. (A special shout out to 'Brown Squirrel' for checking in on the Twittersphere to make sure I'm writing and not just putting on the kettle.) Thank you all for coming with me on this journey and maintaining hope for the families of the missing and murdered.

Stay safe,

Justine

**Name changed*

MORE BESTSELLING TITLES FROM JUSTINE FORD

Unsolved Australia

Follow the twists and turns. Piece together the clues. Weigh the evidence. Assess the suspects. Can you catch a killer?

Australia's most baffling homicides and mysterious missing persons cases are uniquely explored in *Unsolved Australia*, a remarkable true crime book in which you, the reader, are invited to play armchair detective.

Crusading journalist Justine Ford shines fresh light on 18 infamous cases, unearths jaw-dropping evidence via in-depth interviews with police, criminals and families of victims, and introduces the humble heroes who never stop searching for the truth.

Unsolved Australia is a chilling, thrilling and inspiring book full of drama, emotion . . . and hope.

The Good Cop

'A – Assume nothing. B – Believe nothing. C – Check everything.'
Ron Iddles

In an incredible twenty-five-year career as a homicide detective, Ron Iddles' conviction rate was 99 per cent. Yet that only partly explains why Iddles is known to cops and crims alike as 'The Great Man'.

Tough, inventive and incorruptible, Ron has applied his country cunning and city savvy to over 320 homicide cases – some of them the most infamous, compelling and controversial crimes in the nation's history.

Ron Iddles never gave up on a 'lost' cause. He became a regular on the nightly news, he became the dogged face of Australian justice, and to families of victims, Ron was both a shoulder to cry on and an avenging angel.

This is the extraordinary inside story of a real crime crusader. Ron Iddles. The Good Cop.

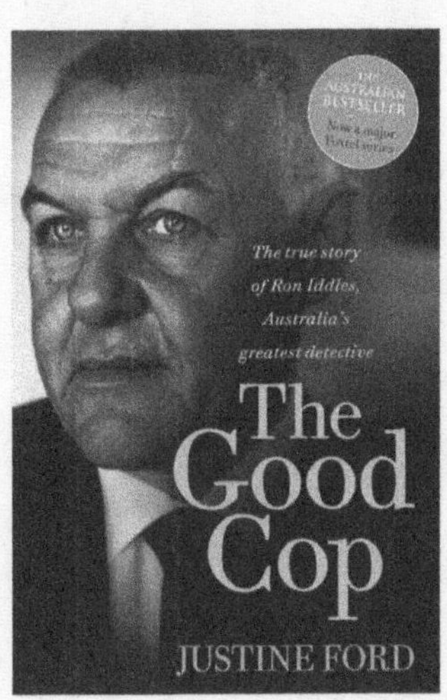